INTEGRATED MANAGEMENT SYSTEMS

Wiley Operations Management Series for Professionals

Other published titles in this series are:

INTEGRATED MANAGEMENT SYSTEMS

A Practical Approach to Transforming Organizations

THOMAS H. LEE
SHOJI SHIBA
ROBERT CHAPMAN WOOD
With contributions by
David Walden and Chris Bergonzi

John Wiley & Sons, Inc.
New York • Chichester • Weinheim • Brisbane • Singapore • Toronto

Library of Congress Cataloging-in-Publication Data:

Lee, Thomas H., 1923–
    Integrated management systems : a practical approach to
  transforming organizations / Thomas H. Lee, Shoji Shiba, Robert
  Chapman Wood : with contributions by David C. Walden and Chris
  Bergonzi.
        p.   cm. — (Wiley operations management series for
  professionals)
    Includes bibliographical references and index.
    ISBN 0-471-34595-4 (cloth : alk. paper)
    1. Management. 2. Management information systems. I. Shiba,
  Shoji, 1933–   . II. Wood, Robert Chapman. III. Title.
  IV. Series.
  HD31.L3727   1999
  658—dc21   99-23516

Printed in the United States of America.

10   9   8   7   6   5   4   3   2   1

Preface

In the fall of 1989, seven companies in the greater Boston area organized a Center for Quality Management (CQM).[1] Their goal was to facilitate mutual learning of Total Quality Management to accelerate its implementation.

Today, it's hard to recall the self-doubt that afflicted American business at the time. Most U.S. companies were suffering from the economic downturn of the late 1980s. But more than that, they were beset by a sense that foreign (especially Japanese) firms were producing better, more reliable products at lower cost—that foreigners knew something about management that they did not.

The senior executives who formed the Center had a special understanding of the problems, since several had personal experiences with Japan and had observed its business practices. At least one had lived in Japan, most had divisions there, and most traveled there with some regularity. Some had studied Japanese business practices through the Massachusetts High Technology Council or the American Electronics Association. They all believed that the concept called Total Quality Management (TQM) could make a difference for their organizations.

Some ten years later, the world has changed dramatically. Now it is American business that is perceived to be on top of the world and the Japanese who are suffering. Yet few managers in the United States have time to gloat. As the economy changes, almost every company finds it faces tougher competition than ever before. Seeking new and better ways of managing and ways of putting new insights to use, 117 companies, including two winners of the Malcolm Baldrige National Quality Award, have joined CQM, which now has four chapters in the United States and two in Europe.

Two of us played key roles in the launch of CQM in 1989. The organization grew out of a seminar that Lee organized and Shiba presented at the Massachusetts Institute of Technology. Lee and Shiba believed that the best of Japanese management had real lessons to offer American companies. Shiba coauthored a book that describes the key philosophies and tools of TQM.[2] But Shiba and Lee also believed that real growth and improvement would occur not from obedience to the exhortations of some "experts" but when managers of many organizations got together to learn—especially to learn from each others' experiences.

Wood became involved with the Center soon after its launch. All three of us have been excited by the progress that some U.S. organizations—both CQM members and others—have made with TQM and similar ideas.

But two facts bothered us. First, more organizations seemed to be failing to progress with the new ideas than were achieving dramatic results. And second, writings on TQM and other new approaches to management were mostly exhortations and assertions supported by handfuls of anecdotes. There was little credible research on what was really happening in organizations and little sustained analysis of a kind that would help a thoughtful manager understand what to do day-to-day in the struggle to change.

To fill this gap, in 1993 we began the study that led to this book. We chose seven sectors of U.S. society where people were passionately working to improve organizations through methods that resembled Total Quality Management. The sectors were manufacturing, education, health care, for-profit service organizations, the military, other government agencies, and community groups.

In each sector, we selected a small number of organizations that seemed like they might be successes. We gathered printed materials and other data, conducted phone interviews, then visited a few organizations in each sector.

Some successful organizations we studied are listed in the table on page vii. In five of the sectors, we found organizations that had without doubt achieved dramatic improvement. In each of these sectors, we studied not only these successful organizations but at least one less successful organization.

Not all of the successful organizations called their efforts "Total Quality Management." And indeed, successful companies that

Successful Organizations Included in the Study

Sector	Organization
Manufacturing	Teradyne Inc.[a]
	Hewlett-Packard Medical Products Group[a]
	Eastman Chemical Co.[a]
Education	Kenmore-Town of Tonawanda Public Schools[a]
Health Care	InterMountain Health Care Services[a]
	Meriter Hospital
The Military	U.S.S. *Kinkaid*[a]
	U.S.S. *McKee*
For-Profit Services	Ritz-Carlton Hotels[b]
	Synetics Inc.
General Government	Ogden, Utah, Internal Revenue Service Center[c]
	Madison, Wisconsin, Police Department[c]

[a] Provided evidence of substantially improved performance for all stakeholder groups at the time of our initial data gathering.

[b] Provided evidence of superior performance for all stakeholders examined; but there was evidence that performance had also been superior prior to management changes, so impact of changes was harder to determine.

[c] Did not provide evidence of improvement as dramatic as the iimprovements in other sectors.

advocated Total Quality never limited themselves to techniques identified with TQM. They were integrators. Organizations that slavishly set out to "install TQM" went nowhere.

Lee's original vision statement for CQM had proposed that it incorporate not just Total Quality but also comprehensive systems science. The participating companies had decided to focus principally on TQM at first because they believed they needed to concentrate initially on the most important new ideas. But by the time we were a year or so into our study, we knew that it was time to recognize that the most successful managers design their own management systems, using TQM techniques and others as well.

The reports on management developments that appeared in leading business magazines during this period were useless. In fact, they were downright destructive to managers who were influenced by them. By 1995, for example, the media was reporting that TQM was "dead" while practitioners were telling us they were just learning how to create real value with it. The media had previously declared strategic planning "dead," and a year or two later they declared it "re-born." But for the successful managers we met, strategic planning was an important tool that they always used as they needed it.

In 1995, the Center for Quality Management made a small but significant change in its TQM-oriented name. It became the Center for Quality *of* Management—an organization dedicated to helping managers learn first-rate methods of all kinds and learn from each other the arts and sciences of creating management systems.

This book is written in the same spirit. It begins with two theories and five principles that many managers have found useful in efforts to create comprehensive real-world management systems for their organizations. The research strongly supported the idea that each is central to any effort to drive a management system with the scientific method.

We then tell how leaders have developed integrated management systems for an uncommonly diverse group of organizations. (Chapters 2 through 7 examine six of the seven sectors we studied. Though we found remarkable work going on in some community groups, we didn't find integrated management systems with the lessons that we thought might be drawn from the other sectors.)

We believe that even the best of today's managers are far from gaining all the benefits that integrated management systems can provide. For example, none of the organizations described in Chapters 2 through 7—and very few anywhere in the world—fully integrate the insights of Total Quality Management with the systems concepts of Russell Ackoff (see Appendix A).

Yet, there's a great deal to be gained from studying the best of today's practice. Looking at six radically different kinds of organizations demonstrates something important about the differences among management systems. But we think the stories are more important for another purpose: They carry out on the largest possible scale the basic mandate that the Center for Quality of Management has now accepted. They teach diverse techniques *and* make it possible for people in one sector to learn from those in others.

We've found that successful management offers important lessons to all kinds of managers, and that each sector offers remarkable lessons to managers outside it. Many of the best managers in nonprofit organizations have long looked to for-profit companies for ideas. We found that remarkable educators could teach for-profit managers terrific lessons about how to manage the diverse, seemingly competing purposes of people within organizations. Health care demonstrates how to deal with complexity. The military suggests what to do when you manage a service for which you can't find anyone to call "the customer."

Moreover, when managers of each kind of organization learn the basic lessons that one or two integrated management systems in each sector can teach, dialogue will help much more learning take place among the sectors in the future.

After we've looked at the widely applicable lessons of different sectors, Chapter 8 describes a process of evolving a system—a process we think can work in a wide variety of situations. We've abstracted it from the experiences of the companies in the rest of the book.

We wanted to call the process described in Chapter 8, "designing an integrated management system." But before we describe it as "designing" a system, we have to offer one caveat: In the real world, people who design things have to deal with a messy process. In the past, many authors who have written about planning and design of organizations seem to have forgotten that. They've prescribed nice rational rules through which a good strategic plan or organizational structure would emerge.

If anyone is looking for that kind of design process here, he or she will be disappointed. People who design things have always known that such neat rational processes aren't how design works. Whether you're designing an electric generator, creating new software, writing a book, or leading the process that will give birth to a new management system for your organization, the final product never looks like the lovely picture you drew in your mind when you started. Analysts of engineering processes or of the process of writing have frequently recognized this. (See Nam P. Suh's *The Principles of Design* for a wise analysis of the engineering process[3] or Kenneth Atchity's *A Writer's Time* for an intelligent discussion of how good writers work.[4]) Chapter 8 makes an effort to describe a process for developing a management system that will work in the real world— to provide managers with the kind of help that Suh has given to engineers and Atchity has given to writers. We believe that real managers will find it helpful.

Finally, Chapter 9 suggests where the profession of management has to go in the future—how it can make a difference for all kinds of people and how we have to advance into the future. And four appendices present ideas and ways of thinking that help managers in creating integrated management systems.

Some readers unfamiliar with methodologies from Total Quality Management or systems thinking may find some discussions in this book are too compressed to allow them to act on the insights presented. The appendices will help with systems theory (Appendix A), as well as providing important ideas about management for breakthrough (Appendix B), collective action (Appendix C), and the management of conversation (Appendix D). For a comprehensive explanation of the ideas and techniques of Total Quality Management, we recommend Shoji Shiba and David Walden's text, *Four Practical Revolutions in Management* (Productivity Press).

Integrated management systems mean not just more sales and profits for companies, but better lives for people. We want to suggest that it's possible for managers to think of management like true applied scientists. The goal is to use careful analysis, social science, and collegial discussion in the way that doctors use biology, chemistry and the great networks of health care practitioners—or as engineers use physics and webs of associates each with different expertise. If managers learn to do that, we can make every kind of organization work better.

Acknowledgments

In the course of a six-year project, you accumulate a stunning number of debts to an enormous variety of helpful people. First of all we have to thank David Walden. It would be impossible to name all the paragraphs that originally came from his hand or his mouth in one form or another. Dave is responsible for compiling Appendix B and Appendix D, and his contributions to the preface and Chapter 1 are inestimable.

Our debt to Chris Bergonzi doesn't go back as far, but in the project's last year he performed outstanding writing and editorial services, without which it's hard to imagine the book could have been completed well.

The whole Center for Quality of Management staff supported the project from the beginning. Gary Burchill was a key source of many crucial ideas. Toby Woll, who was executive director for much of the research and writing period, contributed innumerable good arguments as well as good humor. Ted Walls helped on much of the initial research and planning of chapters. Eric Bergemann and Kevin Young went well beyond the call of duty in taking care of our technology needs; in particular, Eric personally supported Tom Lee's computer needs, and without his help, writing the book would have been nearly impossible. In the corporate world, there are hardly any CQM member companies from whom we have not learned something significant. But special thanks are due to Ray Stata, who urged CQM to emphasize subjects important to the social model of management, and especially to Alex d'Arbeloff, Ben Holmes, and Sherwin Greenblatt for their real-life examples of learning. John Petrolini, Brad Harrington, and Fred van Deusen provided exceptionally helpful guidance. Dennis Gleason and Bill Rose's comments on a late draft were invaluable.

Outside CQM, our indebtedness is equally vast. Russell Ackoff, Jamshid Gharajedaghi, and numerous other thinkers on the subjects of systems and management took a great deal of time to educate us. Many others deserve special thanks, among them Chris Argyris, Victor Aramati, Bob Chapman, Y. S. Chang, Diane Cobb, Rafael Echeverria, Blan Godfrey, Alan Graham, Steve Graves, Warren Harkness, Tom Heller, Fred Kaufmann, Annie Post, Larry Raskin, Clotaire Rapaille, Shoichi Saba, Larry Schein, Peter Senge, John Sterman, and Myron Tribus. A special thanks goes to our editor, Jeanne Glasser. And, of course, to our spouses. Bob Putnam of Action Design first drew a figure on leadership vs. empowerment that we transformed into the figures in Chapter 1. Other helpful people are quoted in the text or cited in the footnotes. And even with that said, this list is woefully incomplete. We ask those whose names we have failed to mention to forgive us.

Much of the content of this book comes out of the general intellectual give-and-take at the Center for Quality of Management. For instance, in 1994 and 1995, co-author Tom Lee along with Dave Walden wrote the first draft of a paper that was eventually published in the *Center for Quality of Management Journal* called "Designing Integrated Management Systems" (Vol. 7, No. 1, pp. 3–18). At the same time, Tom and Dave provided one of several drafts of what became Chapter 1 of this book. Similarly, in 1995 and 1996, Tom and Dave participated in a CQM study group that created the models of conversation described in Appendix D. Simultaneous with the final revision of this book, co-author Shoji Shiba along with Dave Walden were revising their book *A New American TQM* for issue in a new edition under the title *Four Practical Revolutions in Management*. Since their book and ours (and other CQM-affiliated publications) draw on the same work and discussions within CQM, readers may note some similarities in the arguments and the examples used; in Chapters 1 and 2 and Appendices B and D, there may even be identical figures and text.

We deeply appreciate the contributions of everyone who has participated in these debates. None of them, however, should be held responsible for the errors we have undoubtedly made.

Cambridge, Massachusetts
May 1999

Contents

CHAPTER I

The Theory and Practice of Integrated Management Systems

Putting the Scientific Method to Work

One of the twentieth century's most notable characteristics was its obsession with examining and managing human organizations. To be sure, human beings have always organized into functional groups—for war, for religion, for commerce—and the art of managing them has been examined in classics such as Sun Tzu's *The Art of War* (ca. 500 B.C.) or Nicolo Machiavelli's *The Prince* (1513), which are still referenced today. But only in the past hundred years of full-throttle capitalism and runaway technology have our organizations become so bumptious, far-reaching, and unwieldy that how we manage them has become a central issue for our society and a matter of survival for the organizations themselves.

As a result, management theories and techniques have proliferated, from Frederick W. Taylor's Industrial Revolution bible *The Principles of Scientific Management* (1911) to Thomas Watson Jr.'s gray-flannel classic *A Business and Its Beliefs* (1963). Today, it seems there are more approaches to managing than ever before. Who is not at least somewhat familiar with Hammer and Champy's *Re-engineering* the Corporation, Peter Senge's five disciplines or Tom Peters's Wow Management, which have become part of the lexicon of popular management culture? Indeed, the past three decades have seen such an explosion of management ideas that it could be said we are in management's golden age.

So why is it that so many organizations have failed to adapt successfully to the demands of the modern environment? To be sure, some fail because of a lack of resources or effort. But just as often, the problem lies not with a lack of resolve but with a misunderstanding of the challenge at hand and a misapplication of the tools.

Ask any manager what he or she does and you're likely to hear a litany of the tasks he or she performs: "I oversee customer relations," "I do the annual budget," or "I develop new markets." That's because most companies' management structures revolve around functions, and most people—managers included—tend to view their jobs as equivalent to their functions. Although they may communicate and collaborate throughout the organization, few managers rise above the limited perspective of a functional organization.

The essential premise of this book is the notion that an organization can't be merely an aggregation of functions and tasks. It must be an integrated system. Managers, to succeed, must take a systemic perspective. Managers' primary jobs are to design a desirable future for the organization and to orchestrate interactions and align the power of individual purpose to create that future. They must develop a comprehensive portfolio of tools that will unite the organization's people. They must scientifically test those tools for their usefulness to their particular kind of organization. This book shows how the leaders of a few organizations have made enormous progress toward doing all this.

Two Core Theories

Two core theories drive this book. The first is the systems view and the second is the concept of integrated management.

THEORY 1: THE SYSTEMS VIEW

Let's begin with a good working definition of a system: a collection of elements that is configured, via structure and processes, to accomplish explicit or implicit purpose(s).

Two key principles follow from the systems view. They apply to all kinds of systems, from tiny electric motors to enormous corporations and governments:

1. The first principle is that the most crucial cause of success in a system may not be whether each element does "its job" but whether the elements *interact* well.
2. The second is that any single measure of success will mislead you, and you can understand and track the success of the system only by following a carefully chosen portfolio of measures.

These principles flow from some basic characteristics of all systems. Whether it is animate or inanimate, a system can have properties not possessed by any of its individual elements. And it can have an impact greater than the sum of those elements. In the context of a business, for instance, this simply means that a salesperson, a development person, a manufacturing person, a support person, and a financial person, who individually have capabilities mainly in their functional specialties, can together create, sell and deliver a product or service.

Of course a system can also be *less* than the sum of its parts. For instance, if we had ten machinists who could each design, mill, and assemble the parts of a machine, we might hope that together they could make machines at least 10 times faster. However, together they might fail to agree on the design, trip over each other trying to get their tools, and in the end take as long to build one machine together as each would take individually. At most of our workplaces, these kinds of inefficiencies are all too familiar.

The primary difficulty in creating an effective and efficient system (whether that system is a physical product or an organization composed of human beings) is that the parts affect one another in ways that are not predictably cumulative. Interactions may be counterproductive in unanticipated ways. The job of a designer or manager is to design and manage how the parts of the system will interact.

How do you do that? The first step in understanding is to look at the inputs and the outputs and try to figure out the relationships among them: "If we do this, then that happens . . . or does it? . . . suppose we do less of that? . . ."

You can easily measure some characteristics of a system at the component level. For instance, we can add up the number of days we allow the employees to take in vacation time to estimate the total number of temporary replacement hours we anticipate. But, other characteristics of a system are harder to observe because they are a function of interactions among components.[1]

For instance, the product developer may be able to create two new products a year and the support person may be able to release three while providing ongoing support to 20 customers. The salesperson may be able to make 15 sales per year. But, the number of new customers the system can deliver in a year is a function not of any single individual, but of the interactions among them. It is difficult to estimate. Even more difficult to gauge is the degree of customer satisfaction all these people, working more or less together, will engender.

So, there is quite a bit to take into account when designing a system in which the elements will interact effectively. Purpose and the functions necessary to support that purpose are the most obvious. Then, you'll think of how the system will be structured and what processes will be put in place to carry out the necessary functions. You have to consider how each choice will affect interactions.

You also need to develop a portfolio of ways to *measure, monitor,* and *adjust* the system. Thinking about what to measure often leads to a better understanding of what the system's purpose, structure, and processes should be.

General Electric (GE), for example, first attempted comprehensive measurement in the early 1970s. When CEO Fred Borch introduced strategic planning as a key management function, managers soon realized that the real challenge was going to be deciding what to measure and how to measure it to create a plan. In an attempt to measure its market opportunities in light of its competitive advantages, GE invented a matrix with axes labeled "Industry Attractiveness" and

"Business Strength." Unfortunately, the number of variables that had to be considered was very large, and there was no simple best method for measuring them. After almost a year and a half of study, a GE vice president named R. W. Lewis came up with eight key areas with which to measure GE's strength and performance.[2] Still problems existed, such as the difficulty of systematically measuring and balancing long- and short-term goals. GE's system is still being perfected today, nearly 30 years later, but much of the work it began in the 1970s is reflected in "balanced scorecard" approaches to comprehensive measurement used by several of the organizations you will read about later in this book.

THEORY 2: INTEGRATED MANAGEMENT

Systems aren't perfected by following a recipe. They are perfected through a constant process of iterative experimentation, measurement, and adaptation that we call *integrated management*. In this book, we argue that the process can be fundamentally scientific. We provide real-world examples and guiding principles that show how scientifically-based processes of integrated management can work.

One of the greatest causes of lost opportunity in business is the tendency of managers, academics, consultants, and everyday culture to treat management methods as if they were mutually exclusive. Usually, good management methods shouldn't have to compete with each other. But business consultants, perhaps for marketing reasons, seek to differentiate their methods from others rather than integrate them. Business schools are organized into relatively isolated departments that specialize in particular functions. Business managers often replace methods of their predecessors to make their own imprints. Business journalists delight in uncovering the "next big thing," which of course discounts and supplants the last big thing.

This is not the way to help organizations succeed. A top manager will fail if he or she uses one method of managing interactions one month and abandons it for another method the next month. The world is complex and its problems are the result of integrated and interdependent causes. It seems intuitively unlikely that solutions would be any less so.[3] When it comes to designing a management system, there is no single correct, all-encompassing management method. You can be sure that any method touted to be a shortcut, a turnkey package, or a panacea will be none of those things. What it will be is a fad.

But our research showed that successful approaches to management had in common something important and extraordinarily powerful. At The Center of Quality of Management, we believe that management is an applied science and should be approached as such. As with any science, the goal in management is achieving increased predictability—to know we will consistently deliver what stakeholders want. The only way to do that is by applying the scientific method.

Scholars have reached no consensus on how to define the scientific method, but a definition from the *American Heritage Dictionary of the English Language* summarizes what the successful organizations we examined possessed and less successful organizations usually lacked:

> principles and empirical processes . . . generally involving the observation of phenomena, the formulation of a hypothesis concerning the phenomena, experimentation to determine the truth or falseness of the hypothesis, and a conclusion that validates or modifies the hypothesis.

Each of the successful management systems we studied shared one striking component: Each successful organization had developed its own particular way of implementing the scientific method. Each had its own integrated collection of techniques that the organization's people consistently used to gather data on the questions that were crucial to its success, to advance theories about the data, to test the theories, and finally to document and share the results. What was shown to be valid, in whole or in part, could be integrated into an accepted body of knowledge. Beliefs that were disproven could be discarded. The processes were imperfect but nonetheless powerful.

Almost every successful tool the organizations used looked simple. But the integrated systems, capable of evaluating hundreds of competing ideas flying around the organizations, were sophisticated in ways that hardly anyone has understood.

The organizations we studied showed how real organizations can be the laboratories in which management thinking is constantly being tested. Much as each successful discipline within the sciences creates its own methods and applies them repeatedly against its particular problems, so these organizations have created their own sets of tools they use over and over to address the unique types of problems their work calls on them to solve. Moreover, the best managers draw on any and all proven management technologies—from inside and outside their organizations—to tailor customized combinations of tactics to their individual situations.

The long history of Hewlett-Packard provides one comprehensive example. HP has been designing an integrated management system ever since its founders first articulated "The HP Way."[4] Over time, the company has woven many different quality improvement and customer focus methods into its system, eventually creating the HP Quality Maturity System to provide a framework for integrating them. Integrated elements of HP's management system have included:

- *Hoshin kanri*, a planning system borrowed from the Japanese that integrates strategic initiatives with day-to-day operations by focusing each part of the organization on a few key goals each year and the specific means chosen for accomplishing them.
- A process management system based on the best practices of the recognized best project leaders in the company.
- A 10-Step Planning Method that has been a standard throughout the company.
- Elihu Goldratt's Theory of Constraints, which focuses process analysis on key bottlenecks.
- Peter Senge's ideas on systems thinking.[5]
- Up-to-date ideas on teamwork.
- Traditional statistical quality control.

We won't explain all these ideas in detail here; we will provide details of the specific techniques utilized by each organization examined in Chapters 2 through 7. The main point here is simply to give a sense of the kind of elements that go into a mature integrated management system.

Effective integrated management systems promote creativity. If they become too complex, they can impede it. In some parts of Hewlett-Packard that has happened, and it has caused HP Chief Executive Lewis Platt to re-emphasize that most of these well-developed methods are supposed to be optional for the business units. But that's part of designing an integrated management system, too. Some elements of a management system have to be dropped or de-emphasized because they're no longer useful. The point is that at the best-managed firms old ways aren't dropped just because the Next Big Thing has replaced them; they're dropped because dropping them will make the overall management system work better.

HP has had its troubles in the past few years, but we'll bet that its commitment to constantly evolving better systems will pay off in the long run. In Chapter 2, we will describe in detail some Hewlett-Packard initiatives, how they've worked together (in a part of the organization that has recently been spun off), and some of the problems that have developed when ideas haven't been well integrated.

Five Key Practices

To effectively carry out the process of iterative experimentation, measurement, and adaptation that nurtures an effective integrated management system, managers we examine in Chapters 2 through 6 follow five key practices:

1. *Seek continuous improvement throughout the organization.* Adopt a common language and a set of methods and standards for collecting data and for measuring and evaluating improvement.

2. *Pursue and integrate useful information from outside the organization.* Gather and use profound knowledge of needs, best practices, and technologies from customers, the marketplace, and every corner of the environment.

3. *Cultivate and utilize ideas, knowledge, and commitment from everyone inside the organization.* Learn the concerns of the people in the system, work with them to design a desirable future, and find ways to achieve it.

4. *Create infrastructure that supports the organization's vision.* Develop subsystems, structures, and processes that reflect the organization's desired way of doing business and establish its culture.
5. *Join your peers in mutual learning and societal networking.* Connect with a web of other organizations to share information and insights.

The remainder of this chapter examines what these practices mean for managers. Chapter 8 describes the process through which leaders of companies without effective integrated management systems can bring them into existence.

PRACTICE 1: SEEK CONTINUOUS IMPROVEMENT THROUGHOUT THE ORGANIZATION

Adopt a common language and a set of methods and standards for collecting data and for measuring and evaluating improvement.

This practice is simply the application of the scientific method in designing and changing an organization's management system. Try something, digest what this tells you about how the world works, and then try it again to confirm whether or not your presumption was right. Or start with a presumption and test it out.

Using a common language is an integrating strategy that helps researchers in any scientific field see the same things. As we'll see in Chapters 2 through 6, a common language of improvement in an organization helps that organization to get better in the same way that a common scientific language helps doctors treat the sick or physicists analyze the structure of matter. A common language is necessary for a group to pursue the scientific method.

It's true that uncritical use of the scientific method can lead to many suboptimal or incorrect explanations. For instance, a young manager might learn in a specific instance that by better utilizing some fixed resources, a lower cost-per-unit-produced will be possible. As a result, he or she may embark on widespread application of a theory of maximum utilization of all resources. (In fact, this is the theory behind traditional cost accounting.) But this will almost certainly lead the young manager astray at some point, because maximum utilization of all resources is frequently incompatible with overall maximum throughput of a system.[6]

But this kind of problem becomes serious not because a manager is putting too much emphasis on the scientific method but because he or she has adopted some supposedly scientific conclusion as dogma and ceased to test it. When used with the modicum of skill that training programs in the organizations we examine have created, the best approach to building a system to address a real-life situation—the most pragmatic approach—is the scientific method. The scientific method tests theory with experimentation and experiments to get insights about possible new or improved theories. In general, the scientific method seeks to measure and understand cause and effect, including complex cause and effect with many elements interacting.

Managers need to experiment and find out what kind of scientific methods actually work in their situations. When a number of executives visited NEC's Integrated-Circuit and Micro-computer Systems Division in 1992, President Kyoshi Uchimaru described to the visitors the evolution of its product development process through trial and error over a seven-year period. The process had won Japan's Deming Prize for quality. One CEO asked Uchimaru how other companies could copy his methods. Uchimaru's answer was sobering: "I don't think you can adopt our successful methods. I believe you must do your own step-by-step trial-and-error improvement effort over several years until you have developed the system that is appropriate to your business situation and that has become part of your company culture."[7] Our research supported this: Different organizations practiced quite different versions of the scientific method.

Yet almost all improvement processes have a good deal in common. The first step in continuous improvement is *process discovery*: finding out and explicitly noting what is currently happening. We all follow relatively stable processes (patterns of work and behavior) even though we may not have explicitly designed them. The next step is to determine, explicitly and quantitatively, the *desired outcome* of the process and whether the results are within the range of desired outcomes. Amazingly, for most businesses, there is no explicit or implicit specification for most processes. The simple act of process discovery often provides a substantial improvement because we can see inefficiencies or gaps in what we are doing and fix them.[8]

Once you have discovered what the process *is*, the next step is to determine whether or not the results of that process are *predictable* and/or delivering *good performance* ("within spec"). The two do not always go hand in hand.[9] A predictable process may not be performing as well as we would like it to, whereas another process, though unpredictable, may always produce results that are in a specified acceptable range. Each situation may require a different sort of intervention.

The first step in any intervention is, obviously enough, to establish what must be done first. Attempting to work on many things at the same time results in an uncontrolled experiment. A team must first focus on the most important problems, and data must be collected to establish a problem's root cause. A hypothetical solution is formulated and tested in a trial run. More data are collected to see whether the trial solution worked. If it has, the solution is standardized and the next priority is established and addressed.

The plan-do-check-act (PDCA) improvement cycle (Figure 1.1) formally summarizes this process. As you will see, some form of this

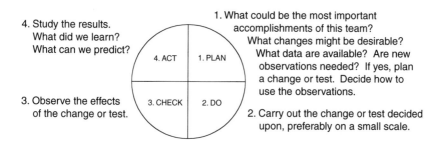

4. Study the results.
   What did we learn?
   What can we predict?

3. Observe the effects
   of the change or test.

1. What could be the most important
   accomplishments of this team?
   What changes might be desirable?
   What data are available? Are new
   observations needed? If yes, plan
   a change or test. Decide how to
   use the observations.

2. Carry out the change or test decided
   upon, preferably on a small scale.

5. Repeat Step 1, with knowledge accumulated.
6. Repeat Step 2, and onward.

Figure 1.1   The Shewhart-Deming Plan-Do-Check-Act Cycle Summarizes the Scientific Process of Improvement

cycle is used in every successful integrated management system we describe in this book.[10] Many people assume continuous improvement applies only to incremental, *reactive* improvements to existing processes. However, the PDCA process applies equally well to *proactive* improvements. In the following chapters, we offer at least two examples. In Chapter 2, we discuss how Teradyne introduced a proactive component to create a nine-step PDCA cycle; in Chapter 3, we show how Synetics employs a portfolio of processes to bring quality to innovation.[11] The history of PDCA as a formal method of improvement stretches back at least to the 1930s, when the statistician Walter A. Shewhart of AT&T introduced a similar technique. W. Edwards Deming helped popularize it, first in Japan and then later in the United States.[12]

It's important to remember that the scientific method and PDCA are not necessarily about finding the "truth." Rather, they are about finding the best explanation that is possible today and replacing it with a better explanation whenever one can be found. The scientific method also is always on the lookout for evidence disconfirming the current theory.

In the following chapters, each of the organizations we offer as an example of an integrated management system has founded that system on the fundamental ethic of continuous improvement. The practice of continuous improvement—which can only be carried out through the consistent application of the scientific method—is the essential characteristic of all learning organizations.

You will further note that these organizations all, to some degree, have adopted the methods of Total Quality Management (TQM). There's good reason for that. First introduced in Japan as an outgrowth of the methods taught by W. Edwards Deming, TQM is a philosophy that encompasses the general practices of integrated management. A focus on quality is not only absolutely predicated on continuous improvement, but it also incorporates each of the other four practices listed below, which are corollaries of continuous improvement. Although it is perfectly possible to build an integrated management system without an emphasis on TQM, we have found that many organizations are drawn to it as an obvious and helpful framework for their efforts.

Common Language Holds Systems Together

Common language was a crucial part of the integrated management systems we observed. In each organization that could be called a success, common language tied purposes, structures, and processes together. Common language is essential because people need ways to talk to each other about problems.

Each of the successful organizations we studied adopted some standard techniques of improvement that they taught to most of their members. Details of the particular methods often seemed illogical to outsiders. Some organizations insisted on use of a certain format for particular reports or required the use of specific words with a meaning that wasn't quite what those words meant in ordinary English.

These shared methods had tremendous power even where they weren't completely logical. Indeed, for an outsider to suggest that a company shouldn't require a particular form for a particular purpose is like a Chinese or Japanese telling Americans that the English language should use less complicated verbs. (The conjugation of the verb "to be" in English— "I am," "You are," "he is," and so on—is much more complex than the verb in Chinese, which uses the equivalent of "I am," "you am," "he am," and so on.) One of the greatest sins that managers and consultants commit against social systems is to introduce new language unnecessarily without regard for the power of an organization's existing language.

It's not principally the logic of a language that makes it useful; it's the commonality. Language ties a society together. And common methods of improvement tied together the successful organizations we studied, enabling them to function like healthy societies.

PRACTICE 2: PURSUE AND INTEGRATE USEFUL INFORMATION FROM OUTSIDE THE ORGANIZATION

Gather and use profound knowledge of needs, best practices, and technologies from customers, the marketplace, and every corner of the environment.

"Focus on the customer." Today this is an article of faith, yet not too long ago, many if not most companies thought they knew best what their customers needed. Even today, some people in product development departments erroneously believe "educating" customers about what they need is more important than listening to them. However, the best companies work hard to focus outside their organizations for input on what they should be doing and how they might be doing it. There are several reasons for this:

1. To paraphrase Peter Drucker, the purpose of business is to get and keep a customer. Without a customer—someone or some entity to serve—an organization has no reason to exist.
2. In these days of rapid change, a company has to constantly look to existing and potential customers so as not to miss signals of a change in the market.
3. Although it is true that customers often don't know what they need (or have a hard time articulating it), a company is inevitably better off learning what current and potential customers have to say. This invariably imparts greater insight than the company likely will have itself. In his book *Sources of Innovation*, Eric von Hippel reports that in 83 percent of the innovations studied in his extensive research, someone outside the company (e.g., a customer or user) created the innovative idea.[13]
4. Hearing from and digesting what the market has to say not only brings in this very valuable external data, it also provides an enormous external energy and aligning force for the company.
5. External focus is not only useful for learning what products and services a company should offer. It is also useful for learning the best methods for the company to use. *Benchmarking*,

around which Xerox built its mobilization infrastructure in the late 1980s, consists of determining the level of performance that is possible from the most masterful practitioners and finding out how they do it. Finding out what others can do provides motivation for change in the company and minimizes discovery effort and counterproductive missteps.

We will see examples of all of these uses of external focus in Chapters 2, 3, and 4 of the book.

PRACTICE 3: CULTIVATE AND UTILIZE IDEAS, KNOWLEDGE, AND COMMITMENT FROM EVERYONE INSIDE THE ORGANIZATION

Learn the concerns of the people in the system, work with them to design a desirable future, and find ways to achieve it.

This practice is the logical complement to Practice 2. Taking an integrated approach to management requires that an organization be open to information and best practices from *all* sources, both external *and internal.*

With today's complexity of business and speed of change, managers are required to orchestrate a vast array of complex interactions. They can't hope to know everything they need to know. The knowledge and skill necessary to take appropriate actions—what Polyani called *tacit knowledge*—is spread throughout the company.[14] To survive, an organization must develop its capacity for rapid adjustment through *collective* action. And that requires the intelligent, engaged participation of individuals throughout the organization, often working in dynamic arrangements across functional or divisional boundaries. This even extends beyond the boundaries of the organization, to suppliers, customers, and other stakeholders.[15]

Managers need not only the collective genius of all the individuals in the organization, but their active cooperation as well. Without cooperation, anyone in the organization can deny it the benefit of his or her knowledge and skill for whatever reason or particular animus that person may have. Some may even resort to what has been called *malicious compliance*: "I know this won't work, but since you didn't ask me, I'll just go along and let you find out for yourself why it's a big mistake."

To elicit the intelligent, engaged participation of all employees, organizations need methods that discover individual concerns and link them to the goals of the organization. In the following chapters, we give examples of integrated management systems that do just that. In Chapter 2, for instance, we'll see how Teradyne focused on organization-wide involvement in the PDCA process from the beginning of its change effort. Another approach is to "force" interaction among individuals and groups by requiring many members of the organization to perform dual, cross-functional assignments. A good example of this occurs at Cisco Systems, one of the highest-performing U.S. companies and a company that is very focused on quality and process. Cisco has given managers in its development organization two jobs: each is responsible for both a functional organization and a specific project. Thus, all share a common interest in giving projects the dedicated resources they need while appropriately utilizing the functional resources. Together, they barter and plan for the staffing of the specific projects so that the work will actually get done.

The progressive integration of these kinds of methods—at Cisco and other companies that employ them—creates what has been called a *social model* management system.[16] The social model is a way of thinking that views an organization as a society of individuals, each with individual purposes, each of whom has the ability to think and learn. Because they depend on one another for mutual adaptation, there should be a great deal of interaction among them. The job of top management is to manage the interactions to create a learning organization: to design a desirable future and to find ways to achieve it by aligning the purposes of individuals with those of the overall society. The social model provides the basis for a flexible, rapid learning system.

The social model assumes the possibility of a level of collective action potent enough to offset problems caused by a multiplicity of purposes. In that regard, it stands in contrast to its historical precedents.

Three Models of Management

Three basic ways of thinking have dominated management thought in the twentieth century.

1. **The mechanical model,** common from the 1800s through the 1940s, presented the organization as a machine. Senior management was supposed to prescribe all details of what the parts of the organization should do, as a designer prescribes what each part of a car should do.

2. **The biological model,** common from the 1930s until today, sees the organization as resembling a human body, with top management ("the brain") giving the parts freedom to handle details on their own—but only within their narrowly defined areas of responsibility.

3. **The social model,** common starting in the 1980s and becoming more common today, sees the organization as like a society, a loosely coupled group of people working together to achieve individual and shared purposes.

See Appendix A for details.

During the early part of this century, for instance, when manufacturing dominated the economy, human organizations were viewed as machines that functioned according to fixed cause-and-effect relationships. From this *mechanical* model arose management techniques that focused on exercising tight controls so that the relationship between an organization's inputs and outputs remained invariant. Then later, as the scope and pace of commerce increased, a new way of looking at organizations came into favor. Management began to view organizations as living organisms. To allow greater speed and flexibility, the component parts of an organization were afforded limited latitude to make their own decisions, much as the heart and lungs regulate their functions without consulting the brain. Management techniques corresponding to this *biological* model tended to emphasize monitoring and feedback rather than tight control.

Management methods consistent with the biological model (with some continuation of the mechanical model) are what most American companies have used for much of this century. Together, those models have given rise to some of our most traditional management tools and measurements: strategic planning, cost accounting and control, functional organization structures, detailed job descriptions, standard procedures, division of labor between those who do the work and those who improve the process, management by objective, and the financial measures we are all familiar with.

Today's information-dense, rapid-fire environment, however, requires a level of organizational intelligence and response that can be found only in the social model. Indeed, it seems that the integrated management approach, when practiced at a high level, inevitably leads to the creation of a social-model system. We believe the social model is the right model for dealing with management today.

PRACTICE 4: CREATE INFRASTRUCTURE THAT SUPPORTS THE ORGANIZATION'S VISION

> Develop subsystems, structures, and processes that reflect the organization's desired way of doing business and establish its culture.

When CQM was formed as a forum for mutual learning, a design team was assembled consisting of senior executives from five of its member companies, a faculty member and a staff member from MIT, and CQM founders (and two of the authors of this book) Tom Lee and Shoji Shiba. Charged with the task of defining what the CQM should be and how it should operate, the team visited many companies. During one visit, Florida Power and Light executive Frank Voehl offered an observation that became a guiding principle for CQM. He pointed out that many managers tend to try to initiate change by focusing first on the company culture. He offered this schematic to illustrate that accepted view of how change originates and cascades through an organization:

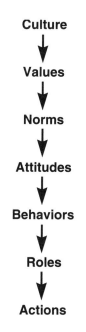

Culture
↓
Values
↓
Norms
↓
Attitudes
↓
Behaviors
↓
Roles
↓
Actions

However, Voehl went on to state that trying to change the culture directly seldom works. Any culture tends to be conservative—to maintain current practice. We have organizational cultures such as the IBM way, the HP way, and the U.S. Marines way. We also have functional cultures such as the accounting culture and the development culture; we have cultures that have developed around the operation of a certain process; and there are others.[17] Culture is simply the set of practices we have learned and follow as our behavioral defaults.[18]

Culture changes over time, but slowly and usually only because of slight variations in adherence to it. In other words, one may be trying to adhere to the culture but get it "wrong" and then teach this wrong behavior to someone else. Over time, the wrong behavior may become the standard behavior. "Culture," said E. O. Wilson, "is created by the communal mind. It is reconstructed collectively each generation in the minds of the individuals." Changing the communal mind is never quick or easy.

The effective way to change an organization's culture, suggested Voehl, is to reverse the hierarchy—to put in place structures and processes that define the roles and actions that in turn will enforce behaviors that ultimately will result in a changed culture:

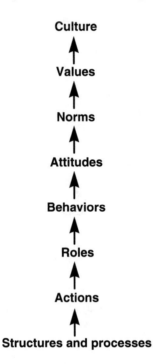

To create this kind of change, managers first must envision a new, desirable culture and articulate it to the entire organization (talking the talk). Then they must make changes to the structures and processes of everyday operation (walking the talk) that will cause people to behave in ways that will bring the desired culture about. "Employees can smell hypocrisy at one part in a million," said Frank Pipp, former vice president of development and manufacturing for Xerox, in a presentation to membership of the CQM. Management has to demonstrate complete integrity with consistency between its words and actions for a very long time before the employees will give it the benefit of the doubt and commit to the articulated culture change.

There is a good deal of interesting research and theory about how collective action in the physical world sometimes results in dramatic, abrupt change—such as the phase change of water molecules into a gas when the temperature is raised to the boiling point. But there are no useful theories or predictable formulas for such phase changes in human organizations. Yet we all know they exist anecdotally. Microsoft, for instance, after years of dismissing the potential of the Internet, turned almost on a dime to embrace it both strategically and operationally. In cases like that, leadership seems to be the catalyst that causes a mass disruption in individual behaviors that then result in accelerated change to a new culture. In other words, the leaders *strongly lead* the engaged participation of the individuals.

We are not necessarily arguing for autocratic management or charismatic management (no CEO can do it all alone), but we are saying that top-down management is required for an organization to change and improve.[19] A naïve interpretation of the evolution from the mechanical model, through the biological model, toward the social model is that as the employees (and other stakeholders) become more empowered, management is required to become more laissez-faire—heading toward the bottom right corner of Figure 1.2.

However, for a system of any size or complexity, laissez-faire management doesn't provide sufficient leadership or management of all of the necessary interactions. You are likely to get something that is much less than the sum of its parts because people are not pulling together and some people are not engaged or pulling at all.

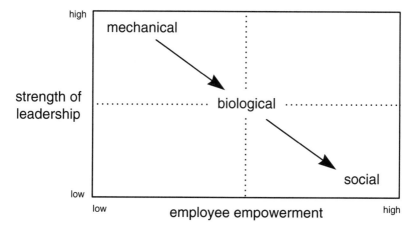

Figure 1.2 The Naïve View

The theory of human nature consistent with the mechanical model is social psychologist Douglas MacGregor's Theory X, put forth in *The Human Side of Enterprise* (1960): that people want and need to be controlled. The theory of human nature consistent with the biological model is his Theory Y: that people are *motivated* to work if certain conditions are satisfied.[20] As you might expect, the more highly evolved social model acknowledges the truth of both theories: Most people want to be led, and they want clear goals and security. But they also want to contribute and some even want to innovate. Innovation requires taking initiative and risk, and that leads to insecurity. Conversely, employees don't want security at the price of not being able to exercise their creativity and self-determinism. Given such ambivalence, maintaining a happy and effective workforce is a delicate balancing act.

To obtain the benefits of a social model, therefore, management has to learn how to design systems that function at the *top right* of Figure 1.3: very strong leadership *and* very engaged and capable participation of all concerned. What is needed is encouragement and alignment of participation without explicit enforcement of participation.

In the case studies that follow this chapter, you will observe the differing styles of some very successful leaders. There is no formula to their success, but there are some common denominators: the ability to develop and promulgate a shared vision, the ability to be receptive

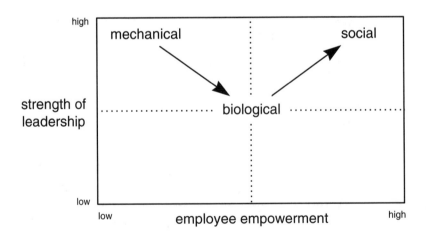

Figure 1.3 The Reality of Effective Social Model Management

to information and ideas, the ability to consistently experiment, and—most enigmatically—the ability to lead by following.

Alex d'Arbeloff's CEO initiative at Teradyne, for instance, provides an example of a leader developing and promulgating a shared vision (see Chapter 2). Intel's Andy Grove accomplished the same end by choosing to speak to society at large in his book *Only the Paranoid Survive*.[21] By discussing in open forum what he had learned about remaking Intel for the new business environment, he was able to speak to his own organization in a reflected way. Undoubtedly, many people at Intel read his words in more detail than they ever would have had he used conventional top-down communication mechanisms.

Once the vision has been disseminated, it is the institution of structures and processes to support it that actually drives the change in culture.

PRACTICE 5: JOIN YOUR PEERS IN MUTUAL LEARNING AND SOCIETAL NETWORKING

Connect to a web of other organizations to share information and insights.

In any collective effort, all transformation depends on personal learning. Personal learning is magnified by teamwork. Team learning is enhanced when it occurs within an organizationwide learning system, and organizational systems are richer when part of a societal learning system. It is no coincidence, therefore, that successful leaders consistently look outside their own organizations for role models and advice when trying to effect fundamental change. You will see examples of this throughout the book, such as Eastman Chemical's Earnie Deavenport and Teradyne's d'Arbeloff.

Large companies such as automobile manufacturers can often lead change within entire industries, encouraging competitors, partners, and suppliers to emulate and coordinate their improvement efforts.[22] Similarly, consumer or competitor pressure for higher quality or different products and services has provided motivation for many manufacturers to improve their management systems.

Also, when companies work together in professional or trade organizations and share experiences as they try to improve, more scientific experimentation can occur faster and on a larger scale. Anytime one company tries something that works, other companies can skip the learning curve and try to reproduce the good result. If they cannot, then they either illuminate the limitations of application of the improvement method or they cast doubt on the method entirely. Either way, the iterative improvement process is accelerated dramatically.

Mutual learning and societal networking are the natural extension of applying integrated management and the social model within an organization. It is simply the expansion of the relevant transactional environment beyond the organization's boundaries to include the entire societal system.

The Challenge of the Journey

This book is not intended to offer a step-by-step guide. Indeed, the notion of a step-by-step guide is antithetical to the premise of continuous improvement, which, by definition, is unscripted and unending. We hope instead to offer a map that shows the lay of the land and the roads that can be taken toward better, more effective management.

Managers have found a few key direction signs on the road to be particularly significant. They help in the implementation of the practices described above. Here are some crucial findings:

- The emergence of an integrated management system absolutely depends on the organization's leader.
- It's the leader's job to listen and study . . . Ask everybody for advice both inside and outside the organization, especially your customers.
- After listening and studying, the leader must pick key elements that will form the core of the integrated system.
- Because problems are complex, the scientific method is the only way organizations can develop reliable answers.

- Developing a structure and a standard set of tools enables whole organizations to apply the scientific method with consistency.
- Common language is far more important than you think. Leaders have to help one to develop in each organization.
- Start by doing something today, but don't try to boil the ocean yet.

Chapters 2 through 7 describe the practical application of integrated management systems, not just in manufacturers and for-profit service companies but also in some of society's most challenging, sectors, including education, health care, and the military. Most of the research for this book began with study of organizations that were attempting to implement Total Quality Management. The ones we focus on, however, went further. They each transcended a strictly TQM approach by integrating complementary methods in a scientific way, instinctively evolving integrated management systems. We hope you will glean from these case studies practical steps for initiating an integrated management system in *your* organization. Chapter 8 offers analysis of how new integrated management systems are launched.

Remember, however, that the integrated systems presented in this book are, for the most part, in relatively early stages of evolution. Many crucial management practices and methods have yet to be integrated. You will see, for instance, how Eastman Chemical Co.—with a strong integrated management system—was nevertheless thrown off stride by unforeseen market changes. Indeed, contingency planning is a concept crucial to systems thinking but, in our observation, usually nearly absent in practice. In Chapter 9, we will discuss how that—and several other elements missing from the systems in our case studies— can be added to the management repertoire.

Finally, four appendices provide detailed discussions of ideas and techniques helpful in creating an integrated management system. Appendix A provides a detailed introduction to the systems theories of Russell Ackoff including the concept of the social model of management. These probably provide the best theoretical basis for thinking about the task of an integrated management system. Appendix B presents some ideas on the management of breakthroughs. Appendix C describes the concept of "collective action"—how not only groups of people, but also groups of atoms in the atmosphere or particles in a magnetic field may suddenly change state in ways that theory cannot predict. Appendix D describes Center for Quality of Management work on conversational competence—how to carry out conversations in organizations for the consistent satisfaction of all parties. Consult these appendices when a reading of the text leads you to suspect that a deeper knowledge of these ideas can help your organization.

We are just beginning a journey toward better management. The arguments in this book are hypotheses emerging at an early stage in the development of true management science. We hope others will test and refine them. But having seen the power of integrated management systems at work, we think we're seeing the rarest of phenomena: a far-reaching opportunity for change that's firmly grounded in reality.

CHAPTER 2

Pioneers in Integrated Management Systems

What Manufacturers Learned from Crisis

Alex d'Arbeloff, chairman of Teradyne, believes that a single key step made the difference in enabling his company to put the scientific method at the center of its management system. That step was the adoption of a well-defined methodology that allowed groups of people to use the scientific method together.

"If you ask someone in a company as an individual, 'Do you use the scientific method?' the answer is, 'I'm a trained engineer. Of course I use the scientific method,'" d'Arbeloff says.

"But when people are in groups, they don't use the scientific method. They say things like, 'Hey, I knew the answer to this already.' Or they say, 'I knew the answer two years ago, but you guys weren't going to listen to me.' They're emotional."

The well-defined methodology that Teradyne adopted so that groups could solve problems together was a form of the "plan, do, check, act" improvement method, which was introduced in Chapter 1. The method's history is long. But d'Arbeloff and Teradyne—the world's largest maker of semiconductor test equipment—have developed a more profound appreciation for the method's significance than most managers who use it.

They have made it one of two pillars that form the foundation of their management system. The second pillar is summarized in two words: "Market In." It is simply a commitment to hear the voice of the customer and act on it rather than trying to sell what Teradyne thinks the customer "should" want. These two ideas drive one of the most elegant integrated management systems we have encountered.

This chapter describes how integrated management systems have emerged in two outstanding U.S. manufacturing companies, Teradyne and the Hewlett-Packard Medical Products Group (HP MPG). And a sidebar at the end of the chapter describes the emergence and challenges of an integrated management system in a radically different, but equally good, manufacturer, Eastman Chemical Co. We're presenting case studies of manufacturers first because manufacturers have borne the brunt of the radical increase in competition in the business world in the past two decades. As a result, their leaders have been forced to work hard on their management systems. The managers of American manufacturing companies have developed some of the best integrated systems in the world.

This chapter and the sidebar describe how good systems have come into existence. They illustrate how managers have sometimes used problems that emerged to nudge toward a better, more comprehensive integrated system. On the other hand, the HP MPG and Eastman Chemical stories also show how managers have sometimes allowed gaps in their integrated management systems that caused big problems. We thus try to provide clear examples of pathways that managers can use in the real world to put the systems and principles of Chapter 1 into practice, and also dangers to avoid.

All the integrated systems we will discuss have enabled large groups of people to use the scientific method together. And d'Arbeloff, for one, believes the gains available from processes that help groups use the scientific method are enormous. In fact, he recently obtained an unusual perspective on the scientific method that provides further support for this view. In 1998, d'Arbeloff was elected chairman of the Corporation that governs Massachusetts Institute of Technology. Now when he talks about private sector engineers ignoring the scientific method when they work in groups, d'Arbeloff adds: "Professors at MIT do exactly the same thing." He finds that professors can often use the scientific method in groups when they address a question in their field, because the field provides methodologies that keep the group on track. But world-class professors, like professionals in companies, tend to argue emotionally rather than scientifically when they deal in a group with other issues, such as university governance or budget.

It isn't easy, but Teradyne's experience and those of other organizations we will discuss suggest PDCA methods can drive the creation of powerful integrated management systems and allow large groups to use the scientific method effectively, producing the benefits of scientific thinking everywhere.

Teradyne

From its beginning in 1960, there was something special about Teradyne. It had a spirit that made it one of the most exciting technology companies in Massachusetts.

Teradyne's leaders never had their own offices. (Today the president, George Chamillard, works in an 8 foot by 8 foot cubicle that looks—from the outside, anyway—exactly like the cubicles in the comic strip "Dilbert.")

And no one ever accused Teradyne of being an old-fashioned bureaucracy. Teradyne knew how to recruit brilliant engineers and maintain a strong, egalitarian company spirit. It produced a continuous flow of thoughtful solutions to semiconductor industry problems. From the time when d'Arbeloff founded the firm in 1960 with fellow MIT engineer Nicholas DeWolf until 1984, Teradyne grew at a stunning 25 percent a year, taking a commanding lead in the business of helping high tech companies test their chips and devices.

THE END OF GOOD TIMES

But then something went wrong. Asian firms began to dominate the semiconductor industry. And Asian semiconductor equipment makers offered equipment in the U.S. that was far more dependable than Teradyne's. "Our equipment did not work as well as theirs," recalls Alex d'Arbeloff. "It was just plain less reliable." Sales fell 22 percent from 1984 to 1986. The company lost money in 1986, 1987, and 1988.

These problems helped to expose other, deeper weaknesses. Customers complained that Teradyne was arrogant. d'Arbeloff recalls that a friend told him customers preferred dealing with one of his American competitors because when there was a difficulty "at least he would try" to find a solution. The comment stunned d'Arbeloff. Everyone at Teradyne was trying very hard. But customers didn't see it. For all the brilliance and dedication of its engineers, the company couldn't consistently fulfill its customers needs when they wanted them fulfilled. d'Arbeloff knew there was no simple solution. "If you do everything your customers want, you're not going to succeed. You will have no coherent program," he says. But the company was far from behaving as he knew it should. "When a customer gives you a problem, there's a tendency to deny the problem," he adds. "Arrogance is wrong."

Two-and-a-half decades of teamwork among Teradyne employees hadn't prepared it for this. For all its strengths, Teradyne had no system that would enable it to solve the problems it now faced.

A THOUGHTFUL RESPONSE TO DISASTER

Some Teradyne people were already doing important work to address the problems that caused the crisis. But before that work could produce a system that would change the company, the senior leaders of the firm had to go through a period of study that involved listening to many people within the firm and outside it. They had to make a few seemingly minor structural changes. And then they had to make big process changes—changes that pushed the plan-do-check-act approach to improvement into every corner of the firm and created innumerable new ways through which the customer's voice could be heard and acted on.

George Chamillard was on the front lines. When disaster hit in the mid-1980s, he had just been placed in charge of Teradyne's manufacturing. He'd created a unit called "the Foundry" to produce all the printed circuit boards used in Teradyne products. And Foundry managers had launched Teradyne's first quality program, based on the teachings of the guru Philip Crosby. It addressed Teradyne's quality problems by demanding that Teradyne's manufacturing processes produce "zero defects."

Teradyne's executives say in retrospect that Crosby's program was "mostly exhortation." The Foundry adopted "policy" of producing defect-free products and sent people to seminars that urged them to do so. The program involved no well-defined problem-solving process, but by persuading people in the manufacturing group that much lower levels of defects were possible, the guru's people inspired them to locate many of the problems that were causing defects and eliminate them. They reduced the share of circuit boards returned to the factory for quality reasons from 1 per thousand to 0.2 per thousand.

But while this sort of effort might keep Teradyne's market position from deteriorating further, d'Arbeloff couldn't see how it would revitalize Teradyne's competitiveness and enable it to penetrate the Asian markets where more and more of the world's semiconductor chips were being manufactured. d'Arbeloff recognized that somehow Teradyne's whole system needed to be changed. By 1989, sales still had barely recovered from the declines of 1985 and 1986. The firm was only marginally profitable. Procter & Gamble chief executive Edwin Artzt, who sat on Teradyne's board of directors, had sent a top quality executive to help Teradyne think through its quality problems, and after a meeting with him Teradyne's management team had promised to reconsider its way of managing.

d'Arbeloff responded by devoting a year to a thoughtful effort to develop new knowledge and new consensus. Teradyne's integrated management system could evolve effectively over the decade of the 1990s because d'Arbeloff and the rest of Teradyne's management team responded so intelligently to the crisis. They took time to listen to each other and to network with others in society who might have solutions to their problems. For Teradyne's upper management, the fourth quarter of 1989 through the third quarter of 1990 represented a full year of wide-open thinking about change.

A SOLID FOUNDATION FOR AN INTEGRATED MANAGEMENT SYSTEM

In late 1989 and the first half of 1990, all of Teradyne's top 42 managers would read and discuss six books on quality management: W. Edwards Deming's *Out of the Crisis*, William Scherkenbach's *The Deming Route to Quality*, Kaoru Ishikawa's *What Is TQC? The Japanese Way*, Shigeru Mizuno's *Company-Wide Total Quality Control*, J. M. Juran's

Juran on Leadership for Total Quality, and Philip Crosby's *Quality Is Free.* Each would attend at least two of the leading seminars on Total Quality.

"You started realizing the complexity of what you were doing," says Chamillard, who by this time was running one of Teradyne's business units. "The problem you have—if you're running a big company—is that you've got a ship in motion. The ship is leaking, so you're bailing water. But you've got to keep the ship moving. So you're trying to keep the ship going, bail water, and change direction at the same time. The value of the seminars and the books was that you step away from that. The phone rings and you're pulled back in. But the seminar lets you pull out."

In April 1990, d'Arbeloff addressed Teradyne's annual sales meeting and said, calmly but firmly, "We've got to be better in everything that we do: the quality of our product, our engineering, manufacturing, finance, administration, marketing, applications, service, and of course, sales." He endorsed Total Quality Management as the answer. But he says now that he was still "not sure what to do."

Two of us (Shiba and Lee) had a chance to work with d'Arbeloff at this point. Teradyne was a charter member of our Center for Quality of Management, and two executives from Teradyne were members of the design team that decided how the Center should work. By spring of 1990, they had helped us develop plans that included a six-day course for senior executives, a course that imparted some techniques that had proved useful in Japan, but that also created a place where senior executives could talk about their problems and solutions with each other. Chamillard, d'Arbeloff, and other key Teradyne executives were among the first students in the course. At least two methodologies taught in the course became key elements in Teradyne's integrated management system.

Figure 2.1 shows the version of the plan-do-check-act cycle taught in the course. It is a seven-step problem-solving process that is routinely taught at our Center. A slightly modified version of this cycle became a pillar of Teradyne's transformation.

d'Arbeloff emphasizes that the PDCA process is simply a way of applying the scientific method in a consistent fashion: "Define the problem, get some data, analyze the data, propose a solution, check whether the solution works, and then apply it." But the well-defined

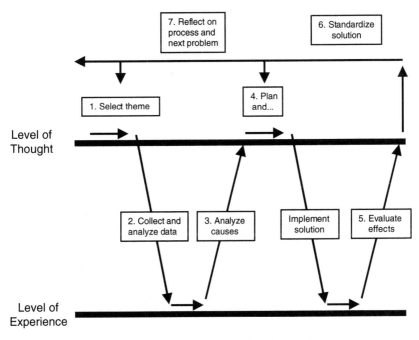

Figure 2.1 The Seven-Step Problem-Solving Process

process guides teams of people to behave in a scientific way as they work together on all kinds of problems, with each member applying his or her own skills.

The well-defined process also provides the common language through which the people of the organization can discuss ideas, data, and problem solving. Soon after the introduction of the seven-step process at Teradyne, an executive named Tom Pursch got up to make a presentation in front of d'Arbeloff. Within seconds of the start of the presentation, d'Arbeloff realized he didn't like what Pursch was saying. He wasted no time in letting Pursch know. He recalls: "I said, 'Tom, I think you have the wrong idea. This is not the way this company works.'"

Pursch, a man known for keeping his cool, responded slowly: "Alex, you're jumping to Step 4."

In the language of the seven-step problem-solving process (diagrammed in Figure 2.1), Pursch was saying that on hearing the theme of Pursch's talk, d'Arbeloff was immediately jumping to the "Plan and implement solution" step. He was making a decision without collecting and analyzing data (Step 2) or using the data to analyze causes (Step 3).

It was quiet in the room. The chief executive said nothing at first. "I thought about it," d'Arbeloff says, "and I said, 'You're right.'"

The clarity of the seven-step process made it apparent that Pursch was the one who was following the scientific method. At the next meeting of the management group, someone presented d'Arbeloff with a T-shirt. It said, "Don't jump to Step 4." "Don't jump to Step 4" became a slogan throughout much of the company.

The seven-step process made a real difference in almost every aspect of Teradyne's performance. Teradyne referred to groups using the seven-step process as Quality Improvement Teams (QITs). On the front lines of the organization, quality improvement teams (QITs) tended to address very concrete, practical problems. For example, when a plant in Nashua, New Hampshire, found its drilling operation couldn't keep pace with the overall production of circuit boards, a group of employees made the improvement of drilling operations the theme of a QIT. In the "Collect and analyze data" phase, they videotaped machine operators on the job. Then, to identify causes of the problem, they broke down the setup process into minute steps and timed each step precisely.

The team discovered that the methods used to set up drilling stations for work were inefficient. For example, some operators performed key setup steps only when the machines were not running. Better planning could save time. Moreover, operators were entering data manually that could have been captured automatically. The team reorganized setup procedures and worked with the programming department to automate data entry.

But the most dramatic impact on Teradyne came from QITs composed of managers, which focused on management issues. In 1992, for instance, a QIT consisting of the operations and administration division's top managers established a standardized methodology for developing improvement goals for the division each year and then mobilizing the organization's people in pursuit of them. As we'll show, this methodology eventually became a significant element of Teradyne's integrated management system.

The Language-Processing (LP) Method

The LP method helps people in a group communicate word data and perceptions and then group similar ideas to provide insight. It involves the following steps:

1. *Agree on a topic question.*
2. *Write down and understand the data.* All participants write one fact at a time on a self-stick note such as a Post-it, aiming to write facts at the lowest possible level of abstraction—that is, facts that are as concrete as possible. In the LP process, the Post-it notes with facts written on them are called "data labels." (Figure 2.2 shows some data labels developed for a problem-solving process in Teradyne in 1991.)
3. *Group similar data.* Participants work as a team to gather the labels into groups of no more than three, each of which represents intuitively similar ideas or information. The goal is to create new connections and new insight. If a label doesn't seem to fit into a group, it is identified as a "lone wolf."
4. *Write summary titles for each idea group.* (Figure 2.3 shows examples of groups of labels with titles.)
5. *Repeat steps 3 and 4,* creating groups of groups and titles for groups of groups. The idea behind steps 3–5 is to organize data based on the data themselves and not on a preconceived categorization.
6. *Vote on which of the groups or lone-wolf labels are most important,* show relationships among the groups, and draw conclusions.

Figure 2.4 shows portions of a completed LP diagram. The titles of the groups and the importance ranking given to groups and lone-wolf labels represent a group's scientific method conclusions. They have to be tentative, like all scientific conclusions, but they are often far more accurate and useful than what would have emerged from a conventional discussion.

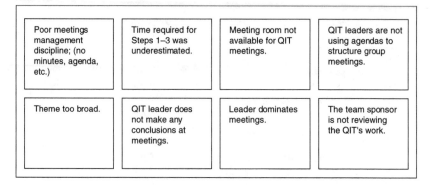

Poor meetings management discipline; (no minutes, agenda, etc.)	Time required for Steps 1–3 was underestimated.	Meeting room not available for QIT meetings.	QIT leaders are not using agendas to structure group meetings.
Theme too broad.	QIT leader does not make any conclusions at meetings.	Leader dominates meetings.	The team sponsor is not reviewing the QIT's work.

Figure 2.2 Examples of Labels Prepared by Teradyne TQM Managers for LP Diagram to Answer the Question: "What are the problems slowing QIT progress?"

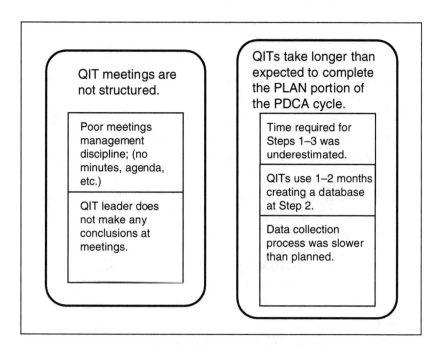

Figure 2.3 Groupings of LP Labels

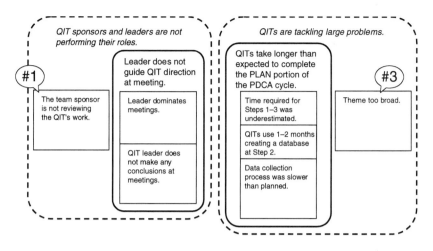

Figure 2.4 Portions of the TQM Managers' LP Diagram, "What are the problems slowing QIT progress?"

d'Arbeloff finds the power of a continuous improvement culture to be amazing. "Of all the things I've learned about management, that's probably the most exciting one," he says. "I wish I had known about it twenty years ago."

The other technique from the Center for Quality of Management that became central to Teradyne's integrated management system was a method of gathering and analyzing data that we today call the "Language Processing (LP) method." Seven-step processes in Teradyne frequently used this method in the "collect and analyze data" phase of seven-step problem-solving projects. A key strength of the method is that it allows data and ideas to be equitably considered without regard for the position in the hierarchy of the people who present them. Thus, it helps teams to think about a question in a more scientific, more consensus-building way.[1] (See box on page 35.)

A DARING SIMPLICITY

The Center for Quality of Management's six-day course is conducted not in six consecutive days but in blocks of two or three days, scheduled four weeks apart. Between the first and second blocks, participants return to their organizations to put what they've learned to work. Then they report on what they've done in subsequent meetings of the course.

d'Arbeloff recalls that students from other companies came back with lists of six to eight initiatives they were undertaking in their companies. They were trying to introduce new integrated systems for their organizations all at once. The majority of the plans succeeded (though in retrospect, in most cases, you could point to at most two or three initial initiatives that accounted for most of the early success).

d'Arbeloff described only two initiatives: Teradyne would teach the whole company to do seven-step problem solving, and it would emphasize "market-in," listening to customers rather than trying to sell them what Teradyne believed they should have.

None of the other organizations succeeded more completely than Teradyne. Ultimately, every successful company including Teradyne needed more than two initiatives to evolve a comprehensive integrated management system. But by focusing on just two to start, Teradyne made dramatic progress quickly. And the two initiatives it launched— seven-step scientific method problem-solving and market-in customer focus—were powerful. Perhaps they were uniquely powerful. They would form a foundation for systems that, over the following decade, have over and over again improved the workings of the whole company for its customers.

"In organizations, if you have to learn twenty tools, you wind up learning nothing," says d'Arbeloff. "Over a ten-year period, we have produced a lot of tools. But the most important thing was to get started with an improvement culture."

LEARNING BY TEACHING

Soon after completion of the Center for Quality of Management course, d'Arbeloff conducted a "CEO crusade" to sell his two initiatives to the rest of the organization. In six sessions held at Teradyne facilities around the world, d'Arbeloff met with some 200 key middle managers. He asked each to do homework before the sessions, and he charged each with carrying the message of the new Teradyne to the people who reported to him or her.

But in delivering a message that called for a new focus on team-work, d'Arbeloff also demonstrated concretely that he himself would act as a team member. He carefully solicited feedback from the members of his audience each time he spoke. He asked each participant in the meeting to write one weakness of his presentation on one Post-it note, and one strength on another Post-it.

Then d'Arbeloff made an LP diagram to analyze the feedback. "I thought I saw a lightbulb go on in Alex's head," says John Petrolini, a manufacturing manager who had been working on quality issues since the first Crosby programs, and who had been named one of the orga-nization's two TQM managers. On the "weaknesses" notes, managers noted that d'Arbeloff's presentation had lacked clear structure and an implementation plan, and that only a minority of the members of the audience had participated in the discussions. After he organized the feedback in an LP diagram, d'Arbeloff understood them in a new way, a way that handled data about actions as a manager more scientifically than he ever could before.

He made significant changes in his presentation based on the LP analysis of his listeners' comments. (d'Arbeloff eventually became so enamored with the LP process and with the underlying understanding of semantics on which it is based that he had all his managers read S. I. Hayakawa and Alan R. Hayakawa's *Language in Thought and Action*.)

It was the start of a real turnaround for Teradyne, a turnaround that showed positive results years before Teradyne's key customers, the U.S. semiconductor manufacturers, turned their own businesses solidly around starting in 1993.

INTEGRATING CRUCIAL NEW PROCESSES

Teradyne named two TQM managers for the organization as a whole. Top executives weren't turning the solution to their problems over to "experts," however. The quality managers were Petrolini and an up-and-coming marketing manager named Mike Bradley. Bradley had been responsible for developing and marketing of a tester that had been one of the most successful products in Teradyne's history. Now he was effectively the first head of the TQM office. But the office consisted simply of Bradley, Petrolini, and a secretary.

The idea was that Teradyne needed someone to oversee learning about quality and other improved methods of management, and thus ensure new ways were integrated into the organization. Though the office was tiny, creating it turned out to represent an important structural change. The TQM managers would schedule and sometimes teach the seminars where Teradyne's people were to learn about change. They would also keep track of progress in implementing the new techniques and sponsor TQM Days, when people who had successfully solved a problem with the seven-step technique would present their work to an audience that would include most of the company's managers. When the TQM managers and their secretary couldn't do everything themselves, they borrowed staff from managers sympathetic to the effort to introduce new practices.

Teradyne believed it needed TQM managers to guide the change, however, it didn't want them to be "in charge" of it. Rather, each of Teradyne's senior manager would be in charge of developing a new management system for his or her own part of the business. Senior managers had been meeting monthly to talk about quality since 1989; they continued to meet monthly as the Corporate Quality Council. Each business group formed its own quality council, consisting of its own senior managers meeting regularly to discuss how to listen better to customers and apply seven-step improvement processes. Each named one up-and-coming manager to serve as TQM manager.

Teradyne's senior executives wanted all the quality directors to spend a year or two in that job and learn the new scientific way of mobilizing the intelligence of the organization's people to solve problems. Then they'd move on to another job in the organization where they would continue to put that knowledge to use. (Bradley is today Teradyne's global sales manager, a job in which he has put his experience promoting seven-step improvement to work, as we'll see below. Five other rising managers have since headed the TQM office, and most have gone on to make crucial contributions as leaders elsewhere in the company.)

Journalists often portray Quality Improvement Teams as equivalent to "quality circles," teams that involve mainly the lowest-ranking people in an organization. But in keeping with Teradyne's emerging understanding that seven-step problem solving was a way of applying the scientific method in groups, Teradyne's QITs were to a considerable extent groups of managers. All Teradyne's senior leaders served on QITs. Some 200 teams were created in the first half of 1991. And when teams seemed to be getting bogged down in the second half of the year, Petrolini, Bradley, and the quality managers of Teradyne's business groups formed themselves into a QIT to figure out why. The result was development of a how-to manual for sponsors of teams, which has helped Teradyne keep QITs exceptionally active to this day.[2]

Teradyne effectively created infrastructure that supported its vision. The Center for Quality of Management believes a good infrastructure of change includes seven elements: an organizational unit to support change, a goal-setting system, promotion methods, a training and education system, methods for diffusing success stories, ways of recognizing success, and methods for diagnosing and monitoring achievements. Teradyne used all these elements in introducing Total Quality Management, and it subsequently utilized them to introduce additional elements of its integrated management system:

- The TQM managers represented the organizational unit that supported change.
- Initially the TQM managers and senior management represented the goal-setting system; later Teradyne adopted a system it called "goal deployment," to be discussed below.
- The TQM managers led training and education throughout the organization.
- Promotion was carried out in every part of the organization through posters and displays showing what could be done with the seven-step process.
- Success stories were diffused through "TQM Days" meetings that involved most of the organization's management.
- TQM Days was also the setting for recognition of good performance.

• Teradyne regularly brought in outsiders (including the authors) for evaluation of its system as well as conducting diagnosis by its president, to be discussed below.

One striking difference between successful and unsuccessful organizations we visited was that every successful one had all—or almost all—the seven elements of infrastructure. Organizations that found change to be difficult almost always lacked several of these elements of infrastructure.

The result of this change was dramatically improved reliability in Teradyne's products and increased satisfaction among its customers. By the second half of 1991, the results were visible on the bottom line. Figure 2.5 shows Teradyne's quarterly profits before and after d'Arbeloff's crusade.

CREATING A COMPREHENSIVE SYSTEM

Teradyne's essentially simple approach to Total Quality Management drove its turnaround. But the Quality Improvement Teams and

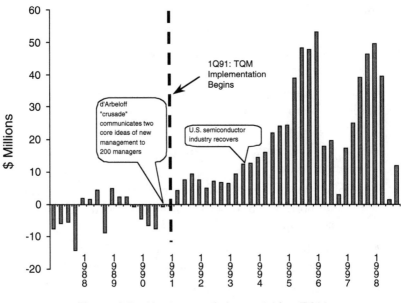

Figure 2.5 Net Income: Before and After TQM

improved communication with customers that grew in 1991–1992 weren't designed to be a complete management system. They were a foundation for change. Teradyne could use its increasingly scientific and customer-focused way of thinking to guide it toward new systems and ways of doing things that built on the core.

From 1990 through 1992, for instance, listening to the market had been a mantra: senior executives constantly talked about the importance of thinking in terms of "market-in" rather than "product-out," of listening rather than just pushing products on customers. They themselves spent far more time with customers than they had in the past. But there was no overall program to gather the market's needs systematically.

Managers in several parts of the organization felt they needed a consistent system, however. The QIT that consisted of the Operations and Administration Division's top managers in 1992 provided the standardized methodology that would manage the social system to achieve the most needed changes each year. Each year, each major unit in the division would first carry out formal visits to customers, then develop goals for the coming year based largely on the needs the customers expressed, and then systematically pursue those goals in the coming year. For each goal, each business unit lists, based on conversations with customers, the same five elements:

1. Desired outcome
2. Focused means
3. Metric
4. Target value
5. Deadline

The "focused means" are typically one or more teams that will use the seven-step process to solve the problems blocking the achievement of the desired outcome. They called the system *goal deployment*. By 1995, Teradyne was using the system companywide.

Another new approach that built on the core was the customer teams system. In 1992, Mike Bradley left the post of TQM manager and was named the national sales manager for Teradyne's core business.

The sales group was already creating customer teams. But Bradley's experience overseeing the management conversion of the whole company proved invaluable in helping the teams transform what Teradyne did for its customers.

The problem that the customer teams system addressed was so common it was hardly considered a problem in the technology industry. At least three different groups of people were serving each Teradyne customer. Account managers sold the goods. But they can hardly be said to have "managed" their accounts. Teradyne's semiconductor testing machines cost from $250,000 to $2 million each, but couldn't do anything for customers till a program was written specifically for each one. A corps of application engineers helps customers to perform that task, and a third group, the service engineers, visited customers to maintain machines and fix them when they broke.

It wasn't that the account managers, application engineers, and service engineers didn't talk to each other. But there was a problem in knowing what the three groups should talk together *about*. The account managers tended to focus on the new accounts they were trying to land. But while they were doing so, they would neglect some of the existing accounts, and account managers for the competition would capture those. Application and service engineers watched all this with no clear sense that they could do anything about it. Some of the work that customer teams would have to do was obvious: keep the focus on each existing customer, and ensure that no one was forgotten. Beyond that, it wasn't clear exactly what the customer teams should do.

Bradley's experience proved useful. "You had to ask, 'What improvement opportunities are there?'" he says. "Service engineers were reactive. They would fix systems that would fail. The metrics of success were how quickly you get it back up (mean time to repair) and inputs to reducing the mean time to failure."

As account managers, applications engineers, and service engineers employed the methodologies of proactive improvement built around the seven-step process, they realized that they could organize dramatic productivity improvements—in essence, work together to make sure the customer needed fewer of Teradyne's machines. Instead of an account manager selling machines, a team was asking, "What is the lowest-cost way for this customer's needs to be met?" The teams quickly produced tens of millions of dollars in capital savings for Teradyne customers. "That's a loss in sales to us, but it strengthens our value added," says Bradley. It also made a dramatic contribution to reducing the number of accounts lost and a substantial increase in market share. At the beginning of the 1990s, Teradyne's share of the semiconductor test equipment marketplace was in the low 20s; today, it is estimated at 28 percent.

The customer teams made use of another extension of Teradyne's scientific method. The seven-step process illustrated in Figure 2.1 is a problem-solving methodology. Team members select a problem to address and discover the solution. It works best for improving an existing process. For problems that require creation of a largely new process, Teradyne developed the nine-step process described in Table 2.1.

New product engineering proved to be an especially complex part of the company where problems were particularly difficult to solve with either seven-step or nine-step problem-solving processes. The

Table 2.1   The Nine-Step Method for Design of New Processes

1. Describe the project
2. Explore
    a. Explore the essence of the project
    b. Examine constraints
3. Define objectives
    a. Determine the objectives
    b. Set up metrics
4. Determine solution
    a. Identify the alternatives
    b. Select a solution
5. Plan
    a. Develop an optimistic plan
    b. Forecast obstacles
    c. Develop contingencies
6. Develop a schedule
7. Confirm the results
8. Standardize
9. Reflect

scientific approach they inculcated in the organization helped the company decide to reach out for an additional methodology from outside. George Conner, Teradyne's corporate Total Quality manager in 1994–1995, organized an engineering council that evaluated product development methodologies. It developed consensus that the methods prescribed in Steven C. Wheelwright and Kim B. Clark's book, *Revolutionizing Product Development,* were the best available ways to improve.[3] Wheelwright and Clark provide methods through which product development teams with strong leaders can define clear objectives and shared understanding of a development project's intent, anticipate future customers' needs, and achieve introduction of products to the market on aggressive schedules. The process of revolutionizing product development is far more complex than most efforts Teradyne has undertaken, and it was not complete in 1999. But dramatic improvements in the engineering group's performance were being seen.

These are only a few of the systematic methods of improvement Teradyne eventually integrated into its management system. (See Table 2.2 for a summary of elements of the integrated management system.)

DIAGNOSIS TO UNDERSTAND WHAT'S REALLY HAPPENING

Since 1994, first d'Arbeloff and now Chamillard have practiced what Teradyne calls "presidential diagnosis." Once a year, the president visits each part of the company not (principally) to review results but to diagnose how well the unit is aligning itself with customers and pursuing a scientific method approach to solving problems.

That doesn't mean that everything in Teradyne is truly guided by the scientific method. Perhaps nothing is harder to continually think about scientifically than the messy flow of data that the managers of real organizations must handle. One of the key teachings of the Center for Quality of Management's six-day course was the importance of understanding the difference between *affective (emotional) language* and the *language of reports.* Statements such as "Engineers live in ivory towers" use affective language; a statement such as, "The product designer omitted four features that customers said they wanted" is in the language of reports. To use the scientific method, people have to find

Table 2.2 Teradyne Integrated Management Matrix

Year	Action or Method	Reason for Integration	The Systems View	Key Practices
1990	d'Arbeloff's vision statement: "Dedication to Quality."	Grabs the attention of and mobilizes the workforce.	Provides "high leadership"; imparts common purpose.	Practice 3: Seek internal engagement. Practice 5: Participate in societal networking.
1990	Management team studies quality, recommends new guiding principles.	Disseminates the vision.	Aligns purposes of individuals with those of the group.	Practice 3: Seek internal engagement. Practice 5: Participate in societal networking.
1990	CEO Crusade.	Disseminates the vision.	Aligns purposes of individuals with those of the group.	Practice 3: Seek internal engagement.
1990	Common language; Semantics; fact-based debate.	Provides basis for goal setting, measurement, and evaluation.	Optimizes interactions.	Practice 1: Seek continuous improvement. Practice 3: Seek internal engagement. Practice 4: Build supportive infrastructure. Practice 5: Participate in societal networking.
1990	Creation of Central Quality Office.	Coordinates quality efforts.	Forces cross-functional interactions; aligns purposes.	Practice 1: Seek continuous improvement. Practice 3: Seek internal engagement.

Table 2.2 (Continued)

Year	Action or Method	Reason for Integration	The Systems View	Key Practices
				Practice 4: Build supportive infrastructure.
1990	7 Elements of TQM infrastructure.[a]	Drives quality consciousness deeper into functional processes.	Facilitates process discovery; team-based mutual learning and alignment.	Practice 1: Seek continuous improvement. Practice 4: Build supportive infrastructure.
1991	QITs.	Creates team-based problem-solving mechanism.	Forces cross-functional interactions; utilizes "tacit" knowledge.	Practice 1: Seek continuous improvement. Practice 3: Seek internal engagement. Practice 4: Build supportive infrastructure.
1991	7-Step PDCA.	Standardizes an approach to problems and processes.	Provides the basis of a learning system.	Practice 1: Seek continuous improvement. Practice 4: Build supportive infrastructure.
1991	Language processing.	Provides a control for language biases in problem solving.	Optimizes interactions; utilizes "tacit" knowledge.	Practice 1: Seek continuous improvement. Practice 3: Seek internal engagement.
1991	Education and training.	Guarantees promulgation of quality ethic.	Optimizes interactions; utilizes "tacit" knowledge.	Practice 1: Seek continuous improvement.

Table 2.2 (Continued)

Year	Action or Method	Reason for Integration	The Systems View	Key Practices
				Practice 5: Participate in societal networking.
1992	9-Step PDCA.	Adds proactive component to 7 Steps.	Basis of a learning system.	Practice 1: Seek continuous improvement. Practice 4: Build supportive infrastructure.
1992	Concept engineering.[b]	Taps into tacit internal and external knowledge to drive innovation.	Forces cross-functional interactions; team-based learning.	Practice 1: Seek continuous improvement. Practice 2: Seek external information. Practice 3: Seek internal engagement.
1992	Goal deployment.	Enables a PDCA approach to strategic planning.	Aligning short-term and long-term purposes.	Practice 1: Seek continuous improvement. Practice 4: Build supportive infrastructure.
1994	Presidential diagnosis.	Closes the loop between vision and implementation.	Provides "high leadership"; aligning purposes of individuals with those of the group.	Practice 1: Seek continuous improvement. Practice 2: Seek external information. Practice 3: Seek internal engagement. Practice 4: Build supportive infrastructure.

(continued)

Table 2.2 (Continued)

Year	Action or Method	Reason for Integration	The Systems View	Key Practices
				Practice 5: Participate in societal networking.
1996	Revolutionizing product development (Wheelright & Clark).	Connects innovation to execution.	Forcing cross-functional interactions; team-based learning.	Practice 1: Seek continuous improvement.
				Practice 2: Seek external information.
				Practice 3: Seek internal engagement.
				Practice 4: Build supportive infrastructure.

ª Shoji Shiba et al., *A New American TQM*, 337–372.
ᵇ To be discussed in the Synetics section of Chapter 3.

the factual information that lies behind affective language, state it in the language of reports, and then make decisions based on the facts.[4] But the daily work of a manager makes that difficult.

Petrolini notes that he recently attended a Teradyne executive committee meeting and found that most senior executives in the company were still using affective, emotional language to discuss problems that could have been addressed in the language of reports.

d'Arbeloff suggests that may not be bad. "I think there has to be a balance between results and process," he says. "You need a balanced view. You can't work all on process with no focus on results."

In any case, the success of Teradyne's integrated management system is undeniable. The company is further ahead of its competitors in the semiconductor test field than it has ever been. Sales tripled in the 1990s, and in 1999, Chamillard noted that 90 percent of the profits the company had ever earned had been earned in the previous three years.

The semiconductor industry remains highly cyclical, and by the time you read this, Teradyne could be in trouble again. But the company's management system contains important lessons for almost anyone.

Hewlett-Packard Medical Products Group

In many ways, the experience of the Hewlett-Packard Medical Products Group resembled that of Teradyne. But HP MPG experienced difficulties that illustrate some of the key dangers and challenges of integrated management systems, especially as companies go through leadership transitions (see Table 2.3).

BUMPS ON THE ROAD

In 1990, Ben Holmes, the chief executive of the Hewlett-Packard Medical Products Group, knew he was facing a crisis. He'd seen sales grow 151 percent in seven years, from 1981 to 1988. In 1989, the Group sold $807 million worth of medical electronics, representing some 7 percent of all Hewlett-Packard sales. Growing at nearly 20 percent annually, Holmes's operation seemed to be a model of excellence.

So what was the problem? The world and the market were changing. The group now sold medical devices such as patient monitors for hospitals in highly competitive markets throughout the world, each with a different approach to hospital care. Moreover, hospitals wanted to network their computers and medical devices. New equipment had to communicate in innumerable ways. Despite the feverish work of design groups in Europe and the United States, the group's new products were late to market, and did not have all the desired features. Customers began to complain that it took too long to get answers from Hewlett-Packard and that even deliveries of older products were behind schedule. Almost every month, executives had to tell the sales force more bad news. Sales stopped growing. Unease in the HP MPG ranks was growing and beginning to turn into panic. Holmes had

Table 2.3 HP MPG Integrated Management Matrix

Year	Action or Method	Reason for Integration	The Systems View	Key Practices
1939	The HP Way.	Philosophical basis for the company emphasizing people and quality.	Provides "high leadership"; imparts common purpose.	Practice 3: Seek internal engagement.
1990	Ben Holmes's TQM research.	Attempt to initiate a formal companywide commitment to quality.	Provides "high leadership"; imparts common purpose.	Practice 1: Seek continuous improvement. Practice 3: Seek internal engagement. Practice 5: Participate in societal networking.
1991	Executive Committee becomes the Quality Steering Committee.	Disseminates vision.	Forces cross-functional interactions; aligns purposes.	Practice 1: Seek continuous improvement. Practice 3: Seek internal engagement. Practice 4: Build supportive infrastructure.
1991	Create a central office to monitor and coordinate initiatives.	Coordinates quality efforts.	Forces cross-functional interactions; aligns purposes.	Practice 1: Seek continuous improvement. Practice 3: Seek internal engagement. Practice 4: Build supportive infrastructure.

Table 2.3 (Continued)

Year	Action or Method	Reason for Integration	The Systems View	Key Practices
1991	Create quality director positions in each division.	Push quality initiatives down the hierarchy to an operational level.	Forces cross-functional interactions; aligns purposes.	Practice 1: Seek continuous improvement. Practice 3: Seek internal engagement. Practice 4: Build supportive infrastructure.
1991	Kawakita/language-processing methods.	Provides a control for language biases in problem solving.	Optimizes interactions; utilizes "tacit" knowledge.	Practice 1: Seek continuous improvement. Practice 3: Seek internal engagement.
1992	11-Step PDCA.	Standardizes an approach to problems and processes.	Provides the basis of a learning system.	Practice 1: Seek continuous improvement. Practice 4: Build supportive infrastructure.
1986, revised 1991	Hoshin management.	Enables a PDCA approach to strategic planning.	Aligning short-term and long-term purposes.	Practice 1: Seek continuous improvement. Practice 4: Build supportive infrastructure.
1991	Predictability initiatives.	Guarantees timeliness and predictability of product development.	Forces cross-functional interactions; team-based learning.	Practice 1: Seek continuous improvement. Practice 2: Seek external information. Practice 3: Seek internal engagement.

(continued)

Table 2.3 (Continued)

Year	Action or Method	Reason for Integration	The Systems View	Key Practices
1992	Phase review.	Coordinate product development efforts companywide.	Forces cross-functional interactions; aligns purposes.	Practice 1: Seek continuous improvement. Practice 2: Seek external information. Practice 3: Seek internal engagement. Practice 4: Build supportive infrastructure.
From 1989; focus at HP MPG from 1992	Quality Maturity System.	Internal, cross-functional review of all TQM goals and processes.	Forces cross-functional interactions; team-based learning.	Practice 1: Seek continuous improvement. Practice 2: Seek external information. Practice 3: Seek internal engagement.
1992	TQM hoshin.	Formalizes the adoption of TQM initiated by Holmes in 1990; closes the loop between vision and implementation.	Provides the basis of a learning system.	Practice 1: Seek continuous improvement. Practice 2: Seek external information. Practice 3: Seek internal engagement. Practice 4: Build supportive infrastructure. Practice 5: Participate in societal networking.

never been much of a rah-rah guy and he wasn't about to start now. But something had to be done.

When colleagues suggested a Total Quality Management approach, Holmes was skeptical: "Gee, here comes another secret of success," he thought. He had always looked down his nose at what he deemed quick or faddish fixes. But the approaches that went under the name TQM would not be out of left field for Hewlett-Packard. The ethic that stemmed directly from founders William Hewlett and David Packard—the HP Way, as it was referred to—was built on the twin pillars of concern for people and concern for quality.

Holmes began his search for solutions by doing a little intellectual networking. He began to discuss management issues with peers outside the company. He attended a seminar at the Center for Quality of Management given by George Fisher, then president of Motorola. At the seminar, a fellow chief executive asked Fisher what advice he would give other CEOs. He offered two suggestions: First, "Start earlier." Though Motorola was one of the earliest U.S. organizations to refocus on quality and had won the Malcolm Baldrige National Quality Award, Fisher felt the company would have benefited by beginning even earlier. Second, Fisher said, "*Put quality first* in your staff meetings." Motorola was making big profits in the viciously competitive microelectronics and telecommunications equipment businesses, but Fisher said that managers should not focus on profits, but on improvement in the activities that served customers. Profits would be a natural by-product.

NEW STRUCTURES FOR PUTTING QUALITY FIRST

The idea of putting quality first resonated with Holmes. He felt the Medical Products Group had always been good at dealing with quality issues in a reactive way. Executive Committee meetings started with discussions of financial statistics: sales, profits, and so on. The executives used the statistics to identify so-called hot quality problems and, once those brushfires reached conflagration stage, they took steps to put them out. Otherwise, management left the organization to tend to its work. HP MPG managers were following the biological model "management by exception" principle, otherwise known as greasing the squeaky wheel. But they had no systemic way to deal with problems *before* they became hot, no ongoing way to ensure quality and continuous improvement.

HP MPG had to change. "Probably the most important thing that we did was to decide to set up a quality steering committee," Holmes said in an interview. "And the most important part of that was that instead of setting up a committee *in addition* to the Executive Committee, the members of the Executive Committee became the Quality Steering Committee."

Each month, Holmes and his Executive Committee/Quality Steering Committee addressed quality first in their meetings, before discussing sales or profits. And they made three key adjustments that affected the overall structure of the firm. First, committee members realized that the only way they could intelligently address quality as a group was for each to take special responsibility—in addition to his or her regular job—for one specific aspect of the quality of HP MPG's operations. Figure 2.6 shows how the structure of the Executive Committee changed. For example, Bob Ford, the controller, wound up in charge of developing data that would tell the group how well it was doing. Ed McDonald, marketing and distribution manager, was in charge of improving customer feedback. Holmes took charge of "quality vision and strategy."

In addition, to coordinate the changes at HP MPG, the committee created a quality office at the group's headquarters. Holmes hired Brad Harrington, formerly the quality manager of Hewlett-Packard's British operations, as HP MPG's quality manager. The British group had had great success implementing quality initiatives, and Harrington had helped Holmes reorganize the Executive Committee along cross-functional lines. Harrington's mission was to help executives throughout the group plan for and manage the coming changes.

Finally, a quality manager was named within each subunit of HP MPG: the Clinical Systems Business Unit, the Imaging Systems Business Unit, and the customer service organization. Along with their regular operational roles, these managers were charged with developing quality initiatives and processes within their units and coordinating with the central quality office.

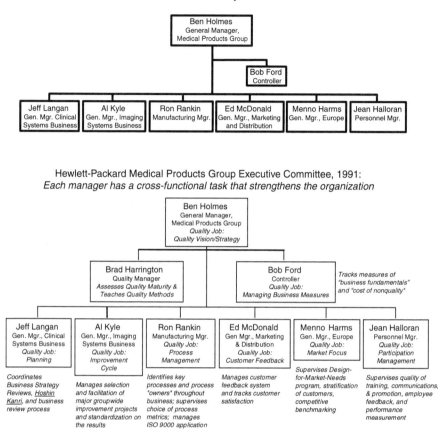

Figure 2.6 Hewlett-Packard's System Change

It's hard to avoid the striking similarity between the above three initiatives and the fundamental structural changes undertaken by Tera-dyne. Indeed, in nearly every successful quality initiative we have found, the organization has taken some version of these three basic steps:

1. Study, define, and disseminate vision at the top management levels.

2. Push change initiatives down the hierarchy to an operational level.

3. Create a small central office to monitor and coordinate initiatives.

Underpinning each step, successful companies almost always create cross-functional roles to ensure maximal beneficial interaction among people and subdivisions. In other words, whether they know it or not, they take a social model systemic approach.

New Processes: Language Processing, *Hoshin Kanri,* Phase Review

With new structures in place, Ben Holmes continued to network, seeking new processes that could drive HP MPG's thinking. Through the six-day course at the Center for Quality of Management, Holmes was introduced to the work of Jiro Kawakita, whose ideas underlie what we now call the Language-Processing (LP) method. (Other organizations refer to techniques similar to the Language-Processing method as the *KJ method.* In the Asian practice of placing the family name before the given name, KJ are Kawakita's initials. However, Kawakita himself prefers that the KJ method be applied only to techniques practiced exactly as taught by him.)

Holmes thought the Kawakita/Language-Processing approach might be exactly what was needed to address what senior managers at MPG had come to believe was the group's primary problem: bringing new products to market. Holmes called a joint meeting of all top marketing and R&D managers to address the simple question "What are the barriers to improving our product-generation process?"

HP managers had a wide variety of ideas about what might be going wrong. The new approach enabled them to get those ideas out in the open and sort through them in a group where it wasn't important *who* proposed an idea. "We were part of an organization that was very judgmental," says Jeff Langan, who was general manager of the Clinical Systems Business Unit. "You got promoted by saying 'Here's the answer.' This gave you another way of working."

Holmes led the process, religiously creating a diagram of the ideas that were being generated. Figure 2.7 shows some of the elements in

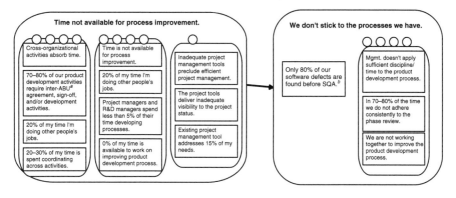

What are the problems that prevent senior R&D Management from improving our product development processes?

We lack the time, discipline, and long-term focus to improve the product development process.

[a] ABU refers to Application Business Unit
[b] SQA refers to Software Quality Assurance

Figure 2.7 Portions of HP MPG Executives Diagram. Circles indicate participants' votes about the most important low-level groups of issues.

the completed diagram. In the final analysis, the managers chose two ideas as the most significant:

1. Management doesn't apply sufficient discipline to the product development process.
2. Time is not available for process improvement.

These observations suggested radical changes that had to be made throughout the organization.

The new understanding of what had to be done was instrumental in making *hoshin kanri,* a Japanese-inspired methodology for focusing on the organization's most crucial needs, work effectively at MPG. Hewlett-Packard had introduced hoshin kanri companywide in the mid-1980s, but the method had made uneven contributions. In the first year it was implemented at the Medical Products Group, fiscal 1986, the Executive Committee established five hoshins supposedly the top priorities the group was to work on. "Nobody was really tied in to them," says Fred Van Deusen, the quality manager of the Clinical Systems business unit during the early 1990s. Management discovered

---

Hoshin Kanri

Hoshin kanri is a Japanese-developed methodology for focusing an organization each year on a few top priorities and mobilizing all parts of the organization to achieve them. "Hoshin" is a Japanese word for "policy" and "kanri" is a Japanese word for management—a rough translation for the term is "management by policy." For each of the top hoshin (policies) of the year, each unit within the organization launches a few well-defined support initiatives, establishing clear measures that will be used to determine whether the support initiatives have succeeded.

---

that it couldn't change in five different directions at once. "You get into 'hoshin gridlock,'" Holmes says. "You don't know what to do."

But in 1990, HP MPG focused on a single, clear hoshin: Improve the timeliness, contribution, and predictability with which MPG brings new products to the global marketplace.

Van Deusen was already leading a team charged with finding a new way to manage the product development process. The team quickly realized that HP's existing process had many problems. For one thing, the objectives that executives established for a project provided only vague guidance to its designers. A list of objectives might include the market share the company wanted to achieve in the new product's niche, the profits it wanted to earn, the target date for introduction, and a short list of the features the company wanted the product to embody. But, during the product-development process, engineers couldn't coherently evaluate whether any particular part of a proposed design was appropriate to meet such targets. Project managers, selected from the Research and Development Department, often didn't communicate consistently well with other departments.

To address these problems, Van Deusen's team proposed adopting a product-development process that other parts of Hewlett-Packard had been using, called phase review. A program manager would coordinate the whole development process, not just research and development, including communications among different departments. Executives would choose for this job a manager known for facilitating and communicating skills. The program manager would ensure that every participant in the introduction of the new product understood its progress at every step. "We can now [define a product well enough] so R&D knows exactly what features are needed," says Van Deusen. "And marketing knows what will be there, and manufacturing knows." The system requires the managers of each function in the organization to review the project's progress and sign off at end of each phase of its development.

By the time Van Deusen's group had come to that conclusion, however, the discussion of the hoshin throughout the organization had caused the entire management team to recognize a broader problem. There was more to improving product development than improving the flow of work among people with "product development" in their job titles. Lack of predictability throughout the organization limited the likelihood of effective product development. Even if a good design emerged on time, manufacturing couldn't predict how long it would take to get it into production, for instance.

MPG management began to insist that every part of the organization establish goals for increasing predictability. Manufacturing, for example, for the first time established a group of new-product engineers and a well-defined process for getting the manufacturing part of product introduction carried out.

The first major product to benefit from the so-called predictability hoshin was code-named Genesis. It was a monitor system capable of tracking numerous patients from a central location. Previous MPG projects had taken two to four years from launch to introduction of the product. Engineers would produce a prototype, discover that the prototype lacked features that someone in the organization considered necessary, and begin time-consuming redesign.

Genesis was completed and delivered to the market in mid-1992, 18 months after the launch of its development. It had all the features promised. The prototype had required no fundamental redesign and there was only a one-month deviation from the planned development schedule.

Once again in 1992, the product development hoshin remained one of the group's key priorities. Every part of the organization was asked to set goals to increase the predictability of its operations and better support an improved product development process. But the committee also agreed it was time to adopt a second hoshin for 1992: Adopt Total Quality Management as the management system for the Medical Products Group. In most organizations that use hoshin kanri, adopting TQM is considered a long process, and some other, more immediate business goal is typically chosen as the hoshin. But Harrington argued that if adopting TQM was the group's key priority for the coming year, it should be a hoshin.

By 1992, the hoshin kanri mentality was cascading throughout the entire organization. Each spring, top management would review the company's situation, its vision, and its three- to five-year objectives. In early summer, the Executive Committee would invite some 60–70 top managers to a management retreat, where they used Kawakita/Language Processing methodology and other tools to examine the challenges facing the group, then wrote a draft of the next year's hoshin. Employees would have one month to comment, then the Executive Committee would make its final decision and, generally, each top manager on the Committee would be responsible for one measurable companywide dimension of the new hoshin initiative.

Next, based on the group hoshin, each business unit and other top-level department wrote its own hoshin using a form (Figure 2.8) to establish its own goals and to define the measures it will use to track its progress in achieving them. The form also required each unit to identify the steps it would take to implement the priorities established by the unit above it.

Goal-setting systems, such as hoshin kanri at HP or goal deployment at Teradyne, tie all the continuous improvement and customer-focus process activities together. The actual work of improvement can remain highly decentralized, often with thousands of people working on hundreds of improvement teams whose individual goals may have been chosen by the team members. "Hoshin kanri is total quality applied to the management planning process," Holmes said. "It's a much

PREPARED BY: MPG Exec Cmte	DATE: 8/24/91	FISCAL YEAR: 1992	DIVISION: MPG	LOCATION: Group Headquarters

SITUATION: MPG competes in a global marketplace with serious competitors who have committed time, people, money and resources to the pursuit of total quality. QMS[a] reviews have shown that MPG is still lagging the Corporation in its execution of TQM. To improve our operating results, we believe that institutionalizing TQM is the key strategy which needs to be employed.

OBJECTIVE	NO.	STRATEGY (OWNER)	PERFORMANCE MEASURE
1.0 Establish TQM as the Management methodology within MPG.	1.1	Develop an MPG Quality Strategy which is integrated with MPG's mission, vision, and BSR objectives. OWNER: HOLMES	1.1 — Document ratified by (Q1) — Communicated to all employees in all-hands meetings (Q1)
	1.2	Implement a customer feedback system worldwide. OWNER: McDONALD	1.2 — Concept defined (Q1) — Start implementation (Q3)
	1.3	Improve the effectiveness of MPG's annual planning process. OWNER: LANGAN	1.3 — Calendar and process published (Q1) — Quarterly reviews conducted
TARGET/GOAL QMS score > 2.5 by end of FY92	1.4	Create an effective infrastructure to support TQM at all levels. OWNER: B. HARRINGTON	1.4 — Quality charter established (Q1) — Quality function resources in place (Q2) — Quality training curriculum developed (Q1)
	1.5	Establish a recognition and reward system which supports TQM. OWNER J. HALLORAN	1.5 — Scope defined (Q1) — Proposals (Q2) — Quarterly reviews
	1.6	Develop an improvement process strategy. OWNER: KYLE	1.6 — Proposal (Q1)
	1.7	Develop an approach for improving MPG's horizontal processes. OWNER: RANKIN	1.7 — % Execution vs. Plan

[a] QMS refers to Quality Maturity System

Figure 2.8 Form Used to Track Goals, Strategies, and Performance Measures in Hewlett-Packard Medical Products Group

more rigorous methodology for management planning than we've ever used before."

"If you had suggested to me years ago that I would leave the decisions to choose major breakthrough projects to other people, I would have laughed at you," continued Holmes in 1994. "Now, that's what we're doing."

THE QUALITY MATURITY SYSTEM

To monitor their efforts at continuous improvement, many of the successful organizations we studied regularly invited thoughtful outsiders to evaluate the effectiveness of the management system and point out problems. Of the ways of doing this that we've seen, the most sophisticated was the Quality Maturity System (QMS) review that Hewlett-Packard carries out for its business units.

In the 1980s, Hewlett-Packard executives realized that parts of the corporation were introducing dozens of quality management techniques that often added up to a hodge-podge. So executives commissioned a team led by Sarv Singh Soin, a Singaporean who had served as quality manager in several Asian HP units, to develop a new management review methodology.

In the Quality Maturity System reviews that had crucial impact at HP MPG, two experienced HP managers from outside the unit being evaluated studied the unit's management system on five major dimensions:

Customer focus

Improvement cycle

Process management

Total participation

Planning process

On each dimension, the reviewers gave the unit a score of 1 to 5 and advice on how it could improve further. The scores were displayed on the chart represented in Figure 2.9 and averaged to produce an overall score. For Hewlett-Packard as a whole, the system can provide a degree of unity of management without the costs of centralization.[5]

The MPG used the score on the QMS reviews as its single most important measure of progress in the first stage of its transformation. In 1991, the first QMS review in MPG had produced a score of 1.8, not an impressive performance. By 1993, the average group score had risen above 3.0 and Harrington reported that reviewers were starting to be at a loss as to what improvements to recommend.

THE STRUGGLES OF A MANAGEMENT SYSTEM

Between 1991 and 1993, the Medical Products Group gained market share, achieved No. 1 ranking in preference surveys of doctors and hospitals, and reduced customer-reported problems with its equipment dramatically.

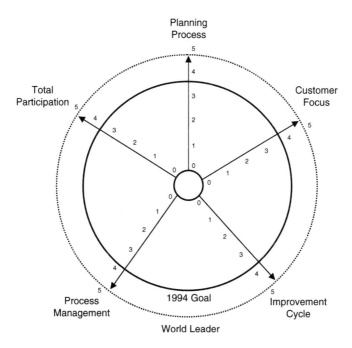

Figure 2.9 Quality Maturity System

But the group was in no position to live happily ever after. When we conducted the largest part of our study of HP MPG in 1994, we were every bit as excited about the group's progress as we were about Teradyne's. Its management system was well integrated and powerful.

The group, however, endured real struggles in the rest of the decade, which illustrate some of the problems in maintaining an integrated management system in a rapidly changing world.

Holmes's vision included not just better patient-care equipment, but information management that would improve the entire medical care system. In 1992, he had the company produce a riveting videotape that imagined the world of medical care in 1997. When a patient in cardiac arrest arrived in an emergency room, instead of having to wait while hospital staff hunted for his chart, he would be transferred immediately to a stretcher cart with a computer terminal attached. The staff would call up his electrocardiograms on the screen through voice commands as they rushed him directly to the operating room.

Holmes retired as chairman of the group at the beginning of 1994 (though he continued to maintain an office there that year). His successor was an executive from another computer company who knew the technologies believed essential to make the vision a reality. The successor attempted to use many of the management systems the group had developed. He hoped to increase the group's sales fourfold by the end of the decade by integrating health care information.

But it's fair to say he never managed to make management methodologies gel as an integrated system for promoting his new agenda. They'd been effective in turning around a medical hardware company. They even seem to have worked well when Holmes used them to begin the transition to what he called "integrated information management." But when Holmes's successor tried to make information networking the core of the business, he didn't create a system that could turn the organization in the new direction. "Ben was patiently trying to work the organization toward it," said one executive. Under the new chief executive, change accelerated without an increase in clarity of what, exactly, was to be accomplished. "People felt, 'Whoa! We've been hijacked.'"

Many of the elements of HP MPG's system had the capacity to make major contributions in a radical change process. But the quality department was de-emphasized, and no new initiative had the effect of showing people throughout the organization what they should do or mobilizing them effectively in the new direction.

The dream of integrated information management was never really realized. The Medical Products Group has recently re-emphasized its strengths and in most respects its management system seems to be performing well again. But its experience (along with recent experience in the Kenmore-Town of Tonawanda public schools, to be discussed in Chapter 4) stands as a lesson. Leaders face great dangers when they attempt major change in an organization without fully understanding the systems that have created its strengths. As we'll discuss in the sidebar at the end of this chapter and in Chapters 8 and 9, there's a great need for leaders to create clear lists of the assumptions they make in their programs and create explicit early warning systems that will show when the assumptions have been violated.[6]

Conclusions: The Scientific Method Is Even More Powerful Than We Realized

The Teradyne experience shows that the scientific method can achieve far more than most managers have previously believed it could if leaders effectively introduce tools and structures to manage interactions in ways that allow people to use it. In Teradyne's case, it is fair to say that the scientific method has driven an entire management system throughout the 1990s, and the results have been exceptional.

HP MPG's experience is also consistent with the idea that the scientific method can guide our integrated management systems. But it also illustrates what can be lost when new managers have a different direction and method than their predecessors and don't evolve an adequate integrated management system to support it. The organization may not respond.

The scientific method is powerful. But it can deliver its power only when leaders design systems in which it can work.

Eastman Chemical: Integrated Management in a Radically Different Manufacturer

In this chapter, we described two manufacturers we know well. They're companies we've worked with, and we've watched them struggle. But readers may wonder if they aren't too much alike to tell much about what manufacturers as a group learned from the crisis of the 1980s and early 1990s. Both Teradyne and Hewlett-Packard Medical Products Group are high-tech equipment manufacturers. How much can other kinds of firms learn from them?

The rest of the book demonstrates striking similarities in a remarkable variety of organizations. But before we leave manufacturing, it's important to show how a very different kind of manufacturer—one that operates huge chemical works—has also struggled and in the process developed an integrated management system.

At first glance, Eastman Chemical Co. would seem to be as different as could be from Teradyne and the Hewlett-Packard Medical Products Group. R&D processes drive the successes of the latter two; Eastman also depends on its technology, but some of its products haven't changed in decades. It is an old-line manufacturer whose five major domestic plant operations (in Kingsport, Tennessee, Longview, Texas, Columbia, Missouri, Batesville, Arkansas, and Rochester, New York) consume the largest share by far of its resources. As a $4.5 billion multinational company with more than 16,000 employees, Eastman Chemical is the tenth largest chemical company in the United States, thirty-third in the world. Its products include more than 400 chemicals, plastics, and fibers for 7,000 customers. Production requires stabilized equipment of long operating life and miles of interconnecting piping for highly instrumented processes. Because of the complexity of the interactions in such an environment, innovation does not come easily.

The central process of management change at Eastman Chemical has taken more than 15 years, a period that Eastman Chemical's executives refer to as the company's "quality journey." The results show continuing improvements in products and processes as well as increasing satisfaction of executives, employees, and, in particular, customers. Eastman Chemical, like Teradyne and HP MPG, has been able to transform itself into an integrated management system based on human potential, continuous improvement, and customer satisfaction. But the results haven't been entirely happy. In the late 1990s, Eastman tripped over what is perhaps the biggest unsolved problem in the creation of integrated management systems: inability to develop comprehensive contingency planning systems.

EVERYTHING IS A PROCESS

George Eastman, founder of Kodak, created the Chemicals Division in 1920 so that he would never again suffer the chemical shortages that plagued his company during World War I. Eastman made Kodak the world leader in photography using technologies that his Chemical Division often knew more about than anyone else in the world. With decades of success came diversification as the division's research moved it into nonphotography chemical technologies.

By the 1970s, one nonphotography innovation was yielding hundreds of millions of dollars a year in sales to just two major customers. Then the unthinkable occurred. One of the two customers informed Eastman that it was switching to a competitor that, in the customer's estimation, made a better product. Eastman management snapped to the offensive, dispatching teams of engineers to focus on quickly improving quality. The teams not only reduced customer complaints by 90 percent, but also sharply reduced costs and achieved a startling increase in productivity. The customer shifted its business back on a dramatic scale. And profits were far higher than they would have been if the customer had never raised the issue. Earnie Deavenport, Eastman Chemical's chairman, recalls that this experience profoundly affected Eastman executives. They realized how much better their organization could be.

But they didn't yet understand how difficult was the task of improvement. In the early 1970s, Eastman had licensed a plant design from Japan and, with Japanese help, it introduced then-emerging quality management processes. The plant began applying statistical process control in its manufacturing and adopting customer focus and the PDCA procedure for continuing improvement. "Then the boss said, 'Move [those processes] to the rest of the complex,'" Deavenport recalls. "We tried to use the problem-solving techniques in other parts of the [Kingsport] facility for three years, and it didn't work. We didn't understand why for ten years more. . . . We found that integrated processes and integrative systems are indeed necessary for a world-class company."

Real progress didn't begin until the early 1980s. "We made a key discovery in 1983," said one Eastman Chemical executive, "that our business was not just a big business. It was really a series of processes that fit together like a puzzle." The word process here is being used in the general, TQM sense: a repeatable sequence of events. "Once we made that discovery," the executive continued, "we realized that even jobs such as closing the books, obtaining pricing response, and measuring customer satisfaction were processes just as much as manufacturing operations were. It was then easy to apply process control and PDCA to those functions in the same way we were doing it in manufacturing."

The real revolution occurred when this approach was applied with a market-oriented mentality, that is, when customer satisfaction, not the product itself, became the goal of work. In 1983, Chemical Division General Manager Toy Reid and other Eastman executives launched a Customer Emphasis Program. And the company adopted its first Quality Policy (the most recent version of which appears in Figure 2.10).

But Deavenport believes that real "from-the-top" leadership began in 1986, when Reid led several new, integrative initiatives, including the introduction of a

Quality Policy

QUALITY GOAL

To be the leader in quality and value of products and services

QUALITY MANAGEMENT PROCESS

- Focus on customers
- Establish mission, vision, and indicators of performance
- Understand, standardize, stabilize, and maintain processes
- Plan, do, check, act for continual improvement and innovation

OPERATIONAL POLICY

- Achieve process stability and reliability
- Control every process to the desired target
- Improve process capability

PRINCIPLES

Customer Satisfaction	Anticipate, understand, and excel at meeting customer needs.
Continual Improvement	Improve the current level of performance of processes, products, and services.
Innovation	Search for and implement creative processes, products, and services.
Process Emphasis	Focus on processes as the means to improve results.
Management Leadership	Create and maintain a shared vision, constancy of purpose, and supportive environment that includes appropriate recognition and reinforcement.
Empowerment	Create a culture where people have the knowledge, skills, authority, and desire to decide, act, and take responsibility for the results of their actions and for their contribution to the success of the company.
Statistical Methods	Understand the concept of variation and apply appropriate statistical methods for continual improvement and innovation.
Employee Development	Encourage and support lifelong learning and personal growth.
Partnerships	Build long-term relationships with customers and suppliers.
Assessment	Assess performance and benchmark against the world's best.

E. W. Deavenport, Jr., President

Figure 2.10 Eastman Chemical's Quality Policy

standard methodology called process evaluation, control, and improvement (PECI). It provided Eastman with a common language for applying the scientific method in the same way that other versions of the PDCA improvement process did for Teradyne and HP MPG. PECI became the key tool of Eastman's Quality Management Process (Figure 2.11).

In addition to PECI and the Quality Management Process, Eastman developed a standard measurement process for customer satisfaction. Using a survey, review, and feedback loop, managers worked with salespeople to build a database of key decision makers at 2,000 organizations that purchased Eastman products. A database scorecard was developed to record key results, process indicators, and potential improvements, tracking elements such as cycle time for order entry,

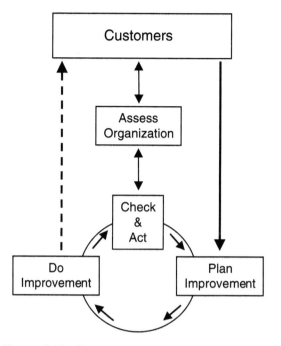

Figure 2.11 Eastman's Quality Management Process

confirmation of requested ship date, and on-time delivery. The company also began to conduct a quarterly survey of a sample of decision makers among its key customers and emphasize continuing daily interaction with customers for relationship building and learning. Company groups such as manufacturing, safety, supply, and research began to regularly keep in touch with customers in person and by telephone. Later, the division created a new way of dealing with complaints, treating them as key data for improvement by ensuring that they were logged carefully and examined for information about process weaknesses. In the final analysis, every bit of customer information, whether gleaned formally or informally, was entered into the database, an ongoing process that has yielded Eastman a rich and potent storehouse of information.

THE MOSES FACTOR

In 1990, Earnie Deavenport was named general manager of the Eastman Chemical Division. Deavenport had an expansive vision of quality. He believed that if every employee could be made to feel a commitment to making Eastman the leader in quality and value, the company would become self-optimizing for customers, employees, and stockholders. He also believed that, at the time, most Eastman executives had not really learned how to lead that kind of thought revolution from the top down. He felt that although Eastman had "begun to work on the tools and the techniques of quality," it had yet to learn that a key element was missing: the engagement and alignment of individual purposes. "We had yet to consider the social aspects of quality as a critical element of total quality management," he says.

Back when he was division president, Deavenport had been sponsored by Kodak to participate in the 1984–1985 Sloan Fellows Program at MIT. His thesis on quality management was based on simple premises: "No limit exists for latent human capabilities" and "Every person wants to do a good job." These became the cornerstone of the management system at Eastman Chemical.

One of the first by-products of Deavenport's approach was the institution of an Employee Development System based on the idea that employees should be continually coached and trained to be responsible for their own development. The new Employee Development System instituted personalized performance measurement, which meant that, for the most part, employees were responsible for compiling data relating to their efforts. Quantitative charting of the data then becomes the basis for performance analysis, hiring, promotions, and transfers. The company sought, in particular, to eliminate any perceived "black box method" for determining pay increases.

Deavenport was the type of leader the division needed at that point. He saw his job (as exemplified by the Employee Development System) as creating norms, processes, and an infrastructure that encouraged optimal interactions among the people in the organization. And he saw continual communication as a crucial part of that job. He referred to this as "the Moses Factor."

"Moses gave his people a vision," says Deavenport. "They believed in him. He led, they followed, across the Red Sea on a very long and a very difficult journey. There is no journey without the Moses Factor." Deavenport is fond of pointing out that, as leaders go, Moses was neither particularly charismatic nor particularly dictatorial. He led followers to the Promised Land through the sheer power of belief and the daily iteration of that belief.

At the heart of Deavenport's communication program was the development of, and continual emphasis on, four "foundation documents." These were the Quality Policy (Figure 2.11, first developed in 1983), The Eastman Way (1984), Responsible Care[7] (1991), and Strategic Intent (1991). Each document consisted of an easy-to-read single-page list of bulleted phrases on policy and operating philosophy, and Deavenport insisted that each be displayed on the walls of Eastman facilities everywhere in the world. They were like the articles of a constitution:

- The *Quality Policy* defines the quality management process (QMP). It highlights statistical process control in three brief statements: "Achieve process stability and reliability"; "Control every process to a desired target"; "Improve process capability."
- *The Eastman Way* is a statement of values. It opens: "Eastman people are the key to success. We have recognized throughout our history the importance of

treating each other fairly and with respect. We will enhance these beliefs by building upon the following values and principles." Next, it lists the nine values and principles: honesty and integrity, fairness, trust, teamwork, diversity, employee well-being, citizenship, and winning attitude. By including it among the four-document group of otherwise more pragmatic statements, the company heightens the focus on these values.

- The *Responsible Care* document expands on the company's stated values of citizenship and employee well-being. Emphasizing policies adopted by the Chemical Manufacturers Association, it offers guiding principles for safe management, handling, and care of chemicals, consistent with sound health, safety, and environmental protective practices. "Responsible Care," says Deavenport," is the bottom line—the very essence of survival."

- *Strategic Intent,* written more recently than its companion documents, was patterned after the ideas in a ground-breaking article by Gary Hamel and C.K. Prahalad.[8] In this article, the authors urge companies to articulate and focus on "an unplanned, ambitious goal." The intentional absence of a plan will almost force employee inventiveness and resourcefulness to fill the vacuum while "allowing for changing circumstances without changing the company's vision." What is Eastman Chemical's strategic intent? "To be the world's preferred chemical company."

A Team-Based Structure

Because invention and creativity require self-confidence and freedom of action, the strategic intent approach can be effective only in a self-motivating, process-oriented environment, the kind of environment that has come to exist at Eastman Chemical only in the past 15 years. Up until the early 1980s, Eastman Chemical had been a traditional organization within Eastman Kodak, structured hierarchically. But then, concurrent with the adoption of its Quality Policy, it began to experiment tentatively with a team-based orientation.

The team structure was not part of the organizational matrix. Teams were instead separately viewed as mechanisms for overt purposeful action. "Many employees also serve on cross-functional teams where experts from different areas come together to work on a specific process or project," said Vicki Wolfe, director of Human Resources at the Texas Eastman Division. "In some manufacturing and services areas, we have even set up new work systems, high-performance teams that are virtually self-regulated. In these situations, employees become their own managers. Common objectives and measures link one team to another. This builds cohesion and an ongoing flow of communications throughout the company. The interlocking team structure encourages employee empowerment by providing a means of contributing ideas, working with peers, and sharing ownership in the workplace."

There is an important difference between the systems in the successful organizations we observed and old-fashioned quality circles: quality circles typically include only workers. Just as Teradyne executives are key participants in Teradyne's Quality Improvement Teams, Eastman executives greatly de-emphasized their traditional role as supervisors, ceasing to attempt micromanagement of process development, and instead came to see their roles as "drivers," "owners," or "stewards." A driver is a member of the team, unifying and directing its day-to-day activities. An owner is a team member and the accountable executive, overseeing team activities to assure its work maintains imperatives consistent with the company's goals. A steward is an executive and non-team participant, serving as coach, nurturer, and ombudsman of the process, encouraging and stimulating both employees and himself or herself to innovate and to take responsibility for their own individual growth. Many executives who became stewards seemed to emerge as a natural part of the system rather than by selection or appointment.

Encouraged by Deavenport's Moses Factor, Eastman executives further refined the team concept. They recognized that successful teams allow each person to find his or her own way of pitching in to do what each does best, and each integrates his or her own actions with what others do best. "We actually really run the plant's day-to-day operations. We no longer park our brains at the gate," said Kenny Evans, filter tow team coach of crimper-dryer operations at the Tennessee Eastman Division.

Courses in scientific analytical skills and statistical principles, emphasizing the concept of variability, enrich the common language for evaluating processes at all levels.

A Four-Dimensional View of the Organization

By 1991, Eastman had built a push-pull management system involving the company's three driving forces: executives, teams, and customers. Teams motivated, sustained, and regulated themselves through process-oriented, self-directed development. Executives *pushed* the teams by means of stewardship, guided by the company's Strategic Intent and consistent with the workers' needs and basic beliefs. Customers *pulled* the teams by making their needs known through direct interaction and the customer satisfaction database. Because executives were members of teams as well, they too got pulled to satisfy customers, even as they were pushed by their own initiatives.

The increasing employment of teams began to reveal that many strategic and process imperatives cut across product lines or resisted product categorizations. Deavenport led a complete reorganization of the company. The new organizational matrix was based on simultaneously viewing the division in four different ways: looking at its business units, its functions, its geographies, and its core competencies.

The *core competencies* transcend the business units and functions. They are, says Deavenport, "bundles of knowledge, skills, and technology that give us advantage over our competition." Eastman executives identified seven such areas of

Table 2.4 Eastman Chemical's Integrated Management Matrix

Year	Action or Method	Reason for Integration	The Systems View	Key Practices
1983	Customer Emphasis Program; learning from Deming and others.	Attempt to customer data to drive strategy and processes; "market-in."	Extends system to include external stakeholders; enlists external knowledge.	Practice 2: Seek external information. Practice 5: Participate in societal networking.
1983	Quality Policy.	Formalizes the adoption of TQM.	Imparts common purpose and common language.	Practice 1: Seek continuous improvement. Practice 3: Seek internal engagement.
1984	The Eastman Way.	Codifies a set of values for the company.	Imparts common purpose.	Practice 3: Seek internal engagement.
1986	PECI/Quality Management Process.	Standardizes an approach to problems and processes.	Provides the basis of a learning system.	Practice 1: Seek continuous improvement. Practice 4: Build supportive infrastructure.
1986	Interlocking team structure.	Creates team-based problem-solving mechanisms.	Forces cross-functional interactions; utilizes "tacit" knowledge.	Practice 1: Seek continuous improvement. Practice 3: Seek internal engagement. Practice 4: Build supportive infrastructure.

(continued)

Table 2.4 (Continued)

Year	Action or Method	Reason for Integration	The Systems View	Key Practices
1988	Customer satisfaction process/ Customer database.	Formalizes and standardizes "market-in" processes.	Utilizes "tacit" external knowledge.	Practice 1: Seek continuous improvement. Practice 2: Seek external information. Practice 4: Build supportive infrastructure.
1989	Adopt Baldrige Quality Criteria.	Standardizes metrics for TQM.	Imparts common language.	Practice 1: Seek continuous improvement. Practice 3: Seek internal engagement.
1990	The Moses Factor (*Earnie Deavenport*).	Reestablishes and disseminates the vision; emphasizes social aspects of quality.	Aligns purposes of individuals with those of the group.	Practice 3: Seek internal engagement.
1990	Employee Development System.	Emphasizes education and training; establishes methods of evaluation, promotion, and compensation.	Aligns purposes of individuals with those of the group.	Practice 3: Seek internal engagement.
1991	Responsible Care Policy.	Codifies a set of values for the company.	Imparts common purpose.	Practice 3: Seek internal engagement.

Table 2.4 (Continued)

Year	Action or Method	Reason for Integration	The Systems View	Key Practices
1991	Strategic Intent.	Encourages a link between long-term goals and day-to-day management.	Imparts common purpose; forces cross-functional interactions; team-based learning.	Practice 1: Seek continuous improvement. Practice 3: Seek internal engagement.
1991	Chemistry of Excellence Program.	Disseminates Eastman's management system to external stakeholders.	Imparts common purpose and common language.	Practice 5: Participate in societal networking.
1991	Four-dimensional organization.	Drives quality consciousness deeper into functional and core-competency processes.	Facilitates process discovery; team-based mutual learning and alignment.	Practice 1: Seek continuous improvement. Practice 3: Seek internal engagement. Practice 4: Build supportive infrastructure.

competitive leverage, some managerial in nature, some technical: large-site management, environmental performance, innovation, customer interface, polymer technology, organic chemistry technology, and cellulose technology. The Eastman executives "own" these competencies and allocate corporate resources consistently so as to maintain and develop them. In addition, specific Eastman executives "own" nine companywide processes, such as supplier relations, internal communications, employment diversity, and inventory planning, to name a few. (See Table 2.4.)

SUCCESS AND DISASTER

Deavenport's stewardship was the catalyst for breakthrough development at Eastman Chemical, the results of which appeared impressively on the bottom line. Sales grew 40 percent between 1988 and 1993, a remarkable record in a chemical industry that was depressed through most of that period. Eastman Chemical consistently outperformed other diversified chemical companies in profit margin.

In 1994, the Board of Directors of Eastman Kodak Company spun the Chemicals Division off to Kodak stockholders, giving Kodak stockholders shares in the new corporation called Eastman Chemical Company. The new company won the Malcolm Baldrige National Quality Award and began life with higher customer satisfaction, better financial performance, and faster, more customer-focused research and development than any of its peers. Eastman was famed as the leading producer of such key products as PET resin, the raw material for plastic drink bottles, a rapidly growing market that produced as much as 25 percent of Eastman's earnings by the mid-1990s. It was a business that hadn't been a focus when Kodak owned the company—and Eastman Chemical invested aggressively in 1995, soon after it became independent, to protect its leadership position in the PET market.

That, it turned out, was a mistake. With demand growing at 10 percent a year as beverage producers around the world switched from other kinds of packaging to plastic, PET had never experienced the radical price swings that other chemical products had gone through. But in the years when Kodak was investing too little, others were noticing the profitability of PET. Competitors were building new facilities before Eastman's burst of investment in 1995. But their attacks would have produced only a modest problem if it weren't for another problem: in the mid-1990s, the market for polyester fibers collapsed, and Asian producers discovered they could easily switch to making PET. The product that sold for up to 80 cents a pound in the middle of the decade was now selling for 40 cents. Troubled Asian producers were probably dumping it for as little as 30 cents. Eastman was losing money on it. Its earnings crashed, and so did its stock. In early 1999, the stock was selling for barely more than the price at which it had been issued in 1994.

Obviously, Eastman deserves criticism for the aggressiveness of the 1995 investments that may well have made a glut—and unprofitable prices—inevitable. "We waited to make some major investments until too late," says R. Wiley Bourne Jr., Eastman's executive vice president. "And once we began to invest, we invested too much."

Eastman's experience points up a common problem in integrated management systems. Managers don't know how to deal with the unknown. The systems thinker Jamshid Gharajedaghi has suggested a partial solution: he advises that when a decision is made, the assumptions behind the decision be written in "read-only memory," that is, in a place where they can't be changed. Then, as business proceeds, reality must be regularly compared to the assumptions. That creates an early warning system for mistakes like Eastman's, and it can enable companies to escape their mistakes with minimal loss.

Such efforts could have done Eastman a great deal of good. At the same time, it's essential that the beauty and power of Eastman's management system not be completely ignored just because of a single strategy error. We're inclined to bet on Eastman's future success.

CHAPTER 3

The Service Industries

Integrated Management for
Radically Different Processes

Early in the development of the Center for Quality of Management, some managers began to notice that people in service businesses were less enthusiastic about Total Quality tools than we'd hoped. New management techniques were working well for manufacturers. But when teachers talked about the PDCA cycle, sales managers would give them skeptical looks that said, "Yes, we believe in standards, but . . ."

We came to realize that the vast variety of efforts called "services" are produced with a profoundly diverse assortment of processes. And service providers within manufacturers often seem far harder to manage than factories. Most office work, for example, just doesn't follow standardizable patterns that can be analyzed with traditional means of process control. The journalist Michael Rothschild, writing in *Forbes ASAP*, noted, "Levels of confusion inconceivable in a well-managed factory are tolerated as unavoidable inside well-run marketing departments, finance groups, and R&D centers. The hit to profits is staggering, but until recently, the inherent complexity of the work in these white-collar domains made productivity breakthroughs all but impossible."[1]

He's right.

A group of managers from CQM companies formed a Service Industries Committee to explore these phenomena. They began by adopting a notion, developed at Digital Equipment with the help of the consulting firm A. T. Kearney, that *any* successful organization requires a palette of many fundamentally different kinds of processes.

The committee then identified at least three different kinds of basic processes:

Operational processes: predictable and repetitive, such as the processing of invoices

"Moment of truth" processes: reactions to unpredictable, immediate requirements generated by customers or a changing environment

Innovation processes: adaptive, longer-term reactions to requirements generated by customers or a changing environment

The Service Industries Committee made no claim that this represented a comprehensive list of types of processes. But it suggested that most organizations can improve by thinking carefully about differences in the basic processes they must manage, and then evaluating whether different basic processes need to be managed differently.[2] Table 3.1 illustrates the differences among the three kinds of processes the committee identified.

Our research on service industry companies strongly supported the committee's analysis. In this chapter, we look at two service-based organizations, the Ritz-Carlton hotel chain and Synetics, a $50 million-a-year systems engineering company based in Wakefield, Massachusetts. In each case, their experiences demonstrate an awareness of the three kinds of processes identified by the Service Industries Committee and a willingness to apply different kinds of process management to each. That approach turned out to be crucial to both companies' success. The different processes that these service companies must manage result in different methods of continuous process improvement, but ultimately, the integrated systems evolved by the Ritz-Carlton and Synetics are remarkably similar to those we've observed in other sectors.

Ritz-Carlton: Systematically Preparing for "Moments of Truth"

Horst Schulze, president of the Ritz-Carlton Hotel Co., arrived in Singapore seven days before the opening of the Ritz-Carlton Millenia there in January 1996. His primary job: To train every new employee.

Table 3.1 Types of Processes and the Management Methods That Guide Them Effectively

Type of Process	Observable Characteristics	Basic Structure	Nature of Process to Be Managed	Employee Skills for Improvement	Management Skills for Improvement	Needed Management Methodologies
Operational process (factories, services, e.g., check processing).	Customer not present; processes repeat fairly predictably; measurable output; applying statistical tools is relatively easy.	A chain of successive steps.	Steps in process repeat as planned and are improved.	Process control, teamwork, scientific problem solving.	Delegation, including delegation of authority to stop process; coaching.	Standard improvement process used by teams at all levels.
Innovation (new product development, design of education for a student).	Something genuinely new is produced; process takes time; powerful communication is required with customer or other stakeholder who is being served.	Partnership of different units in an organization, requiring rich information flows.	Overall process repeats, and subprocesses can be predicted, but content of each step in each iteration of process is probably unique.	Sensitivity to customers' latent needs; creativity.	Delegation of authority to shape outcome.	Overall design of innovation process conducted at high level; individuals and work teams create own processes suited to overall plan.

(continued)

Table 3.1 (Continued)

Type of Process	Observable Characteristics	Basic Structure	Nature of Process to Be Managed	Employee Skills for Improvement	Management Skills for Improvement	Needed Management Methodologies
"Moment of truth" service (airline steward, business consultant).	Employees serve customers or other stakeholders in real time, and requests can't be easily predicted.	Frontline people interact with customers when customers want them; other processes provide support.	Elements of process repeat over time, but timing and order in which actions must be done is not predictable; employees have complex information needs.	Presentation, empathy, sensitivity.	Delegation of authority to alter system to satisfy customers or other stakeholders right away.	Frontline people empowered to change system to satisfy customers' immediate needs; improvement processes conducted at high level.

RITZ-CARLTON: "MOMENTS OF TRUTH" ■ 83

"In the first hour of employment, I teach them who we are, and where we're going," Schulze says. "Then, I teach them the most critical process in the hotel industry: how you interface with the customer. And I give it to them in three steps." In fact, each employee receives a wallet-size laminated plastic card enumerating those "Three Steps of Service":

1. A warm and sincere greeting. Use the guest name, if and when possible.
2. Anticipation and compliance with guest needs.
3. Fond farewell. Give them a warm good-bye and use their names, if and when possible.

These three steps represent how Ritz-Carlton intends all employees to deal with customers, all the time. The card also contains the company motto: "We are ladies and gentlemen serving ladies and gentlemen."

Under Schulze's leadership, the Ritz-Carlton has developed many techniques for achieving quality service, but the key to the company's success remains the handful of basic principles that appear on the card each employee receives in his or her first hour or two on the job.

THE CHALLENGE OF PROVIDING COST-EFFECTIVE LUXURY

Patrick Mene, the Ritz-Carlton's quality director, notes that prior to the 1980s, most hoteliers believed "superluxury hotels were not feasible, not economic." The best hotels, locally owned institutions such as the Carlyle in New York and the Bel-Air in Los Angeles, were inevitably labor-intensive operations. The only way they knew to achieve the highest standards of luxury—beyond the standards of a Hilton or a Marriott—was to hire more employees.

At Ritz-Carlton Hotels until recently, for instance, after a housekeeper prepared a room, an inspector would check to see if the work had been done correctly, and then a manager would review the work of the inspector. Obviously, this was expensive. No superluxury hotel can charge enough of a premium over the rates at a Hilton or a Marriott to cover all the extra labor required and still match the profit margin of the chains. Consequently, no chains attempted to achieve superluxury standards in the United States between World War II and the founding of the Four Seasons in the late 1970s and then the Ritz-Carlton chain in 1984.

The idea of a superluxury chain, however, is an old one. The roots of the Ritz-Carlton go back to the nineteenth century, when Cesare Ritz, a European hotelier, established a policy of serving hotel guests with the same luxury provided to European kings and queens in their courts. In the 1920s, soon after Ritz's death, the Ritz group in Europe licensed Americans to establish Ritz-Carlton Hotels in Boston, New York, and other U.S. cities. The term "ritzy" remains a synonym for superluxury. But first the Depression, then World War II, and finally rising wages made Cesare Ritz's style of hotel far more difficult to manage profitably. Today, several of Cesare Ritz's hotels still provide superb service in European cities, but all the licensed Ritz-Carlton hotels in the United States except the Boston hotel had closed by the 1970s.

W.B. Johnson, an Atlanta real estate developer who had made his fortune as owner of franchises from Marriott, Holiday Inns, and Waffle House (a Southern restaurant chain), believed that a superluxury chain could succeed in the late twentieth century. "He had a stroke of genius," says Mene. "Why not buy the Ritz-Carlton Hotel and name, which communicates a clear quality commitment, then build, and find the people that can lead and manage, a chain that will deliver that quality?"

Johnson bought the Ritz-Carlton Hotel in Boston and the Ritz-Carlton name in 1983, then hired Schulze, a German hotelier who had worked at leading hotels in Europe and North America. First, as vice president for operations and later as president and chief operating officer, Schulze was charged with creating a Ritz-Carlton chain that would deliver both unsurpassed quality *and* a healthy profit.

THE RITZ-CARLTON QUALITY SYSTEM OF THE 1980s

From the beginning, Schulze understood the unique aspect of managing customer focus in the hotel business. He instinctively knew that quality service revolved around successful management of employee-customer relations on the front lines. All employees had to be ready and equipped to make the right decision or take the right action to meet customer needs as they occurred and at a moment's notice. With little influence from quality management efforts outside the hotel industry, Schulze created a careful approach to quality management.

Chain hotels, whether they bear the name Ritz-Carlton, Marriott, Hilton, or another, are partnerships between two companies: an entrepreneur develops and owns the hotel, and a management company supplies the brand name and runs it. From the launch of the Ritz-Carlton chain, the management company's staff worked closely with local developers and with design professionals to produce true superluxury hotels.

A distinctive aspect of the Ritz' quality system is the way new hotels are "launched." Starting about a month before opening of a new hotel, a team including top performers from every level in existing hotels traveled to the new hotel's site. They recruited people who shared the organization's values. Schulze, the company's president, personally taught the company's vision and values to all new employees. Then top waiters from other hotels train waiters, top housekeepers train housekeepers, etc.

The company also evolved a scientific approach to recruitment and training. A series of interviews with prescribed questions provided extensive data on each potential employee's attitudes toward customers. Starting about one month prior to the opening of a new hotel, Schulze and a team of top Ritz-Carlton managers and outstanding performers from every level in existing hotels traveled to the new hotel's site where they personally inculcated new employees with their vision and values. Those employees hired after a hotel opened would be given similar training in a two-day orientation program.

To reinforce its values, the Ritz-Carlton adopted a chainwide policy called "the lineup," a five-minute briefing at the beginning of every shift during which all employees received reports of successes or complaints (and discussed any necessary corrective action). In addition, the employees received miniature refresher courses in one or more of the 20 Ritz-Carlton Basics (Figure 3.1).

To complement these human resource techniques, the chain developed a computer tracking system for guest histories. Guests who

<table>
<tr>
<td>

**THREE STEPS
OF SERVICE**

1
A warm and sincere greeting.
Use the guest name, if and
when possible.

2
Anticipation and compliance
with guest needs.

3
Fond farewell. Give them
a warm good-bye and use
their names, if and
when possible.

</td>
<td>

*"We Are
Ladies and
Gentlemen
Serving
Ladies and
Gentlemen"*

</td>
<td>

THE RITZ-CARLTON

CREDO
•
The Ritz-Carlton Hotel is a place
where the genuine care and comfort
of our guests is our highest mission.
We pledge to provide the finest
personal service and facilities for our
guests who will always enjoy a warm,
relaxed yet refined ambience.
The Ritz-Carlton experience
enlivens the senses, instills well-
being, and fulfills even the
unexpressed wishes and needs
of our guests.

</td>
</tr>
</table>

THE RITZ-CARLTON BASICS

1 The Credo will be known, owned and energized by all employees.
2 We are "Ladies and Gentlemen serving Ladies and Gentlemen".
3 The three steps of service shall be practiced by all employees.
4 "Smile" - "We are on stage". Always maintain positive eye contact.
5 Use the proper vocabulary with our guests. (Eliminate - Hello - Hi - OK - folks).
6 Uncompromising levels of cleanliness are the responsibility of every employee.
7 Create a positive work environment. Practice teamwork and "lateral service".
8 Be an ambassador of your hotel in and outside of the work place. Always talk positively - No negative comments.

9 Any employee who receives a guest complaint "owns" the complaint.
10 Instant guest pacification will be ensured by all. Respond to guest wishes within ten minutes of the request. Follow up with a telephone call within twenty minutes to ensure their satisfaction.
11 Use guest incident action forms to communicate guest problems to fellow employees and managers. This will help ensure that our guests are never forgotten.
12 Escort guests, rather than pointing out directions to another area of the hotel.
13 Be knowledgeable of hotel information (hours of operation, etc.) to answer guest inquiries.
14 Use proper telephone etiquette. Answer within three rings and, with a "smile", ask permission to put a caller on hold. Do not

screen calls. Eliminate call transfers when possible.
15 Always recommend the hotel's food and beverage outlets prior to outside facilities.
16 Uniforms are to be immaculate; Wear proper footwear (clean and polished) and your correct nametag.
17 Ensure all employees know their roles during emergency situations and are aware of procedures. (Practice fire and safety procedures monthly.)
18 Notify your supervisor immediately of hazards, injuries, equipment or assistance needs you have.
19 Practice energy conservation and proper maintenance and repair of hotel property and equipment.
20 Protecting the assets of a Ritz-Carlton Hotel is the responsibility of every employee.

Figure 3.1 The Ritz-Carlton Basics

visited the hotels were listed in a central computer that would tell the staff of any particular preferences. If a guest always wanted a fruit basket in the room or a nonallergenic pillow, the computer would notify the chain each time he or she reserved a room. Finally, Schulze instituted a chainwide system of regular and thorough inspections to ensure that any problems were promptly corrected. He also instituted a policy of allowing any employee to spend up to $2,000 to satisfy any customer without seeking approval from above.

Schulze's approach had given his company strong purpose, some good structural elements, and a strong customer focus. It was enough to give the Ritz far better service than most other hotel chains and garnered it some travel writers' awards as the best hotel chain in the United States. But, although profitable, the chain still didn't earn the same return on investment as other leading business hotels. In the terminology of the CQM Service Industries Committee, the Ritz-Carlton was doing a world-class job of managing moment-of-truth quality, but it had learned little about managing operational quality.

In all moment-of-truth activities, it's the frontline person's purpose and understanding of each unique job, not his or her scientific analysis of work processes, that lead to quality. The scientific analysis of processes that leads to operational quality has to be performed by higher-level teams—but teams that deeply understand both customer needs and the needs of the organization's service providers. So, in the late 1980s, Schulze looked outside the hotel industry and started studying some of the process-improvement techniques of the growing quality movement.

SYSTEMATIC PROCESS IMPROVEMENT INTO THE MOMENT-OF-TRUTH-ORIENTED SYSTEM

Schulze had heard that quality methods in other industries produced excellence while cutting expenses. He assigned staff to investigate, and in 1991 hired as quality director Patrick Mene, an experienced hotel operations manager, who at the time was working for the recently opened Los Angeles hotel of the Hong Kong–based superluxury Peninsula Hotels, as quality director in 1991.

The Ritz-Carlton Hotel Company was already pursuing the Baldrige Award. It applied in 1991, but did not win. In part, that seems to have been because the Ritz's approach to quality bewildered the judges. "They basically said to us," recalls Mene, "'You've got great quality values, you've got a great approach to human resources, and you've got the results, but we don't see a system.'"

Ritz-Carlton hadn't learned how to manage operations as well as it could. Mene was hired to learn Baldrige-style quality and then teach it to top management. He focused on the teachings of the quality expert J. M. Juran.

Juran and his consulting firm, the Juran Institute, showed Ritz-Carlton how to measure the *cost of quality,* costs that occurred because the Ritz's operational systems weren't set up to deliver what customers wanted without mistakes that later had to be caught and fixed. Schulze-trained employees were more sensitive to customer needs than those at other hotels, but the Juran techniques demonstrated that such processes as taking reservations, preparing rooms for guests, and doing laundry still lacked the consistency of repetitive processes found at Baldrige Award winners.

Mene also credits Leonard A. Seder's essay, "Quality in a Job Shop," which appears in Juran's *Quality Control Handbook,* for presenting a picture of how a business like the Ritz could use quality control techniques.[3] Job shops, unlike typical factories but like the offices described by Rothschild in *Forbes ASAP,* rarely do the same work over and over in a predictable sequence. Seder provided detailed guidance for ensuring improved processes even when the process might not repeat in exactly the same sequence for years.

The Ritz-Carlton began experimenting with PDCA improvement. By 1992, it had introduced what it calls its "quality production system," a method of tracking defects reported in each hotel and taking action to eliminate them. It had also begun replacing its inefficient inspection systems, which frequently resulted in excellent housekeepers' work being reviewed twice, with better-designed inspection systems based on scientific sampling. The new systems focused inspections on the work of newer employees and enabled experienced employees to be certified to inspect their own work.

The Ritz-Carlton won the Baldrige Award in 1992, but Mene now says, "We were given the award on the basis of our excellent results and our rapid improvement in process. But we were not a classic TQM company when we won the Baldrige." Even as Baldrige examiners were studying the company in a review that would result in the Ritz's receiving the award that autumn, the company was already launching a new and more profound effort to change its systems.

First, Ritz executives instructed each hotel to name a quality director. They provided a book written by Mene, *Ritz-Carlton Hotel Company Guide to Quality Improvement and Cost Reduction.* It described techniques based principally on teachings of the Juran Institute (similar to those used by the manufacturing organizations Teradyne and the Hewlett-Packard Medical Products Group) for tracking areas that needed improvement and then creating the improvements, project by project.

In addition, management identified 19 key processes in hotel operation (valet parking, front-desk check-in, housekeeping, conference services planning, etc.) and assigned each hotel in the chain to focus on improving *one* of them. The Ritz-Carlton in Dearborn, Michigan, for example, worked on improving housekeeping, which was perceived as high in cost and lower in quality relative to other processes.

In Dearborn, the staff examining housekeeping included managers from all over the hotel. They quickly confirmed what most managers in the chain already believed: the housekeeping process produced many "defects" (mistakes made by housekeepers). It involved excess travel time as housekeepers walked around bedrooms performing their many chores in ways that weren't efficient. And, says Mene, there were "a lot of downstream mistakes because of the way housekeeping was interfaced with laundry and the front desk."

"Guest rooms had been cleaned the same way for a hundred years," Mene notes. One person would go from room to room. A housekeeper was required to perform 150 separate tasks every day in every occupied Ritz hotel room: make the beds, clean the ashtrays, put out fresh soap in the bathroom, and so on. But the work was boring, and often the housekeeper would be so bored that he or she would turn on the television while working. A housekeeper could easily neglect some of the jobs. And because the Ritz had traditionally organized its hotels hierarchically into departments—Sales, Reservations, Housekeeping—the housekeepers had no dependable way of communicating with people outside housekeeping.

The system delivered dirty linen to the laundry in a way that made it extremely hard to process, and it didn't effectively communicate to the front desk what rooms were clean and ready for occupancy. Moreover, the order in which housekeepers cleaned rooms had nothing to do with the order in which guests were scheduled to arrive. As a result, a guest with a special need (say, someone who wanted an extra-large nonsmoking room) might be forced to wait on arrival even though that guest had told the hotel staff what time to expect him or her.

The Dearborn group analyzed the system using the processes in Mene's book. It reached an important conclusion: the hotel could provide much better service at much lower cost if it completely redesigned the work of the housekeeping, laundry, minibar, and front desk departments, merging them into one big department that the Ritz-Carlton eventually called the stayover team. Where previously, a single housekeeper cared for a room in 30 minutes, the new, redesigned process took only eight minutes for the team of three. In addition, the housekeeping teams began coordinating their work with the front desk. They received a schedule of when rooms would be required every day so they could prepare them when they were expected to be needed. When a guest showed up unexpectedly early, the room he or she needed could be prepared under the new system in as little as eight minutes.

Dearborn piloted the new system, achieving substantial savings and dramatically reducing defects and other problems for guests. In addition, the portion of housekeepers reporting they were highly satisfied with their jobs rose from 75 percent to over 90 percent. The Ritz had successfully applied a fundamental principle of integrated systems, effectively *managing* interactions among people that had gone largely unmanaged before, and the results were excellent.

By 1998, the Ritz had introduced throughout the chain this and other new guest systems piloted at individual hotels. It estimated savings of $30 million in a business that had grossed $750 million a year, as well as improved service throughout the system. The heart of the Ritz's system remained the method of managing moments of truth that Schulze developed when the company began. But the new process-management techniques improved operational processes that, in turn, provided the foundation for even more successful, more *cost-effective* moments of truth (see Table 3.2).

Synetics: Developing Systems for High-Quality Innovation Processes

If the Ritz gives us a good picture of how to manage moments of truth, Synetics tells us a great deal about how to manage an

Table 3.2 Ritz-Carlton Integrated Management Matrix

Year	Action or Method	Reason for Integration	The Systems View	Key Practices
1984	"The Three Steps of Service"; "Ladies and gentlemen serving ladies and gentlemen."	Philosophical bases for the company emphasizing the importance of moments of truth.	Provides "high leadership"; imparts common purpose.	Practice 3: Seek internal engagement.
1984	Horst Shultz's personal training of employees.	Attempt to initiate a formal, companywide commitment to quality.	Provides "high leadership"; imparts common purpose.	Practice 1: Seek continuous improvement. Practice 3: Seek internal engagement.
From nineteenth-century	"The lineup"; 14 Ritz Basics.	Formalizes moment-of-truth processes at employee level.	Aligns purposes.	Practice 1: Seek continuous improvement. Practice 3: Seek internal engagement. Practice 4: Build supportive infrastructure.
Late 1980s	Use of customer database.	Formalizes and standardizes "market-in" processes.	Utilizes "tacit" external knowledge.	Practice 1: Seek continuous improvement. Practice 2: Seek external information. Practice 4: Build supportive infrastructure.
1991	Juran's Quality Principles; Seder's "Quality in a Job Shop."	Build operational processes to support moments of truth.	Taps into external knowledge.	Practice 5: Participate in societal networking.

(continued)

Table 3.2 (Continued)

Year	Action or Method	Reason for Integration	The Systems View	Key Practices
1992	Quality Production System.	Systematically tracks and eliminates service "defects."	Provides the basis of a learning system.	Practice 1: Seek continuous improvement. Practice 4: Build supportive infrastructure.
1992	Naming a quality director for each hotel.	Pushes quality responsibility down the hierarchy.	Optimizes interactions; utilizes "tacit" knowledge.	Practice 4: Build supportive infrastructure.
1992	Defining and analyzing 19 key processes.	Focus on operational process improvement.	Forces cross-functional interactions; team-based learning.	Practice 1: Seek continuous improvement. Practice 3: Seek internal engagement. Practice 4: Build supportive infrastructure.
1995	Instituting "stayover teams" and other structures companywide.	Standardizing operational process improvement.	Team-based learning.	Practice 1: Seek continuous improvement. Practice 4: Build supportive infrastructure.

organization whose primary business is a different type of service: that of innovation.

Bahar Uttam and William O'Halloran, two engineers who together had worked nearly 14 years providing technical services to the U.S. government, formed Synetics in 1984 in O'Halloran's one-bedroom Stoneham, Massachusetts apartment. Originally, the company sought to evaluate and broker complex technology purchases by the U.S. military.

Building on the reputations of both men, the company quickly won a contract to evaluate rival bids to build the Global Positioning System for the Department of Defense and to create a mouse-based point-and-click decision-support system for the U.S. Coast Guard. The GPS was a complex of satellites and communications equipment that would tell airplanes, ships, and land vehicles precisely where in the world they were at any instant. As the GPS became functional, every fighting unit in the U.S. Armed Forces had to integrate information from the system into its existing data systems. Synetics learned to combine the right hardware and software to accomplish that. Partially as a result of Synetics's work, by 1991 the GPS was a formidable system supporting United States forces in the Gulf War, guiding missiles through the streets of Baghdad with a precision that amazed television reporters who watched missile flights from their hotel.

These successes led Uttam and O'Halloran to consider expanding their scope. "Why can't we take what we've done with the military and apply it to everyone who's got a lot of data but no information?" they wondered. By expanding beyond the military, the company could achieve rapid growth. Synetics started to bid on similar technology management jobs outside the military, first in the U.S. government and later in state governments and private industry. By 1996, it was working for 10 of the 14 cabinet-level departments in the United States.

The company went international in 1990, working with the Ports Management Association of West and Central Africa, tracking all the ports' resources, scheduling their use, planning the loading and unloading of ships, and billing the shipping lines for services rendered. With its extensive experience in managing information, Synetics suggested putting all the information on PCs, linked by Lotus Notes, rather than employing a minicomputer system that would require centralized management and a centralized database.

Synetics trained local people to run the Notes-based system. Each PC ran a separate database program tracking just what its particular office needed to track, but, at the same time, the Notes system would give each office in the network access to all the data on each computer. The system was cheaper and more effective than the minicomputer option, more easily scalable and upgradable, and ultimately far more flexible.

Synetics began to build such systems for other ports, often winning awards for them, and garnered a reputation for having an unusual ability to listen to customers' real needs.

CREATING A MANAGEMENT SYSTEM FOR INNOVATION PROCESSES

Synetics's business requires it to innovate continually. Government agencies and companies become customers because they want to do something new. Usually, it's not something that anyone on Synetics's staff, now 500-strong, has done before. In situations like this, even brilliant people can frequently fail to understand what customers really need, how long projects will take, and how well they'll function at the end.

When Synetics entered civilian markets, one of its first projects involved designing a new Medicare/Medicaid payments system for the Department of Health and Human Services. A previous contractor had attempted the task and failed. To tackle the daunting assignment, Synetics developed a process it now calls Joint Application Design, a set of steps that helped Synetics clearly understand the problems with the existing system that the Department of Health and Human Services' staff wanted solved. In Joint Application Design, a client's key staff members are required to meet with Synetics designers in a workshop that is several days long. The workshop forces Synetics and all the key people who are buying its service to agree on what Synetics is to deliver.

The Joint Applications Design methodology forced Synetics staff to obtain clear and complete explanations from customers even when the customers resisted. In a later application, preparing an information systems project for the Massachusetts Water Resources Authority, for example, project managers had to insist on full-time participation of all the organization's top executives in three days of meetings. Synetics considers the art of attracting customers to workshops where they are needed to be crucial to the application design process.

The same degree of participation was also considered essential to designing the company's internal systems. All officers met once every month, and virtually no one was allowed to skip the meetings regardless of how important other business might be. Uttam visited each office in the company four times a year, and Chief Financial Officer Paul Pakos visited each office twice. Ann Orlando, chief technology officer, traveled to each office twice a year both to learn of new technologies each office had developed and to set up workshops to communicate ideas others in the company had devised.

As the company diversified and grew—sometimes adding nearly 100 people a year—it became a challenge to maintain the same high degree of interaction, not to mention a high level of quality control. Seeking a way to address those issues, Uttam, O'Halloran, and Jack Fagan (who ran the sector of Synetics's business that served the military's command-and-control technology needs) began to examine Total Quality Management programs in other industries. What they observed inspired them to redesign their management system.

FIRST ATTEMPTS TO REDESIGN THE MANAGEMENT SYSTEM

Synetics changed its management in several ways. As a first step, they attempted to clarify their mission, adopting five core values: customer satisfaction, technical excellence, employee growth and development, integrity, and business growth and profitability. They then established a Rewards and Recognition Committee that redesigned annual performance reviews so that employees were measured on their contribution to achieving these values. An annual banquet was instituted to recognize outstanding contributions.

The firm shifted Fagan from his job as head of the command-and-control group and made him quality director for the entire company. It established five companywide committees, one to promote each of the values.

After Uttam, O'Halloran, Fagan, and other top managers took the Center for Quality Management's six-day course for senior executives, they launched companywide training in seven-step process-improvement techniques. But, like Ritz-Carlton employees, Synetics professionals worked directly with customers and with unexpected situations every day and had to be ready to respond creatively to customer requirements. They were doing moment-of-truth work, and the courses were designed to help people working on operational processes. They couldn't establish standards in the ways recommended or carry out the usual kind of seven-step improvement work on most of their processes. In fact, the five committees and the seven-step process-improvement training produced virtually no valuable results. Few employees created substantial improvements due to the training, and the training was unpopular.

However, Synetics' application of another Total Quality Management methodology, Concept Engineering, did begin to produce the desired improvements.

A PORTFOLIO OF DISCIPLINED INNOVATION-MANAGEMENT METHODS

Concept Engineering was developed by U.S. Navy Commander Gary Burchill as part of his doctoral studies at MIT. It provides a well-defined process for developing customer-focused new products. Figure 3.2 shows the five stages of concept engineering.

Concept Engineering resembled the Joint Application Design process, but it was a far more extensive system. For example, in the first stage, "Understanding the Customer's Environment," Concept Engineering includes careful preparation during which participants sensitize themselves to the nature of innovation and the kind of understanding of the customer that's needed for real innovation. Along with a visit to the customer, it includes developing *images* of the customer's environment and needs.

Concept Engineering is based on the idea that customers often can't tell you what innovations would benefit them. If you simply conduct interviews, you're like an observer standing outside a fish tank trying to determine what it's like to be a fish. By creating mental images of the customer's environment and needs, the concept engineering process puts developers in the customer's world. It's like diving into the fish bowl and swimming with the fish.

As a project for the creation of the concept engineering process, for example, Burchill developed a stripping basket for saltwater fly fishermen, a container for holding loose coils of fly line retrieved after a cast. Burchill used a Language Processing diagram to organize 30 different

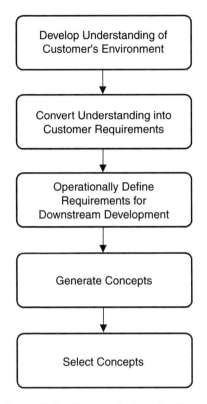

Figure 3.2 Concept Engineering Stages

images gleaned from his conversations with fishermen, images such as: "Standing in a riptide casting to a school of bluefish" and "No time to wait a second; you miss your opportunity, adrenaline goes to 200 percent." These fragmented, experiential images helped him gain an intuitive feel for the processes and problems of fly-fishing. Using that, he was able to design a product that managed fishermen's line in all situations they were likely to encounter. *New York Times* outdoors columnist Nelson Bryant called it "the best stripping basket I have ever used."

When O'Halloran and Fagan took the CQM six-day course, one homework assignment involved using concept engineering to create a solution to a fictitious new product problem. They rebelled against the idea of working on something fictitious. "We decided, 'Why not do something real?'" says O'Halloran. "If I'm going to spend 40 hours, why not make it productive for my company?"

Marty Wapner, the head of Synetics's Government Systems Group and one of the company's most skeptical managers on the subject of using new Total Quality methods, was seeking funds to launch a service bureau that would take advantage of new high-density digital storage devices just then coming on the market. It would maintain vast files of electronic images from government agencies, making the images readily available when the agencies needed them but sparing the agencies the cost of developing new electronic filing systems themselves. Before the next scheduled meeting of the six-day course a month later, O'Halloran and Fagan flew to potential customers in Michigan, California, and Washington, D.C. At each site, they performed each step of the "Understanding the Customer's Environment" process.

The project they turned in at the next session of the six-day course was the first phase of the Concept Engineering of an entirely new business. Using the Concept Engineering methodology, O'Halloran and Fagan made numerous important discoveries about the proposed business. They learned, for instance, that different potential clients wanted very different kinds of service bureaus. Law firms were highly price sensitive, allowing them to put up with occasional errors in the storage and retrieval process if the price could be kept down. Many government agencies, on the other hand, insisted on perfection. The IRS couldn't tolerate an error in a form kept on file, but it was also willing to pay higher prices. This discovery led to the decision to launch an electronic filing service bureau aimed at the high end of the market.

O'Halloran and Fagan felt they might be on to something—Concept Engineering might just be the tool that created standardized improvement of the innovation processes that were Synetics's bread and butter.

PROJECT LIFE-CYCLE METHODOLOGY

Today, Synetics has a suite of standard innovation methodologies that its people can use in a variety of situations and for a variety of customers. Key elements are the Concept Engineering methodology (for major innovations), the Joint Application Development methodology (for simpler innovation processes), and a process Synetics calls Rapid Application Development (See Figure 3.3). Rapid Application Development jump-starts innovation by quickly producing a prototype of a system, which the customer can criticize and comment on.

Combining aspects of each of their main methods, Synetics also created what it calls the Project Life-Cycle Methodology (Figure 3.4). This system gives a fuller picture of the development process than the Joint Applications Design methodology without requiring all the steps of Concept Engineering in cases where they may not be appropriate.

In 1996, the State of Massachusetts hired Synetics largely because officials felt the Project Life-Cycle Methodology gave them a good picture of exactly what the company would do to reinvent the state's process of placing citizens in private industry jobs. The existing system at the state's Department of Employment and Training had real problems. Employers would telephone their needs to the state agency, where a staff member would attempt to describe the jobs using forms

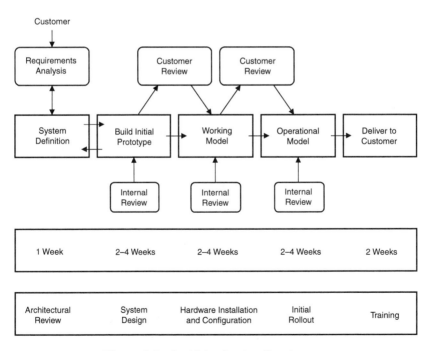

Figure 3.3 Rapid Application Development

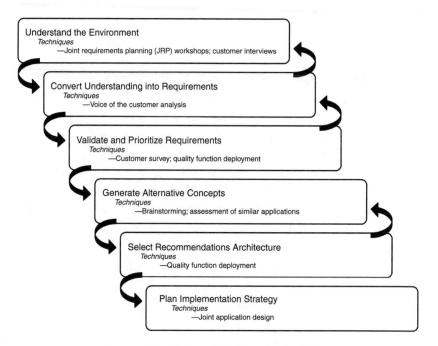

Figure 3.4 Project Life-Cycle Methodology

in an old database program that allowed only a few characters for each data element. The state wanted employers and potential employees to be able to list their job or their credentials with any center and have it available everywhere, on the Internet as well as at job centers.

At the same time, the state wanted to turn much of the function over to private companies who it felt would have incentive to do a better job than did government employees. But merely hiring a private contractor would not create efficiency or higher performance. The state wanted a number of privately operated matching centers to compete with one another.

The entire project followed the Project Life-Cycle Methodology. In working with state officials and potential operators of job-matching centers, Synetics staff conducted a complete Concept Engineering process, developing a clear image of what it would be like to support and run job-matching centers that effectively benefited employees.

But of course, those weren't the only customers. The ultimate test would be how well the system filled the needs of employers and potential employees. Synetics people conducted workshops using the simpler Joint Applications Development process to obtain employers' and employees' understanding of how the system should work. Then they used the Rapid Application Development methodology to provide prototypes of computer screens that showed how the proposed system would look and work. Only when a well-defined process of matching had been defined did Synetics design the information system that would support it. The State of Massachusetts was delighted with the performance at the first centers to open, and other states are now seeking to implement similar systems.

Synetics is finding that the Project Life-Cycle Methodology greatly benefits the organization because it shows potential customers exactly what Synetics intends to do, making them more willing to employ the firm. Work using the Project Life-Cycle Methodology has subsequently produced highly successful projects not only for the State of Massachusetts but also for the FBI, the Internal Revenue Service, and Sainsbury, the leading food distributor in the United Kingdom.

LEARNING TO APPLY THE SCIENTIFIC METHOD TO MANAGEMENT OF INTERACTIONS

Equally important, the Project Life-Cycle Methodology has become a model for defining, clarifying, and managing other major processes within Synetics. Much of the thinking about quality originated in factories, where processes are linear and predictable. Synetics executives, on the other hand, can never prescribe exactly what will happen when.

"A systems engineering firm [like Synetics] functions as a network, not according to a process flow of work," says Uttam. Rather than talking about "managing people," a phrase often equated with telling them what to do, or prescribing narrow "objectives" for them, he encourages the concept of "managing interactions" among people or "managing processes." Synetics's leaders try to give definition to the general processes employees should follow, but leave employees freedom to innovate and create within those processes.

Although few Synetics processes are so consistently repeated that they can be standardized and improved with simple process-improvement techniques used in factories, many can be managed in the same way that the Project Life-Cycle Methodology manages innovation for a customer. They can be defined with a chart such as that in Figure 3.4 that helps the whole organization understand itself, control its work better, and improve service for customers. In short, an understanding of the process of innovating gave Synetics the knowledge it needed so its executives could use the scientific method to manage other processes in the organization.

Much of Synetics's management system today derives from two one-day workshops that were conducted for the company's nine top managers in 1993. Two facilitators from Bose Corp. led the sessions by arrangement of the Center for Quality of Management. Synetics had grown to 400 employees, and it was continuing to expand at 25 percent a year. Its leaders realized they were losing touch with parts of their organization. And in many ways, they weren't prepared to compete as a large organization for systems-integration jobs that would cost tens of millions of dollars.

After the sessions, the management team addressed several of the barriers by creating new, formalized processes. For example, one problem that the workshops identified was that Synetics had no process to manage the preparation of large bids, an extremely expensive endeavor. (Synetics estimates that, on average, preparing a bid for a $25 million project costs one to two percent of the cost of the project. Unless the company has at least a one in five chance of winning, preparing a bid isn't worthwhile.)

Synetics now defines the steps from the day the organization starts work on a proposal to its submission. The program manager has to defend why he or she has the capability to bid, whether he or she fully understands the customer's requirements and has the resources to satisfy them, and whether Synetics is uniquely different from and better than competitors for this job. Synetics can't define a process like this with the precision that could be applied to a manufacturing process, but it can achieve roughly the same level of clarity and precision that the Project Life-Cycle Methodology brought to the creation of innovations.

Synetics Chief Engineer Ann Orlando headed a group that created a similarly well-defined marketing process for the company.

Another team created a clear definition of the personnel development and promotion process and the career ladder within Synetics. These process-definition efforts created an organization that could achieve excellent performance in a more controlled way than could otherwise have been realized.

In addition to these top-management efforts, Fagan launched a suggestion system called IMPROVE (IMproving PROcesses Via Employees) that produced more than 100 ideas, about half of which have been implemented so far. One employee, development engineer Lee Romero, suggested that the company use Lotus Notes to create a standard project notebook that would track every project's development in a uniform way. A team was set up to design the online notebook system, and now Synetics employees can understand each others' projects significantly more easily. The company is even beginning to sell the notebook methodology to its customers.

To ensure that all the new tactics were coordinated, Synetics's nine top officers began to meet monthly as the steering committee for the company's Total Quality Management effort, tracking how the organization's processes were functioning and examining how they could be improved.

SYNETICS AS A SOURCE OF MODEL FOR MANAGING INNOVATIVE SERVICES

Synetics's management changes are by no means perfect or complete. Nonetheless, the company's changes offer important lessons for companies that live by providing innovative services. It has learned to routinize innovation without restricting creativity or forcing clients to accept prepackaged solutions. Recognizing that its early effort to train every employee didn't work, Synetics created a just-in-time system that provides training when a part of the organization has a specific problem it wants to solve.

Even as the number of its original clients in the military shrank, Synetics continued to grow rapidly and accumulate an ever larger order backlog. In the mid-1990s, the company created a system to certify, inspect, and regulate 140,000 clinical laboratories for the federal government's Health Care Financing Administration. It helped the FBI launch its national DNA database. It created a voter registration system in Massachusetts. It developed a laptop computer system that salespeople for Guinness in the United Kingdom could use to promptly negotiate and close deals with pubs. (In 1996, the company sold a large part of its business to Science Applications International Corp., a systems design company that is the third largest employee-owned business in the United States. Some of these projects, though originated by units that were part of Synetics, went to Science Applications in the sale.)

Managing Each Kind of Process

When we look closely at the Ritz and at Synetics, we find strong evidence that the basic scientific method approach that is used in the manufacturing sector can be applied to service businesses. Moment-of-truth and innovation processes, although greatly benefiting from standard plan-do-check-act process-improvement techniques, also involve unpredictable interaction with customers and with new ideas. The Ritz-Carlton's experience suggests a way of managing moment-of-truth processes: Establish a small number of clear rules and an ethos that will guide employees in their interactions with customers. Synetics's experience suggests a way of managing innovation processes: Establish basic processes of innovation that can consistently guide people in hearing the customer.

Table 3.3 presents how operational, moment-of-truth, and innovation processes are encountered and managed at the Ritz and at Synetics. When the kind of process is understood, each kind can be improved using the scientific method.

The service industry represents the largest and most rapidly growing part of the world economy and the opportunity for improvement is enormous. Indeed, it may be that an integrated system approach to management can deliver change in the service sector that is more dramatic than that in manufacturing. Most manufacturing organizations have understood that processes need clear analysis, but, as Rothschild noted, many crucial service activities have never even been analyzed

Table 3.3 Three Management Processes at Ritz-Carlton and Synetics

Type of Process	Example at Ritz-Carlton	Management Method at Ritz-Carlton	Example at Synetics	Management Method at Synetics
Operational	Housekeeping.	Use of statistical systems for inspection and large team effort to map radical new process.	Payroll.	Quality group teaches process-management skills in sections of the company where process problems are identified.
Moment of truth	Guest interactions.	Teaching a basic three-step process of service and constant reinforcement of an ethos.	Sales, consultant interaction with customer.	Definition of a clear marketing process, teaching of "customer first" principle.
Innovation	Creation of new services.	*Not studied by us.*	Creation of new systems to fulfill client's needs.	Project life-cycle methodolgy defines a controlled, step-by-step, customer-driven innovation process.

as processes. And although most of them can't be controlled as tightly as can an assembly process, the experience of Ritz-Carlton, Synetics, and other service organizations strongly suggests that process analysis and forms of standardization can have wide-ranging and demonstrable benefits.

CHAPTER 4

Achieving
Diverse Purposes

Integrated Systems in Education

Basic education in America faces a real crisis. Myriad studies and a torrent of statistics indicate that the weaknesses of our educational system are overwhelming—and worsening. According to the late American Federation of Teachers president Albert Shanker, "Ninety-five percent of the kids who go to college in the United States would not be admitted to college anywhere else in the world."[1] And to a significant extent, this underachieving continues in college. Each year in the United States, on average 600,000 first-year college students take calculus; some 250,000 fail.[2]

Today's schools clearly aren't good enough for today's Americans. Can integrated management principles solve this problem? There's a good deal of evidence that they can make a large contribution. But for them to do so, the process of introducing and maintaining integrated management systems in education will have to be understood considerably better than it is today.

We found at least one powerful example of a well-developed integrated management system that made an enormous difference for students, faculty, and society as a whole in a school district. We found other examples where principles relevant to integrated management systems were being used to great effect. We concluded that the best educators could teach all kinds of managers important lessons about managing the diverse, often competing purposes of

106

people in organizations and presiding over complex processes that can never be fully understood.

But we also found that people within education seemed to understand the processes by which effective integrated management systems are created and maintained even less than people in other sectors. The systems we examined didn't survive transitions to new leadership, and the leaders who made them work weren't able to explain them in ways that would allow others to duplicate their successes.

Thus, this chapter has a double goal. On one hand, we want to show the work of a few leaders who have dealt with a challenging sector in ways that offer lessons for managers everywhere. But on the other hand we want to show the methods of these leaders clearly enough so we can help educators and everyone interested in education begin to develop a clear understanding of just what educational management requires.

Schools can achieve outstanding performance in a decentralized environment that serves all stakeholders—students, parents, faculty, and society—much better. But it will take careful analysis—undoubtedly more than we will be able to provide in this chapter—before educators will be able to do this with consistency.

Kenmore-Tonawanda School District

Just outside Buffalo, New York, we visited a school system that was achieving great things. With nearly 9,000 students, 640 teachers, and 960 nonteaching staff, the Kenmore–Town of Tonawanda Union Free School District is one of the largest suburban school districts in New York State. Situated in the inner ring of Buffalo suburbs, it is overwhelmingly white but economically diverse, containing pockets of rundown housing as well as neat, middle-class homes. When John Helfrich arrived in 1981 as superintendent, the district suffered from considerable distrust between the teachers' union (a local of the United Federation of Teachers) and the administration. By the time he retired in 1994, Helfrich had developed a remarkable integrated management system. The school improvement program he initiated contained, in fact, all the elements of effective Total Quality Management systems and the elements of effective management of a human society whose members have diverse purposes. In particular, Helfrich introduced practices that pushed a good deal of the system's goal-setting down to broad-based teams in individual schools. In essence, his systems said: People, your schools have to pursue and achieve high goals, but *you* can have the primary say about which high goals you'll seek. The result was dramatic improvement by all the yardsticks we examined.

Though the system fell into decline after Helfrich's retirement, during his tenure, the effect could be seen in key measures such as test scores, dropout rates, percentages of students continuing their education, and state and national recognition. Kenmore-Tonawanda (commonly known as KenTon) became the first U.S. educational institution ever to win a major Total Quality Management award, New York State's Excelsior Award, in 1990. Statistics strongly supported the award. For example, between 1982 and 1990, scores had risen from 91 to 98 in New York State Pupil Evaluation Program tests on fifth-grade writing, from 87 to 95 on sixth-grade reading, and 88 to 97 on sixth-grade math. The percentage dropping out of high school had fallen from 4.6 to 2.5. The percentage of high school students winning New York State Regents Scholarships had risen from 15 to 23. The percentage of high school students continuing their education had risen from 72 to 88. Six of Kenmore-Tonawanda's thirteen schools had been named New York State Schools of Excellence.

By the time Helfrich retired, almost all of the district's 13 schools had received the School of Excellence designation at least once.

Kenmore-Tonawanda made most of its progress without help from the quality movement or any management "experts" from outside education. In fact, until William D. Keasling, administrative assistant to the superintendent, read about the quality award in an education publication and suggested that the district apply, no one in the district had even had any formal contact with quality methods or "gurus." Nonetheless, Helfrich introduced an integrated system of great power. Educators can learn from studying KenTon. Many superficially similar programs in other districts have failed, and the details of the methods Helfrich used to keep the system genuinely participatory deserve close scrutiny. But businesspeople and leaders from other sectors can also learn from the story. Most businesspeople must not only manage profit and loss, but also manage the diverse purposes of stakeholders whose common interests aren't always clear. Under Helfrich, KenTon did that supremely well.

The Origins of KenTon's System

Soon after Helfrich came to KenTon in 1981, he launched the school improvement program. He was influenced by principles he'd learned in the 1960s working for the Institute for the Development of Educational Activities (IDEA) in Dayton, Ohio. IDEA had been founded in 1965 by the Kettering Foundation and in its first decade had used the foundation's resources to promote a complex approach to excellence called individually guided education (IGE). A glance at IGE might suggest it was a perfect, comprehensive integrated management system. It broke down large schools into smaller minischools called learning communities, which mixed students of differing ages, practiced team teaching, and, at least in principle, allowed administrators and faculty to jointly share decision making. The program sought 35 specific educational outcomes and provided a detailed road map to achieve them using techniques supported by what seemed to be solid educational research.

But the effort to create a comprehensive integrated system centrally and promulgate it in dozens of districts couldn't really succeed. As Helfrich now says, "It worked, but it was too complicated for people to learn and implement." Some of the underlying principles were powerful. Few districts, however, could get whole schools to buy into the entire program and make it succeed.

Moreover, even where IGE seemed to work splendidly it often didn't make people feel empowered as its promoters expected. John Goodlad, then dean of education at UCLA, had pointed out a simple fact: research showed that educational programs worked best when the people implementing them felt involved in developing them. Goodlad said that change should occur through a dialogue-decision-action-evaluation (DDAE) cycle, ensuring consensus.

But with 35 outcomes and innumerable specific techniques on the IGE agenda, local educators rarely felt competent to "dialogue" and "decide" on the program. IDEA Vice President Jon Paden recalled in an interview that administrators often acted as if efforts to become a "good" IGE district were more important than shared decision making. When IDEA staff visited extraordinarily successful districts, Paden says, they'd often find that "Administrators would act very guilty. They would act as if they had let us down, because they hadn't implemented all the processes IDEA had in the program."

IDEA changed direction sharply in the late 1970s. It began to promote school improvement programs by promoting the DDAE cycle, but refraining from advocating specific types of improvements. It advocated the creation at every school of a school planning team, including teachers, parents, community members, administrators, and support staff such as custodians or secretaries, and, in the high schools, students. Team members would be trained in the processes of how to create and implement their own vision of a good school. To encourage the formulation of that vision, IDEA developed a list of nine very general guiding principles along the lines of "Education is increasingly used to prepare students for successful life transitions."

At KenTon, Helfrich built on IDEA's new approach, transforming the DDAE cycle into a version remarkably similar to the plan-do-check-act (PDCA) cycle we have seen at work in so many successful companies. The central idea of Helfrich's school improvement program was simple: Get each school to develop a vision statement summarizing what the people associated with the school want it to become in three to five years. Then, each year, implement the DDAE cycle to move ever closer to the vision.

Each winter, planning team members canvassed other teachers, parents, staff, and students to decide what aspects of the vision the school should work on implementing or what problems the school should work on solving that year. The planning team commissioned design teams—groups of about six people with special knowledge of the issue, usually drawn from faculty, administrators, parents, staff, and others—to work out implementation strategies in the spring and summer. In the fall, the school implemented the improvements. Then, each winter, a monitoring team studied whether that year's improvements were working. When the monitoring team had largely completed its analysis for the year, the annual cycle started again. Every few years, the monitoring team also conducted comprehensive studies of student and parent satisfaction.

Facilitators made the system work, and Helfrich always insisted that facilitators, including teachers, administrators, parents, and support staff, be trained for each school. KenTon sent more than 250 teachers, administrators, parents, and support staff to weeklong out-of-district IDEA facilitator-training courses. It seemed like an extravagance; many other districts that implement improvement programs send only a few people to outside programs, then have those people train facilitators within the district. But facilitator skills were perhaps the single most important resource in Helfrich's program. And even including the cost of sending facilitators out of town for training, the direct costs of the school improvement program were still only about $250,000 in a total school budget of $80 million. Helfrich was probably wise not to skimp.

During the IDEA courses, participants role-played a school planning team in its first 40 hours of existence. This is the period when a planning team learns group skills and creates a vision of what its school should become in the next three to five years. The participants learned how to conduct a get-acquainted session that will force participants to actually listen to each other, how to run a brainstorming session, and how to create a pyramid group that will enable a small number of people to communicate in a personal way with many constituents.

As we have seen in many of the companies we've studied, the catalyst that sparks the evolution of an integrated management system is usually the leader himself or herself. The leader cares deeply about total involvement and about hearing the ideas of every person in the system. The successful leader believes strongly in the bottom-up movement of ideas, but to make that movement happen, he or she disseminates a new approach to leading in top-down fashion. The infrastructure of Ken-Ton's system of disseminating the vision and mobilizing for its implementation strikingly resembled those we observed in corporate settings (introduced in Chapter 2):

- The *school planning teams* in each school served the same function as the *quality councils* and similar broad-based coordinating groups in many departments of companies.
- *Facilitator training* and an extensive staff development program served the same function as the best parts of company *training programs*.

- *Posters, pins, and speeches* by Helfrich and others in the community extolling quality served the same function as *promotion for new management initiatives* in companies.

- *Diffusion of success stories* through monthly administrators' meetings, presentations to the Board of Education, and retreats for school planning team members served the same function as mechanisms for diffusion of success stories in companies.

- *Nonmonetary awards* such as a "wall of fame" for staff who've taken leadership in in-service education served the same function as nonmonetary incentives and awards in companies.

- *Monitoring and diagnosis* through surveys, interviews, and the continual application for School of Excellence awards from local and national bodies served the same function as monitoring and diagnosis mechanisms in thoughtfully managed companies.

With all these parallels to systems in companies, you might expect KenTon's goal-setting system to parallel those in companies, too. But it was very different, and that difference revealed a way of serving diverse stakeholders all at the same time. In successful businesses, top managers establish basic goals and insist that department goals support those basic goals. In education far more than business, however, there are many diverse purposes, a wide variety of stakeholders, and grave difficulties in trying to control an entire system from the center. An integrated system bent on continuous improvement would be unwise if based on unnecessary conformity.

A New Wrinkle: Decentralized Goal Setting

Kenmore-Tonawanda's system decentralized goal setting far more than any successful corporation we know. The most important parts of the goal-setting infrastructure are in each individual school: the vision statements and the annual goal setting of the planning teams. Indeed, the KenTon Board of Education had no vision statement of its own for several years after the school improvement program started.

Superintendent Helfrich and the central administration also played important roles in goal setting. Principals said, for instance, that if a school's test scores lagged, staff from the central administration would remind them of the need for improvement. But the annual improvement goals in some schools might have no direct connection to Board goals.

Let's examine an annual school improvement cycle at KenTon's Benjamin Franklin Middle School and how it solved a complex, important problem: the isolation of special-needs children who couldn't keep up with regular classes. New York, like most states, mandates that schools develop a customized program for each special-needs child, who may be learning disabled, emotionally disturbed, or physically handicapped. Schools must educate those who can't keep up with regular lessons in classes of no more than 15, taught by certified learning adjustment teachers. In the late 1980s, though research was demonstrating that special-needs children did best when integrated with the rest of the school, the three special-needs classes at the back of Benjamin Franklin had become an isolated subculture. Few special-needs students learned enough to reenter the regular classes in their grades. At the same time, Benjamin Franklin also faced similar problems with their gifted-and-talented students programs. At each end of the educational spectrum, the challenge was to meet the special needs of a minority of students while not isolating those students in a disruptive and counterproductive way.

Figure 4.1 shows the annual planning cycle at KenTon. At the January 1992 meeting, the school planning team began by brainstorming a list of about a dozen issues the school could address in the coming year. Then, the team broke into three small groups, and each of these independently identified the special-needs problem and the gifted-and-talented students problem. The planning team created a single design team to address both. It was called the Meeting Diverse Student Needs Design Team and was composed of MaryAnne Kermis, an assistant principal, and five teachers. In an effort to gather information from all sources, both internal and external (two key practices of integrated management), they used the pyramid group technique in which each team member became the leader of a subgroup of teachers, parents, support staff, and student council members. They were told to bring back at least one specific idea from each. In addition, team members sought suggestions at meetings with guidance counselors, parents, special-needs teachers, non-special-needs teachers, and others.

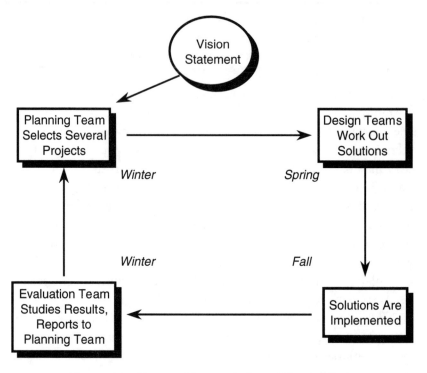

Figure 4.1   Kenmore-Tonawanda Annual Planning Cycle

When the members of the school planning team and the design team gathered to report the results of their pyramid group data gathering it became clear that the more than 100 people they'd interviewed were in remarkable agreement. None of the requests of the non-special-needs parents contradicted the desires of the faculty or the special-needs parents. The solution adopted essentially encouraged a greater integration of students of all abilities while paying greater attention to their individual needs. For example, each grade would have a Connections Team that would include the top students and special-needs children, a learning adjustment teacher dedicated to that team, and the school's resource room teacher (a special teacher responsible for helping lagging students who didn't require special-needs classes). The Connections Team would be able to offer improved opportunities to non-special-needs students as well as special-needs students. The presence of the learning adjustment teacher and the resource room teacher would give it a lower student-faculty ratio than any teams had had in the past. These two special teachers would now be assigned to help not only students who needed remedial aid under traditional criteria, but also any student who felt—or whose teacher felt—he or she would benefit from special assistance.

The new system was put into practice in September 1992. In winter and spring of 1993, Franklin Middle School's monitoring team interviewed students, parents, and teachers and reviewed test scores to evaluate how well the system was functioning. More than 85 percent of special-needs student comments supported the new arrangement. "I like being with more people," said one. "I'm not made fun of now," said another. "Now I know what everyone is talking about," said a third. "Last year, no one would sit with my child at lunch; this year, he has friends," said a parent.

Special-needs students' test scores had improved significantly. Non-special-needs students on the Connections Team also performed well. For both special-needs and non-special-needs students, discipline referrals decreased. Attendance rates increased. And the faculty was thrilled with the placement of the graduating special-needs students when they entered high school. Of ten special-needs graduates, all but one entered mainstream high school math classes and all but three entered mainstream social studies classes. The previous year, only 40 percent of special needs graduates had entered mainstream classes.

Supporters of the Kenmore-Tonawanda school improvement program acknowledge that its success varied from school to school. The system depended on each principal's active commitment, and occasionally, the commitment wasn't there. Moreover, participants emphasize that pieces of the Kenmore-Tonawanda system can't simply be plugged into other districts. The New York State Board of Regents, the highest educational authority in the state, has recently ordered schools throughout New York to create planning teams. Educational authorities in other states have taken similar steps. But these programs make little provision for a supporting infrastructure.

DDAE and the infrastructure that supported it represented a coherent approach to the scientific method for a school system. (Compare the DDAE cycle described here to the dictionary definition of the scientific method described in Chapter 1.) But, neither Helfrich nor anyone else seems to have made the extremely careful effort that might have been required to teach others what it would take to keep a system like his operating in his absence. He assured us shortly before his retirement that others in the district understood the system and "it will just get better and better." Many in the district had come to share his respect for all the district's stakeholders, his belief in continuous improvement, and his commitment to decentralized decision-making. But our interviews suggested Helfrich wasn't good at talking about the nature of the infrastructure he created for managing interactions or about theories and principles like those in Chapter 1 of this book. IDEA didn't seem good at this either. The leaders of private companies like Teradyne, Hewlett-Packard Medical Products Group, Eastman Chemical, Ritz-Carlton, and Synetics each had access to people who thought about this kind of issue in the outside organizations they talked to about management. (These included not only the Center for Quality of Management, but also the MIT Center for Advanced Engineering Study, the Malcolm Baldrige National Quality Award committee, and the Juran Institute). IDEA does not appear to have provided the same kind of guidance for KenTon. The principles taught in its seminars were deliberately vague, and IDEA did not discuss with us a well-developed set of overall management principles for leaders.

To manage a system with 9,000 students and 1,600 staff members requires more than a belief in participative decision-making. It requires an understanding of some principles of management.

We have not studied the problems that developed after Helfrich's departure. Opinions differ on what happened. Many people in Kenmore and Tonawanda believed that some school officials spent money with unnecessary extravagance (both during Helfrich's tenure and after), and we're not in a position to question that argument. We can suggest that spending on out-of-district training for facilitators, which subsequent administrations discontinued, was worthwhile. Heavy focus on facilitators and facilitator training is not surprising in a system that manages interactions as complex as those in a 9,000-student school district. A facilitator, after all, is simply a person who manages interactions in a group.

Since Helfrich's retirement, test scores and other measures of success in KenTon have not continued to improve as they did in Helfrich's tenure. The key lesson from the decline of the system seems to be the need for developing principles of management that can support both rising standards and participatory decision-making at the same time in school districts. The KenTon experience shows that principles borrowed from the for-profit sector will require significant adaptation. But still the for-profit sector can probably offer schools useful lessons.

Mt. Edgecumbe High School

The KenTon experience represented the best example of an integrated management system we encountered in education at any level. But the work of two other groups suggests integrated management systems can be pushed even further—in two quite different directions. A small, state-operated public high school in Sitka, Alaska, managed to engage nearly everyone connected with the school in the school's management. And a study centered at the University of Texas in Austin has shown how much education can improve from careful industrial engineering-like management of the actual process of education.

PROGRESS TOWARD TOTAL INTERNAL ENGAGEMENT

Let's look at the total involvement process first. Mount Edgecumbe High School is located 12 hours by ferry or 40 minutes by air from Alaska's capital, Juneau, on a stunning island connected by bridge to the main part of the town of Sitka (population 8,500). Eighty-five percent of Mount Edgecumbe's 280 students are Native Americans, largely Eskimos, Aleuts, and Athabascan, Tlingit, Haida, and Tsimpshian Indians. Many come from remote rural areas without high schools.

Larrae Rocheleau, the school's first superintendent, resembled Teradyne's D'Arbeloff, HP MPG's Holmes, and Eastman Chemical's Deavenport, in that he was a leader who learned. He created the school with state government funding in a building that had housed a recently closed Bureau of Indian Affairs school. Surveys of graduates suggest that the school provided an excellent education from the beginning.

But David Langford, a teacher of music, business, and computer skills, found the school didn't satisfy him. His dissatisfaction and his effort to practice mutual learning with the students in his classes ultimately played the key role in creating something startlingly new. Disheartened by what he perceived as disengagement of the student body and infighting among the faculty in Sitka, Langford decided to enroll in a training program for potential district superintendents during the summer of 1988 at Arizona State University. He hoped that by becoming a superintendent in a small Alaskan town, he could be his own boss.

Teachers in the Gilbert, Arizona, school district brought him to a local McDonnell-Douglas factory, where he became entranced by Deming-style quality philosophy and techniques. "I was dumbfounded. I'd never seen anything like this before," says Langford. "They were teaching everyone in that plant to think. And they'd already saved hundreds of millions of dollars."

As he watched videotapes of W. Edwards Deming, two lightbulbs went on in Langford's head: first, that failure to achieve good results doesn't mean that the person who has failed isn't trying to do a good job; second, that neither praise nor criticism nor incentives can cause a person to improve if he or she lacks understanding of the mechanism of improvement.

Langford believed that these points were true about teachers and students as well as company employees. "I didn't see it as a business philosophy at all," Langford recalls. "I saw it as a philosophy of life."

Langford's classes in educational administration now bored him, and he began telephoning quality managers all over the United States, seeking more information about the Deming approach. He would need more than one summer program before he could apply for a job as a superintendent. So he returned to Mt. Edgecumbe that fall, and he tried to explain what he'd learned to Rocheleau and to Bill Denkinger, the school's principal. But he didn't know how.

"Deming said you had to get top management committed. So I thought that was my job," Langford says. Then one day, as Langford was telling some of his students about quality and systemwide improvement, he had what he now calls a revelation. "I had been saying, 'It has to start at the top.' Well, here in the classroom, maybe I was 'the top,'" Langford recalls. "So the next day in class, I said to the students: 'Will you help me apply this philosophy here?'"

The students agreed, but Langford couldn't tell how much they understood. The following day, he tried to focus on *constancy of purpose* (the first of Deming's 14 points for the reform of management) by asking them: "Why are you here?"

They said, "To get good grades."

Clearly, that wasn't the kind of purpose that Langford wanted to encourage. So he took out his grade book and, for all ten students in the class, wrote an A for their end-of-term grade. "They were all stunned," Langford says. The next day, he asked again, "Why are you here?" They were defensive. It was clear that they still weren't attending out of a commitment to learning. To emphasize that he only wanted them as participants in a committed effort to learn, Langford told them, "You don't have to come." Langford resolved to spend the time he would have spent in grading on making the educational system better. And in a few days, he asked the students, "What should we do to change the system?"

The students had no profound replies right away. But the next day, a student asked, "Wouldn't we want to know what are the most-asked system questions?" The idea appealed to Langford. The movie *Dead Poets' Society* was at its peak of popularity, so Langford conspiratorially asked the students to join him in founding the Dead Quality Society to study improvement of the system at Mt. Edgecumbe. He told Denkinger, but he ordered the students not to tell anyone. The students were intrigued by the clandestine tone of the project. Naturally, they immediately told all their friends. But they didn't tell the other teachers.

Langford's methods may not be for everyone. But the resulting series of student achievements suggest that students, at least from the high school level up, have far more ability to contribute to the management of their own educations than they're usually given credit for.

After two weeks of data gathering, the students concluded that the three most common questions were:

1. What are we going to do today?
2. Why do we have to do this?
3. Will it be on the test?

The class decided to focus on the reasons why the students asked these three questions. First, they created an Ishikawa diagram to ana-lyze why students asked, "What are we going to do today?"[3] They con-cluded that the most important reason students asked this question wasn't surprising: because the teacher does all the planning, the stu-dents don't know what the class is doing.

Langford's class decided that teacher and students together would plan their course in advanced computer applications. Langford ex-plained what he had planned to teach and discussed with the students what they wanted to learn. Soon, the class had created flowcharts to show what they would be doing for the rest of the term. The question "What are we going to do today?" was eliminated. The students would come in, start to ask, "What are we going to . . . ," and then catch themselves, realizing that they already knew.

To address, "Why do we have to do this?", the group focused on Deming's point: "Create constancy of purpose." The class wrote a vi-sion statement and a statement of purpose.

To deal with "Will it be on the test?", Langford and the class talked about the purpose of testing. The class decided that the stu-dents themselves would decide when they needed a test and what would be on it. Deming had said, "The only reason you give a test is to find out what to do next." Langford claims the students take tests without putting their names on the test sheets. He used the results simply as a diagnostic tool. Langford claims that at the end of the school year, he found that every student in the class had mastered the material at a level that would traditionally have justified an A. There's considerable subjectivity in this, but in a high school class in "advanced computer applications" (i.e., spreadsheets, databases, etc.) subjective evaluations may be as good as any.

In the second quarter of the year, Langford taught methods for studying Mt. Edgecumbe High School as a *system*. One group tracked how many students were sleeping in each class. Members compared the numbers to the time of day, the day of the week, and so forth. Another group tracked the average time it took from the official start of each class until the class actually started working. Then it analyzed the factors that caused the delay: late students, the signing of tardy slips, the time teachers spent taking attendance, and so on.

Langford's classes, which by now shared at least some of his own strong sense of purpose, proposed improvements. Langford stopped accepting tardy slips. When tardy students arrived, Langford would already be teaching. He'd just motion them to sit down. Generally, they responded by coming to future classes on time.

The student-proposed changes weren't exactly revolutionary. "We'd worked for years on maintaining the sanctity of the classroom time," says Denkinger, and there were no reliable data by which to judge whether Langford was more successful than other teachers.

But the impact on the students *was* revolutionary. "The students had vocabulary like *imagineering*. They understood random samples, and they were the only people who understood random samples," says Denkinger. "They were able to contribute in ways they never had before."

Eventually, Rocheleau and Denkinger saw the achievements and set out to make Deming's philosophy the norm for the school. They used the school's computer network to gather students' ideas, taught problem solving to the whole school, and used nominal group technique to set priorities each year.[4] How successful they were is a matter of some debate. Mt. Edgecumbe students made impressive presentations at a series of educational conferences in the mainland United States and attracted a considerable following. But the Alaska Department of Education eventually made changes in how the school was run that left some supporters feeling betrayed.

Mt. Edgecumbe's story tells us a good deal about what our schools should ultimately look and feel like. It also shows how an individual who isn't the chief executive can launch a powerful transformation. Langford's work had power because he truly respected his students. "The students aren't 'customers,'" says Langford. "They're *colleagues*. We're all learners together."

University of Texas at Austin

Whatever problems they had in the long run, KenTon and Mount Edgecumbe were able to find ways to improve their educational systems, the environments in which learning takes place. The other half of the challenge lies in improving the actual *process* of learning, the day-to-day operations, if you will.

MANAGING THE PROCESS OF LEARNING

In any endeavor, careful process management can achieve profound advances. Consider the work of Uri Treisman, professor at the University of Texas at Austin, who has used very old-fashioned business techniques to help students excel in math. Treisman describes his method as a mixture of "ethnography and the 1920s 'industrial style' time-and-motion study." Treisman's work points to a way that we can apply the plan-do-check-act cycle at the national level, and thus solve many basic educational problems.[5]

In the 1970s, Treisman, who was then a graduate student and trainer of teaching assistants at the University of California at Berkeley, confronted the fact that more than 60 percent of Black freshman calculus students were receiving a D or F. He did something very unusual: he conducted a study comparing 20 Black and 20 Chinese-American students. "We decided literally to move in with the students and to videotape them at work," Treisman recalls.

Treisman found two differences that distinguished the two groups: *how* they studied and *how much* they studied. Black students worked alone. Chinese-American students got together in the evening, made a meal, then went over the homework assignment. If one student got a different answer from all the others, that student would recognize that he or she was wrong, and in the group meeting, there would be plenty of opportunity to pick up the right way of doing the problem from the others. Faculty had told students the course required eight hours of homework per week. The average Black student was doing exactly eight hours. The successful Chinese Americans were doing eight hours of work on their own plus six hours of work in groups.

Now Treisman and his coworkers had an understanding of how students succeeded in calculus. Next, they tested their understanding by rigorously managing the process of learning. The teaching assistants set up workshops to help students from all ethnic origins learn to study in groups. They advised workshop students to spend eight hours a week studying by themselves and another six hours in groups. They developed special problem sets suitable for group study. The results were stunning: Black and Latino workshop participants substantially outperformed not only other minority students, but White and Asian classmates as well.

Next, Treisman and associates sought to apply the lessons to other subjects. First, teachers of other courses tried mechanically copying the workshop method that had helped students learn calculus. It didn't work. Old-time industrial engineers could have predicted this failure. Mechanically applying lessons learned by studying one process (the process that leads to success in calculus) to the management of a completely different process (e.g., the study of physics) isn't good quality management.

When teachers carried out a separate process analysis of success in physics, however, they showed that good operational management *could* result in successful learning in physics, too. The key problem was to collect and analyze data so the group would understand the process by which successful students succeeded in each particular discipline. When Treisman's group collected data on the process of learning physics, they found that it differed from the process of learning calculus. In physics, students succeeded not only through group study but also by becoming interested in physics at an early age in high schools that provided excellent preparation. In top universities, introductory physics classes moved at a painfully rapid pace. Students could survive only if they had extensively studied much of the same material in lower grades—and that opportunity was simply unavailable to most minority students.

The evidence suggests that Treisman's underlying methodology—the PDCA cycle executed through a combination of ethnography and old-fashioned time-and-motion study—seems capable of addressing the problems of failures in physics and many other disciplines as well as math.

At the Local Level: Consensus-Driven Improvement

Treisman's work raises serious questions for quality management at the local level. There, educators don't usually have time to carry out the kind of large-scale studies that Treisman and his colleagues are performing. Where operational processes can be made predictable through a standardize-do-check-act (SDCA) cycle, it's hard to understand the actual process by which students learn without Treisman's kind of research. There were sharp limits to how much successful school leaders we interviewed tried to control the process of teaching. The experiences of Kenmore-Tonawanda, however, suggested that analysis and wise management of education as a process could be done at the local level.

At Kenmore-Tonawanda, the district insisted on standards development by consensus, with teacher initiative playing a key role. Such participative management of standards is extremely time-consuming, but at KenTon, there was evidence that it resulted in real quality control and effective process management.

Consider how KenTon introduced the whole-language method of teaching reading, for instance. The whole-language method is a program based on the use of beloved classic children's stories for education in all subjects. Students read famous stories such as "The Three Bears" and then answer questions about them, write compositions about them, perhaps even do math problems based on them. In early grades, the emphasis is on communicating and thinking about the stories, not on making sure that children always spell words correctly or master perfect handwriting.

The district wouldn't order teachers to adopt these methods, however, until the changes had been reviewed and agreed on through the district's consensus-driven improvement methodology. A districtwide committee set out to identify what outcomes the schools were then achieving in reading and writing in the elementary schools, and to learn faculty's and parents' opinions on what skills ought to be learned at each grade level, how they could be assessed, and how progress (or the lack of it) could be communicated to parents.

After talking to parents of children in one school, the district ran a pilot program in one first-grade class in the 1990–91 school year. After data there showed the students were doing well, the pilot program was extended in the following year to all kindergarten, first-, and second-grade classes in the district. At the end of that year, the district asked every parent what he or she thought of the new progress reports the school was issuing. When asked to agree or disagree with the statement "The progress report provides more information than the computerized progress report" (the old report card), 81 percent of those answering either agreed or agreed strongly.

Based on the data, the Board approved the agreed upon skills and the assessment of them districtwide. These were adopted for all the elementary schools of Kenmore-Tonawanda in the 1993–1994 school year.

The Challenge of Integrated Systems

Despite their problems, Kenmore-Tonawanda demonstrates that schools can improve radically. Mount Edgecumbe shows that every student and teacher can be involved in improvement. Uri Treisman's work shows that we can fix failing curricula through analysis of process.

Unfortunately, few of the hundreds of schools where educators are talking about things like continuous improvement and Total Quality are achieving anything of the kind. Despite good intentions and best efforts, in all but a few schools, so-called quality revolutions have fallen short because, as in many fields, the notion of quality is adopted without designing an integrated system to foster and reinforce it.

One such case was George Westinghouse High School, a vocational school that stands in the shadow of the Brooklyn Bridge on the Brooklyn side of the East River in New York City. Its student body reflects some of the worst of America's problems: disinterest, disadvantage, violence, fear. When Principal Lewis Rappaport and Assistant Principal Franklin Schargel came to Westinghouse in the mid-1980s, they recognized that the school wasn't reaching many of its students.

Schargel had been exposed to the quality movement through such companies as Digital Equipment, Motorola, NyNex (now part of Bell Atlantic), and Marriott, and when he heard Larrae Rocheleau of Mount Edgecumbe High School lecture on the improvements that were underway there, he thought he saw a solution for his own beleaguered school.

Schargel and Rappaport held a faculty training day in early 1991 based on the 14 points of W. Edwards Deming and on Philip Crosby's principle that "Quality is free." They asked the staff to list reasons why Total Quality wouldn't work at Westinghouse. They received a list of 23 obstacles, including lack of communication, large numbers in classes, and lack of clearly defined goals. Most important, the faculty felt the school wasn't communicating the seriousness of education. Students would proclaim their disinterest in school by listening to radios in the hallways and wearing baseball caps backwards. "Students don't care what's happening here," said a faculty member.

The faculty created an action plan to show that school was "a serious place." They began to confiscate hats and seize radios in the hallways and in classes. They continued to identify inhibitors to quality and worked on eradicating them as best they could.

Rappaport had his teachers give workshops on creative ways they had developed to involve their students. A cabinet-making teacher showed how he had helped his students set up their own tiny companies to make and sell gift items for Christmas; a social studies teacher showed how he had used a stock market simulation game; an English teacher showed how his students had analyzed poetry in teams; a math teacher used weekly graphic report cards to help students monitor and track their own progress.

Westinghouse began to survey parents as customers to learn what they wanted from PTA meetings. It held a three-day "quality academy" at the start of the school year to teach students how to study, how to take tests, how to think, how to listen, and how to solve problems. It established a mentoring program where seniors help freshmen. It developed a special program for the many Westinghouse students who were flunking every course. Parents were required to attend conferences and troubled students had to attend lunch-hour tutoring.

Despite all this, most statistical measures of the school's performance did not show clear improvement. Things were, in some ways, getting even worse. In the average class at Westinghouse, approximately 35 percent of the students still failed; about 10 percent of the student body continued to flunk everything. Many Westinghouse students seemed to lack any clear goals and many still didn't show up for classes. Of 151 who were failing all their courses at the start of the program, 54 left Westinghouse High School. Of the 97 who remained, only 11 were still flunking every course one semester later. However, 110 other students—students who hadn't been flunking every course at the end of the first term—were flunking every course at that point. Thus, the total number flunking every course was 121. The following fall, the number flunking every course rose to 168.

The Mt. Edgecumbe experience and the quality courses Schargel had taken in companies gave Rappaport and Schargel a fairly clear idea of *what* they want the school to accomplish. But they hadn't received a clear picture of *how* to manage the system for change. At a meeting to plan a faculty conference in 1994, the school was still using the same brainstormed list of items of concern that the faculty had produced at the 1991 faculty meeting where Rappaport and Schargel originally introduced the program. No clear priorities or goals had ever been established. No systemic methods had been added, subtracted, or refined. Nothing had evolved. Westinghouse was all tactics, no strategy.

When we last visited Westinghouse, we found that it still didn't have a system that could be relied on to achieve the extremely difficult but also extremely urgent task of changing this situation. For example, the school had no coherent goal-setting system, no infrastructure of systems to support improvement, and no agreement on any common language to discuss solutions.

Unfortunately, that is a common situation among schools, and many other organizations, that try to practice Total Quality and other improvement methods. Many lack dedicated leaders. But even more, they lack know-how. Organizations don't achieve transformation because they don't know how to manage the process of transformation.

Principles for Transformations in Education

The causes of success and failure of total integrated system efforts in education seem to mirror the causes of success and failure of such programs in general. No program will succeed if its leaders expect to follow a cookbook. Magic formulas will never transform anything.

Programs like those at KenTon and Mt. Edgecumbe, however, do point to some common ingredients for success. Although these principles and the relationships among them don't add up to a magic formula, we think they can help educators—and the parents, businesspeople, and others who want to support them—understand the *how* of Total Quality. The five practices introduced in Chapter 1 provide a reasonable guide.

1. *Continuous improvement.* A well-defined improvement system such as DDAE or another variant of PDCA appropriate for education and a common language of improvement.

2. *Reaching outside.* Learn needs and concerns from parents, employers, and others in the environment.

3. *Ideas, knowledge, and commitment from everyone inside.* Build systems that take account of goals and purposes of the people in the system, work with them to design a desirable future, and find ways to achieve it.

4. *A mobilization infrastructure.* Create methods and structures that reinforce organizational goals, including a reward and recognition system and a system for diffusing information and success stories.

5. *Societal networking.* Work with leaders of other organizations to learn techniques of improvement, remembering the special needs of educational systems.

At the same time, change in education should be built on the special characteristics of educational institutions. Goal-setting should be decentralized, participative, and concrete. Students and parents are colleagues of the faculty—all learners together in the community.

CHAPTER 5

Managing the Most Complex Processes

Integrated Systems in Health Care

"Whether or not we have reform in the way we pay for it, you're going to see a transformation in American health care," insists Dr. Brent James, director of the Institute for Health Care Delivery Research at Intermountain Health Care in Salt Lake City. "We're learning how to design processes that can achieve levels of care we didn't believe were possible before, and at reduced cost.

"You get physicians who truly have dedicated their lives to serving patients, and you show them what's happening, and they get excited. . . . So there's no way anyone's going to be able to stop that change."

James may be overly optimistic. He admits that LDS Hospital, the flagship of Intermountain Health Care, is still at an early stage of improvement. Health care transformation is harder than the transformation of most for-profit companies. But he argues plausibly that LDS can practice better medicine than many traditionally managed hospitals largely because it has implemented plan-do-check-act improvement in many of its operations. Indeed, the same kind of new systems that have increased profits at service companies or reduced cycle time at manufacturers have improved not only cost control but also the quality of care at a handful of health care institutions.

This chapter examines how integrated management systems at Intermountain and at Meriter Health Services, a smaller institution in Madison, Wisconsin, have created benefits for both patients and society. In both cases, it will be clear that health care systems differ from those of most for-profit organizations in at least three ways that make a management transformation different—and perhaps more difficult:

- *Complexity.* The actions of hundreds of people and systems in a hospital affect the survival of a patient. James and his staff estimate 1,600 processes that must be managed to achieve excellent care in a hospital. "A number of different studies show the typical hospital is 10 to 100 times more complex than a factory even for a product as complex as an automobile," James notes.

- *Flat organizational structure.* The independent spirit and deep knowledge of medical professionals limit the power of any hierarchical approach to change. The leaders of a medical care system head a corps of professionals whose skills and knowledge make them the final judges of what should happen in their specialties. Dr. Alan Morris, head of Intermountain Health Care's highly regarded adult respiratory distress syndrome research project, which has increased survival rates for a usually fatal condition by carefully standardizing the care, emphasized this point. "If I had been an engineer or an economist or a government agent, there wouldn't have been a chance of getting this off the ground," he says.

- *Divided leadership.* The chief executives at health care institutions are usually administrators, not doctors. They often see doctors as their *customers.* Doctors, on the other hand, look to other doctors rather than to professional administrators as their leaders. Hospital chief executives can lead changes in noncritical areas such as admissions, routine nursing, and billing. But the core processes of health care—the actual treatment of patients—can improve only if an institution has leadership on two fronts: professional administrators *and* top doctors.

James says that when he began studying new management techniques, he felt that health care organizations' claims of uniqueness were really masking a basic reluctance to change. Now, he emphasizes that, "Health care really is different."

Intermountain Health Care

Intermountain Health Care was formed in 1975. The Church of Jesus Christ of the Latter Day Saints (Mormon), which had created 15 hospitals in Utah and nearby parts of Idaho and Wyoming, decided that running hospitals should no longer be part of its mission. It established Intermountain as a nonsectarian, nonprofit organization to take over the hospitals, and selected a board of trustees composed of aggressive local businesspeople. The board hired Scott Parker, an administrator who had held key positions at hospitals in Arizona and California, as president.

Because of its heritage, the corporation had, from the beginning, a key ingredient necessary for designing an integrated management system: a strong, articulated, clear mission. "The corporate mission statement really drives top management's decisions. IHC exists to be sure that good health care is given to people in the intermountain West," says James. The board emphasized such community concerns as cost control even before market pressures made that necessary. Says Greg Poulsen, vice president for planning and research, "We want to infuse the kind of drive for excellence that you would find in an aggressively managed small company."

That had always been the organization's agenda. Back in 1960, Homer Warner, a young cardiologist, returned to Latter Day Saints Hospital (as LDS was then known) from a residency at the Mayo Clinic in Minnesota. At Mayo, he'd learned about an important new idea: the use of computers in medical diagnosis. A few doctors and computer scientists had shown that clearly specified decision rules, programmed into computers, could sometimes produce better diagnoses than doctors' personal judgment. Warner proposed that Latter Day Saints Hospital develop a computer system to improve diagnostic procedures.

It took seven years to get a system running that provided modest support for the diagnosis of heart problems. But gradually, over the years, IHC added capabilities.

The Process of Change
at Intermountain

By the early 1980s, Intermountain Health Care's HELP (Health Evaluation through Logical Programming) system tracked patients from arrival to discharge in several of the system's larger hospitals, and it helped doctors make decisions about diagnoses and medications at numerous points. Perhaps more important than its contribution to medical decision making was the improvement in the quality and accessibility of patients' records. A system to track patients meant that personnel could instantly obtain complete records on a patient anywhere in the hospital. And they could update the records from anywhere. Because they were easier to access, records could be far more complete than in old-fashioned paper systems.

The HELP system provided a culture of disciplined evaluation and improvement that would be a foundation for Intermountain's evolving management system. In 1986, Intermountain's medical director, Dr. Steven Lewis, hired Brent James, a professor at Harvard School of Public Health, as assistant vice president for research. James, who holds an M.D. as well as a masters degree in statistics, had done a residency at the University of Utah Hospital in Salt Lake City and knew that the HELP system had given Intermountain databases that were probably better than any others in the United States.

James launched several studies of variabilities in medical practice based on the HELP system database. The studies indicated that practice decisions varied enormously from hospital to hospital and from doctor to doctor. As a result of the studies, Intermountain added some additional practice guidelines to its HELP system.

James soon met Paul Bataldan, then quality director of Health Corporation of America. Bataldan suggested that if James wanted to work on measuring variation in medical practice, he should examine the work of W. Edwards Deming. In 1987, James attended a Deming seminar in San Diego aimed at businesspeople. "I realized that if I chose, I could think of what we were doing as what Deming called, 'quality improvement,'" he says.

With that in mind, James began working with an ad hoc group of professionals interested in improving Intermountain's key processes of clinical care. Steve Busboom, a financial analyst, played a key role; other leaders came from Intermountain's clinical research programs. "We believed quality improvement theory was very similar to the principles of clinical research," James says. Both the PDCA cycle and traditional medical research protocols are forms of the scientific method. In traditional clinical research, doctors propose an improvement in medical care, collect data, implement their proposed improvement on a trial basis, examine whether it really works, then publish their findings so other doctors can copy them.

But traditional clinical research is usually separated from the day-to-day work of the hospital. Unfortunately, many aspects of medical care never get studied in this way, and the results of many studies never get adequately communicated to practicing physicians. There's very limited scientific data to help health care providers with most of the decisions they have to make in hospitals. James cites several studies that suggest medical research has clearly identified the best therapies for less than 20 percent of what doctors do in routine medical practice.[1]

Hospitals have had quality assurance programs for decades, of course. Accrediting bodies require them. But traditional quality programs in hospitals almost never have enough data to make change on a genuinely scientific basis.

James describes the traditional approach to quality control in hospitals as "Sort and shoot." Doctors on quality assurance committees review questionable performance to try to sort out what is substandard; then they are charged with disciplining those responsible. Naturally, that approach makes doctors in many hospitals reluctant to cooperate when quality control committees investigate their work. The committees rarely develop enough data for credible decisions on whether the performance they are studying was appropriate.

Using ideas from Deming, James's group sought to introduce PDCA improvement processes that were completely different from traditional hospital quality assurance. The improvement processes would also differ from ordinary medical research, which is usually aimed at producing papers that can be published in medical journals. Journals seek to publish statistically significant analyses of major medical questions. They often don't address all the details on which a doctor must make decisions in treating a patient. Yet, small decisions have major impact on both the cost and the quality of care. Intermountain's PDCA improvement processes, like those of other organizations we've examined, were aimed at improving all the details.

Lewis, the doctor who was Intermountain's vice president for medical affairs, worked with James, Busboom, and others interested in PDCA improvement to choose what to study. They chose hip replacement because it is a common, high-volume, high-cost operation, and data showed a large variability in costs among hospitals. That suggested different doctors were treating similar patients differently.

It is striking how the process of improvement followed a process that paralleled that used in for-profit companies. Figure 5.1 puts the work of the hip replacement project in the framework of the seven-step process used at the Center for Quality of Management.

James and Busboom started the project by taking a different approach with the surgeons from traditional quality assurance investigations. "If we work on this," they told them, "we can be the best in the

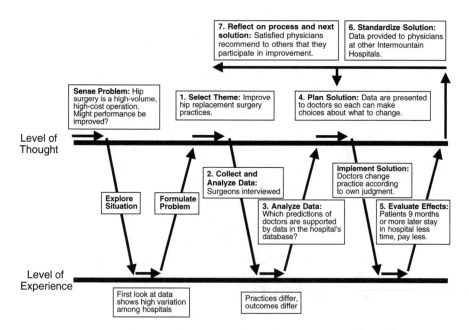

Figure 5.1 Improvement Process for Hip Replacement Surgery. Plan-Do-Check-Act improvement parallels improvement in manufacturing.

country." But that didn't initially impress most of the surgeons, many of whom were independent practitioners choosing to conduct their operations at Intermountain hospitals, and who in many cases had the option of switching their practice to another hospital outside Intermountain's system if they chose. Even many good surgeons feared that data from the experiment might be misused to make them look bad. Without strong support from Lewis, the project would have failed. He needed to disseminate his message and seek internal engagement.

Lewis, James, and Busboom worked with a small group of senior surgeons to identify key factors in the surgery process. The research team knew that doctors had to base many of their decisions on personal judgments about the best medical practice. The team found that doctors made some decisions based on what they were taught in a hospital residency. But they made many based on anecdotal reasoning: "I tried this once, and here's what happened." The team wanted to determine which approaches led to the best patient outcomes at the lowest cost.

To do that, the team gathered data on what different surgeons did on each of the key factors in surgery that had been identified. For example, how long each chose to leave a catheter providing intravenous food and medicines in the patient after surgery. They also identified the problems doctors sought to address by, for instance, leaving the catheter in longer. Then they used the HELP system database to determine whether those problems actually occurred in patients whose catheters were removed earlier.

The results showed that the majority of physicians had areas of strength, where they had something to contribute, and other areas where they could learn from their colleagues. The data showed that some doctors were good at managing medicine or choosing what tests to order; others followed postoperation practices that seemed to improve patients' recoveries.

At each major Intermountain hospital, James presented these data at meetings of the surgeons who conducted hip operations. The name of each physician studied was disguised.

"There were no smiling faces," James says. "They were very threatened, and some of them were angry."

However, the research team carefully avoided any claims that the research proved more than it really did. "We're not interested in attacking physicians," says James. "All we did was take the data back to the physicians and say to them, 'You're really different on some of these points. Why do you think that is?' "

The doctors now took the results seriously, and acted on them. When the research team analyzed another group of patients who received artificial hips nine months or more after completion of the first report, it found dramatic reductions in length of stay, 25 percent lower cost, and improved—or at worst, unchanged—patient health. Moreover, James says every doctor participating in the study improved. In general, the doctors whose performance was weakest before the study remained the weakest, but in many cases, they improved to a level comparable to that of the average doctors before the research project.

The key result, however, was that physicians—including those who'd originally denounced the study—came away believing in the method. Intermountain publicized the results of the study in numerous newsletters, and Brent James and other participants went on speaking tours of most IHC hospitals. Doctors published some of their results in the medical research literature. Many smaller groups in the company set out to do similar work, often after problem-solving training from James's clinical practice improvement group. "We had a culture that believed in quality, and when we started to make heroes of people that were making breakthroughs, it led other people to get involved in improving the quality of care," Poulsen says.

Clinical research often finds some high-cost methods do not produce superior results. In one study of surgical techniques, for instance, some surgeons were meticulously removing very small amounts of tissue as little-as half as much tissue as some of their peers. Their meticulousness led to longer operations. That led to higher costs for operating-room time and longer stays in the hospital for recovery. But the doctors believed that the removal of less tissue would lead to better mobility and general health for their patients. When the researchers studied data, however, they found that meticulousness did not seem to benefit patients. When patients had smaller amounts of tissue removed, the proportion readmitted to the hospital later was actually *higher*. (The researchers suspected that the longer operations caused the increase in later problems.) This kind of knowledge allows better care at lower cost. But such data is only rarely gathered in most hospitals.

At Intermountain, however, carefully managed early studies led to success, and the clinical quality improvement program grew rapidly.

Intermountain also gradually developed an infrastructure to support change.

BUILDING STRUCTURAL SUPPORT

In 1989, James, Poulsen, and other leaders of the quality movement within IHC set up an ad hoc quality leadership group. The quality movement leaders had a list of people they wanted to involve: all the hospital's top operations people. Those who were convinced included Lewis, the head of medical affairs, and the heads of planning, nursing, information systems, human resources, professional services, traditional quality assurance, and Intermountain's health maintenance organization, together with the top administrators of each of Intermountain's largest hospitals. On a summer day in 1989, they met at the nearby Snowbird ski resort, developed a quality mission statement, and declared themselves to be Intermountain's quality council.

One key player who wasn't invited to the meeting was Scott Parker, Intermountain's chief executive. James says that at this point, the participants hadn't considered his participation in the quality council to be necessary. They thought quality was a grass-roots operational issue. But after the Snowbird meeting, several participants went to Parker and asked him to declare support. Parker embraced the idea of the council, and even reoriented the work of the quality assurance department on the administrative side of the hospital. Then in 1991, he mandated that all senior managers go through James's course in quality improvement techniques. The next year, it was determined that the hospital's Executive Management Council—its top 30 executives—should be the quality council. James and other key quality "experts" were made part of a staff organization known as the Clinical Practice Improvement Group.

As head of the Clinical Practice Improvement Group, James was in charge of teaching improvement methodologies and initiating annual programs to improve performance in key areas of medical process. At the start of their quality effort, James and other top managers made a list, based on data from the HELP system and the impressions of LDS's leading doctors, of medical conditions that might be causing problems—either producing substantial excess costs, causing poor outcomes, or both. Then James's group chose a few conditions from the top of the list to work on while also attacking a few simpler problems where the hospital had either exceptionally good data or a "clinical champion," a highly regarded doctor who wanted to lead an improvement project. Quality teams in many areas of IHC hospitals included nurses and technicians on an equal footing with doctors.

James emphasizes the difficulty of clinical process improvement in health care. In many cases, people who wanted to improve quality found that to improve one aspect of the hospital's performance, "You find you have to convert processes to new methods across every system in health care," says James. He says that "Baldrige-quality work" is more common on the administrative side than on the clinical side, because the processes are less complex. For example, like many hospitals, IHC until the 1990s issued illegible bills filled with incomprehensible abbreviations. Even doctors couldn't figure them out. A team was assigned to totally redesign both the billing system and the bill itself, and the results have been a dramatic reduction in both the cost of collections and in the hospital's accounts receivable, along with a dramatic improvement in patient satisfaction.

The HELP system computer network has continued to provide an unusual level of quality control and coordination of both clinical and administrative processes, tying together all aspects of treatment. The system today is a network of Tandem minicomputers and special software, with terminals throughout the hospitals. It keeps patient records and tracks patients throughout their stay. It provides expert-system advice. For example, it helps doctors deduce the most likely pathogen infecting a patient and the best drug for treating it based on the patient's medical record, and data from 13,500 microbiology cultures stored in its database. It checks for evidence of hospital-acquired infections, allowing the hospital to identify 90 percent of these infections while the patients are still in the hospital and the problem can be effectively treated. It prompts the hospital pharmacist to visit a patient's bedside, check papers there, and decide whether to administer or stop administering certain drugs. It helps nurses effectively monitor adverse drug reactions by allowing them to enter only the symptom into the computer rather than requiring the nurse to identify the drug that caused the reaction. The HELP system is also tightly linked to the computers that run the hospital's financial system. When hospital personnel enter a test in a chart, this immediately causes the financial computer system to add the test to the patient's bill.

THE RESULTS

Data suggest that Intermountain's system has had substantial impact on its patients and on the employers who pay their bills. By the mid-1990s, surveys showed that both doctors and patients believed IHC performed better than other hospitals in Utah. State Department of Health statistics showed that charges in Intermountain hospitals averaged 14.7 percent lower than those statewide, which were already 25.9 percent lower than the national average.[2] James is careful not to overstate Intermountain's progress, however. Health maintenance organizations get even lower prices for their patients in America's most competitive health care markets, such as southern California. And James notes that transformation on the clinical side of the hospital has to get "much better and more coordinated." Still, Intermountain's experience leaves little doubt that the same integrated management approach that works in business will garner positive results for a health care organization.

Meriter Hospital

The experience of Meriter Hospital in Madison, Wisconsin, a smaller institution struggling in a difficult market place, parallels Intermountain Health Care's in many respects. Meriter has not produced the definitive evidence of success that Intermountain has developed. But Meriter's work may be easier to learn from because it has built a working management system without depending on a unique asset like the Intermountain's HELP computer system. Meriter has also designed a management system that integrates the purposes of the hospital with the management of two entirely separate but intertwined entities: the physicians' group practice that includes most of the doctors working in the hospital, and the health maintenance organization that the doctors own and operate.

More Scalable Change

The management approach that changed Meriter started modestly enough. It was driven by two instances of societal networking in the mid-1980s. First, in 1983, Mary Zimmerman, director of nursing for the medical units at what was then known as Madison General Hospital, and Chief Operating Officer Robert Coats were exposed to, and became passionate about, the teachings of W. Edwards Deming. When they and other hospital administrators attended a Deming lecture the following year, they were inspired to establish a quality steering committee at the hospital in hopes that the principles of Total Quality could be applied there.

In 1986, they took their quality commitment a step further and started working with a local consulting firm, Joiner Associates. Pilot projects established with Joiner soon demonstrated substantial success in improving patient education for new mothers, decreasing errors in documenting medications, and decreasing waiting time and errors in the outpatient admitting process.

The initial quality programs, however, had little impact on the hospital's overall management system, and when Madison General merged with Madison's Methodist Hospital in 1987 to form Meriter Health Services, progress stalled. No one knew how to use the methods of the quality movement to handle the problems of the merger. The merged hospitals had no corporationwide quality steering committee and no comprehensive approach to creating an integrated management system until 1988. By then, the focus on and passion for quality-driven change had flagged.

A new spark was provided, however, when Meriter's 15 top leaders and 40 department directors each took a five-day quality management course from Joiner. Although many of the Meriter executives were indifferent or even negative about pursuing a new management system, the Joiner course accomplished one important goal: it provided a common language with which to discuss and measure improvement. And it introduced Joiner's version of the PDCA improvement process, which was suitable for use in all parts of the organization.

It was the follow-up to the five-day course, however, that turned out to be a key step in changing the management system. Each of the top leaders and department directors was assigned a "quality coach" from *outside* the organization—people experienced in the PDCA cycle from other organizations in the Madison area, including the consulting firm Joiner Associates. "Their role was to work with us, help us plan out time for projects, and through coaching, keep us on track," says Terri Potter, Meriter's chief executive. Potter points out that key people in organizations have worked hard and often made great sacrifices to reach a stage in their careers where they are considered "experts." This is especially true in health care, where doctors and other professionals are among the most highly trained individuals anywhere, and become accustomed to a high level of respect from both patients and lower-ranking members of the system. It's especially difficult for such people to learn dramatically new ways of working. "People move from novice to expert," says Potter. "If you want to help people who've gotten to the expert point to go back down and learn new skills, you have to bring them back down that slope." The coaches made it easy for hospital personnel to become novices.

"It created a safe way for the learning of new skills," says Zimmerman, who was named quality director at this point. "It reduced the fear of making a mistake or looking foolish."

Many physicians, however, were still skeptical about the application of quality movement methods to what they felt were the unique aspects of practicing medicine. They began to change, however, when they recognized that the dissemination of a standard improvement cycle allowed them to apply the scientific method to areas where, to a significant extent, they had been guessing before. Zimmerman observes, "Physicians gravitate to the use of databases to create improvement. With physicians, a key early finding was that a way to help them get involved with quality was to provide them with new tools to manage data."

All five-day course participants were expected to conduct a personal quality improvement project. Potter focused on the health care corporation's boards of directors. "My project was a soft thing," says Potter. "The question was how you take something very soft—the functioning of the boards of directors—and break it down so we could analyze quantitative data. We had to take qualitative information and convert it into quantitative. And we learned that it was possible." Dr. Carl Weston, the hospital's medical director (Meriter's equivalent of Steven Lewis at Intermountain), selected a clinical activity for his personal quality project. His team, including four non-employee physicians and three other members, developed new guidelines for cesarean sections, and the rate quickly declined from 18.4 percent to 15.9 percent.

Potter, Weston, and other top executives began encouraging doctors affiliated with the hospital to take quality management courses from the Boston-based Institute for Healthcare Improvement. Dr. Geoffrey Priest, a pulmonary care physician, went to Institute training after serving for several years on Meriter's traditional quality control committees. He, like many others, came back persuaded that medicine was "not so unique that the ideas of quality improvement can't be applied."

At Meriter, Priest led a project to improve pulmonary critical care. One focus was on the administration of the anticlotting drug Heparin. If the level of Heparin in the patient's blood stream can be stabilized at the appropriate level within 24 hours of admission to the hospital, it dramatically reduces the likelihood of complications. Preliminary studies found only 30 to 40 percent of patients were getting the right level of Heparin stabilized in their blood within that time. "In a quick poll of 20 doctors, we found 20 different ways of giving Heparin," recalls Priest. His group created a sheet with a standard flowchart for the administration of Heparin. They didn't mandate following the procedures, but made sure that nurses understood those procedures and doctors knew that following this standard process was likely to result in dependable administration of the drug. "The level of follow-up doses is automatic," Priest explains. "If you want a blood level of 50 and you get 40, the sheet tells you what to do." Doctors throughout the hospital accepted the new procedure enthusiastically. Six months after it was introduced, a follow-up study showed that the share of patients who stabilized at the right level of Heparin had risen to an average of 90 percent.

That was the kind of improvement Meriter wanted to create throughout the care processes of the hospital: demonstrable, quantifiable, and aimed at bettering the care of the patient. Meriter's leaders believed that the concept of *internal customers* could tie together the complex health care system. The hospital began to see each part of the medical care system as related to one another in a customer-supplier chain. To emphasize that quality was a goal integral to the practice of medicine, the quality resources group headed by Zimmerman reported to Weston.

AN INTERLOCKING MANAGEMENT STRUCTURE

As at most U.S. hospitals, few doctors at Meriter are hospital employees. Potter, Weston, and other leaders of the change effort quickly recognized that to achieve dramatic improvement, they'd have to work closely with nonemployee doctors like Priest.

Some Meriter physicians are independent practitioners, but to deal with change in the health care marketplace, the majority of Meriter physicians had organized themselves into a large group practice, the Physicians Plus Medical Group, which in turn had established its own health maintenance organization, also called Physicians Plus. Physicians Plus marketed complete, managed medical care packages for the employees of Madison-area organizations. The packages included outpatient care provided at the doctors' clinic and hospital care provided principally at Meriter.

The leaders of both the hospital and Physicians Plus felt that the key challenge was to provide excellent, cost-effective care that was "seamless," that is, to enable the hospital, the doctors, and the support staff of the HMO each to do their parts in the care of the patient with excellent coordination and a minimum of bureaucracy among them. To accomplish this, they designed an "interlocking" management system that would operate on several levels:

1. The management committee of the hospital itself, functioning as the hospital quality steering committee, was in charge of quality improvement in hospital administration areas such as managing nursing, improving patient rooms, and controlling cost.

2. Meriter extensively utilized quality assurance committees of doctors for its clinical quality improvement projects, such as an effort that established clinical management guidelines for deep vein thrombosis.

3. The group practice and HMO had their own quality management systems. Physicians Plus belonged to the Group Practice Improvement Network, through which leading group medical practices consult with one another to improve their care.

4. A medical management council composed of key leaders of the hospital, the physicians group, and the HMO worked to coordinate annual business plan projects that involved all three organizations. In 1994, for instance, this included a team to improve the hospital's services for outpatients, a team to improve cardiac surgery, and a team to improve total hip replacement. Several years later, the projects had shown significant success, with both lower costs and increased satisfaction from the hip replacement project, for example.

The relations between the systems of Meriter and the Physicians Plus Medical Group are represented in Figure 5.2. The memberships of the different teams overlap considerably, but managers believe each is essential if Meriter and Physicians Plus are to deal effectively with the complexity of the health care process.

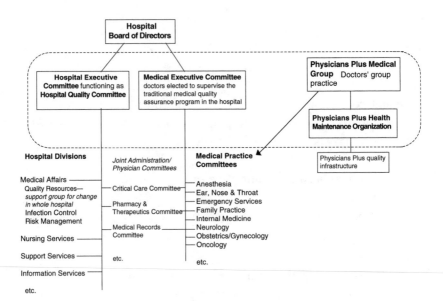

Figure 5.2 Interrelationship between Meriter and Physicians Plus Quality Organizations

Through a well-defined annual planning cycle that bears similarities to hoshin management, the Meriter hospital quality committee
establishes a business plan theme for each year and picks the key projects they will focus on. In 1993, for example, when cost-control pressures were especially intense, the business plan theme was "Reduce
our internal cost structure." The ratio between Meriter's average
charge and its lowest-cost competitor's average charge (adjusted for
differences in diagnostic-related groups) went from 116 percent in
the second quarter of 1992 to 103 percent at the end of 1993. During
this period, one Meriter team focused on cardiac surgery. Meriter's
cost was $29,000 per case, and competitors' ranged from $21,000 to
$30,000. The team's work reduced average cost to $20,000, and took a
full day off the average stay. All quality indicators, such as the number
of complications suffered by patients, improved.

MERITER RESULTS

Meriter's leaders didn't claim that they revolutionized the way the hospital operated, but they could show a structure and a series of real improvements that would make radical change possible. By 1995, the
hospital had more than 35 improvement teams registered with Zimmerman's office, plus additional, unregistered teams dealing with smaller
issues. The 12 medical practice committees of the hospital's doctors
also carried out improvement projects that the quality resources group
tracked separately. The Information Systems staff participated on many
of the improvement teams, which resulted in progressive, intelligent
computerization of Meriter's operations.

Surveys of physician satisfaction also showed significant improvement. The Physicians Plus HMO, the second largest in the Madison
area, consistently began achieving its growth and market-share goals.
Meriter's hospital, retirement center, and home health center were all
achieving their growth targets. The portion of employees saying there
is "good communication between your department and other hospital
departments" rose from 60 to 72 percent.

The clearest measures of the hospital's success were financial. The
hospital's net income had regularly fallen behind budget in 1990 and
1991. The hospital's cash on hand was, on average, enough for only 10
days of the hospital's needs, and it actually held as little as three days

of cash on hand at one point. Starting in 1992, the hospital closed the gap in rates between itself and lower-priced competitors while improving net income; that year, the hospital's bottom line moved ahead of budget, and it has generally stayed on budget since.

This has not totally protected Meriter from the ravages of the changing American health care system, however. Facing its own budgetary pressures, the nearby University of Wisconsin Hospital began broadening the services it offered. The Physicians Plus medical practice chose to affiliate itself with the university physicians group in addition to its affiliation with Meriter. That made it easier for patients of the Physicians Plus HMO to go to the university hospital, which in turn put pressure on Meriter's growth. The result was a period from 1995 through 1998 when cost control got more attention than medical innovation. The year 1999 was the first since the middle of the decade when Meriter could balance its focus as it wanted on improving care as much as on controlling costs.

The Health Care System and Integrated Management: Work Still to Be Done

Thousands of hospitals, clinics, and health maintenance organizations today are working to create effective integrated management systems. There has been real, even dramatic progress, but, as yet, no single institution that could be described as completely transformed. To some extent, health care is slow to improve for the same reasons other sectors are slow to improve: no one seems to understand the process of improvement in any sector as well as we'd like. But health care also faces special circumstances.

Until recently, health care faced relatively little pressure for improvement. Insurance organizations paid health care bills without much emphasis on quality or cost. Once pressure for change appeared in the 1990s, those pressures created enormous turmoil, such as that seen at Meriter—including shifts of power to health maintenance organizations, insurance companies, and corporate payers, and mergers of institutions that couldn't survive on their own. In the long run, such structural shifts may turn out to be essential, but as the effect of the Madison General–Methodist Hospital merger and later turmoil around the growth of the University Hospital system showed, structural change often interferes with efforts at operational improvement.

"We've shown we can get improvement *within* systems," says Donald Berwick, chief executive of the Institute for Healthcare Improvement. "We don't know yet whether we can get improvement *of* systems." Then he amends his comment: "Slow improvement is quite common in the industry," he says. "How many hospitals are improving at the rate of Motorola or Xerox? None. How many are building toward that rate? Very few. I would say there are perhaps 100."

Table 5.1 delineates how Intermountain's and Meriter's efforts compare with the elements of transformation we found in other sectors. It shows that both Intermountain Health Care and Meriter Health Systems possess the majority, but not all, of the elements of new management we found in transformed manufacturing and service companies. Intermountain and Meriter use integrated methods that help each part of the organization achieve customer focus, total involvement, continuous process improvement, and better learning. They have developed organizational infrastructures that support change throughout their organizations. To a significant extent, they've developed new common languages that help organization members become a close-knit team, all behaving in similar ways to bring about change.

However, the table shows two dramatic differences between these health care organizations and the successful organizations we visited in other sectors.

First, their leadership differs significantly from leadership in other sectors. In every successful organization we visited outside health care, the chief executive clearly led and guided the transformation throughout the organization. But few organizations in health care have anybody or any group both willing and able to redesign the entire system and introduce the common language, new methods, infrastructure, and managed program of diffusion necessary for dramatic change to take place. Medical professionals' sense of uniqueness may make it more difficult to involve them in change. Perhaps most important, the divided leadership of most health care institutions makes it difficult to plan and execute systemic change.

Table 5.1 Comparison of Elements of Transformation in Non–Health Care Sectors to Intermountain and Meriter

Elements That Produced Transformation in Other Sectors	Intermountain Health Care System	Meriter Health Services
Believing leadership, willing to act on faith in the possibility of change.	*Both physician and non-physician leadership:* Clinical research department took key lead role, CEO strongly supported.	*Nonphysician leadership* began program; *physician leadership developed* with encouragement from nonphysician leaders.
A new *common language* enables management and ultimately all kinds of employees to become a tight-knit team.	Clinical research tradition, long use of a computer system for hospitalwide diagnosis and monitoring provides basics of common language.	A consultant's proprietary training materials provided a common language.
New methods for: -listening to customers, -communicating priorities, -solving process problems, -learning better from people and data.	*Listening to customers:* new surveys. *Communication of priorities:* annual management conference is partial solution, but communication throughout the organization remains inadequately defined. *Solving process problems:* addition of simple quality management methods to traditional clinical research techniques; HELP computer system ensures processes are applied. *Learning from people and data.*	*Listening to customers:* new surveys. *Communication of priorities:* interlocking leadership teams from hospital and physicians' group practice communicate priorities. *Solving process problems and learning from people and data:* Joiner *Team Handbook* provides techniques.

At both Intermountain and Meriter, the chief executives see leadership from key doctors as being just as important to transformation as leadership from themselves. At Intermountain, CEO Scott Parker has delegated leadership for the whole management transformation effort. At Meriter, Terri Potter clearly leads the quest for quality but

Table 5.1   (Continued)

Elements That Produced Transformation in Other Sectors	Intermountain Health Care System	Meriter Health Services
A well-designed *infra-structure* supporting change: -organizational setting for planning and support of new management, -goal-setting system, -training and education - promotion, -diffusion of success stories, -awards and recognition, -diagnosis and monitoring.	*Organizational setting:* executive committee of Intermountain is the quality council; separate quality promotion organizations for medical and administrative work. *Goal setting.* *Training:* extensive program for both physicians and others. Promotion and diffusion of success stories: Newsletters, collegial meetings with doctors, talks by the CEO. *Recognition.* *Diagnosis and monitoring:* HELP computer system used to track and diagnose processes throughout organization.	*Organizational setting:* interlocking leadership teams guide the transition to new management; quality resources group, providing support, reports to vice president for medical affairs but supplies help to both doctors and administrators. *Goal setting:* well-defined process of establishing both long-term and annual goals. *Training:* extensive program; physicians urged to take training from Institute for Healthcare Improvement in Boston. *Promotion and diffusion of success stories:* well-attended monthly forums, newsletter. *Diagnosis and monitoring:* no system yet.

relies on doctors to lead the transformation in their part of the Meriter system.

Second, despite the real and important progress that both Intermountain and Meriter have accomplished, neither has evolved into a truly integrated management system that can be relied on *throughout* their organizations. So far, at least, the complexity of health care and the circumstances of divided leadership seem to have made it harder for the leaders of Intermountain and Meriter to create diffusion programs.

Intermountain and Meriter haven't even diffused a new common language of management to the extent that organizations in other sectors have. In Teradyne and, to a lesser extent, the Kenmore-Tonawanda schools, a new language was clearly articulated. Standard books and courses tell how everyone in those organizations should solve problems and prescribe language to use in discussing the process.

Meriter has followed the same model to some extent, but even there, doctors take courses from an organization (Institute for Healthcare Improvement) with a different dialect of quality improvement from the organization that provided the language that the organization as a whole uses (adopted from Joiner Associates). This doesn't seem to create problems at Meriter; doctors seem able to function multilingually.

Weaknesses of common language at Intermountain seem more profound. In his introductory course on quality improvement, James offers several different languages that people in charge of improvement projects can choose from, including Bataldan's and Juran's. The lack of a unifying language may contribute to the slowness of diffusion of new management methods in the organization.

In any organization we studied, regardless of size or sector, strong leadership from someone or some group is essential to address the issues of divided leadership and impaired diffusion. It may be that the leader in health care needs to be even more collaborative than the leader in other sectors, but that leader will still have to take charge of the process through which the management system will be designed. Berwick suggests all health organizations will have to develop a unified, CEO-driven model. It's the CEOs who are willing to learn—who seek knowledge external to their organization and their field and then seek internal engagement—who will achieve change, Berwick predicts. "Watch the CEO. Look for curiosity," he says. "Is this CEO telling you what he knows, or asking what you know?"

In the final analysis, one thing is clear: The processes that improve other sectors have been shown to be effective in improving health care, and that bodes well. Dr. Terry Classen, the head of Intermountain's Intensive Care Unit, suspects that if integrated management techniques and the use of computer-aided decision making continue to improve at their current pace, in another 15 years Americans' need for physicians will decline substantially even as Americans' health improves. In that context, he believes that current successes, limited though they may be, make the hope for better medicine at lower prices entirely reasonable.

Better Lives for Sailors and Continuous Improvement Processes

Integrated Systems in the Military

It was 7:10 on an August morning when an SH 60B LAMPS helicopter took off from North Island Naval Air Station and headed west out of San Diego Bay. It turned north. Forty-five minutes later, as it began to descend, the passengers saw only water, and rising rapidly toward them. A hundred feet above the water the descent slowed. Then suddenly, a tiny gray patch of metal, about half the size of a tennis court, appeared and the helicopter came to rest on the fan tail of the destroyer U.S.S. *Kinkaid*. As the passengers climbed out, the deck rolled with the 12-foot waves. Still, the copter rested precisely in the middle, its tail extending 15 feet over the ocean. On either side, there was a distance of about ten feet to the edge of the deck and then a sheer 60-foot drop to the sea.

The ship's executive officer met the passengers and took them to the bridge, where they found a remarkable scene. The *Kinkaid* was in the midst of a Joint Expeditionary Force exercise, a war game in which the destroyer and a group of Marines practice seizing a piece of land.

On San Clemente Island, visible to the north, training personnel had established simulated enemy positions. The previous night, as the destroyer's guns fired giant flares to provide light, Marines had landed. Now, the Marines were radioing to the destroyer for heavy artillery barrages against the "enemy" as the Marines tried to take control.

For the typical U.S. Navy commander, this is a tense time, a time to take charge and be visibly *in* charge. Even in a simulated exchange, any serious mishap when U.S. service personnel are in harm's way is likely to seriously damage the career of the commanding officer. But on the *Kinkaid*, Cmdr. Scott Jones was standing calmly to one side, saying very little, as the busy crew dealt with both the aiming of the guns and the departure of the helicopter. He offered his guests cups of coffee and some freshly made donuts, and pointed out on a map where the ship's five-inch guns would be firing. Then he invited the guests onto the open-air portion of the bridge just as the guns began booming.

Jones gave no direct orders. But he did occasionally coach his crew, once telling the officer in charge of the firing that he didn't need to check his bearings so frequently. The *Kinkaid*'s shells were striking close to the "enemy," and as the guns continued firing, Jones left the bridge entirely and invited his visitors to his office below decks. The crew and the Marines together completed the capture of the island without him.

The *Kinkaid* was managed according to an integrated system that compared favorably with the best of those we'd found in any other sector. Jones's willingness to leave the bridge while the ship's crew performed some of their riskiest tasks illustrated the confidence he had in that system. And, as with many of the successful systems we've seen elsewhere, the unifying and driving force was enlightened leadership—in this case, that of Jones himself.

Jones is one of a handful of U.S. military commanders who have made dramatic progress in implementing what the Navy calls Total Quality Leadership, a management method based on lessons learned from W. Edwards Deming and others in industry. With TQL, the Navy hopes to project U.S. military power more reliably with less money—a necessity in these times of relative peace—and at the same time, compete more effectively with other sectors for human resources. The *Kinkaid* under Jones was one of a few ships where dramatic change can be clearly demonstrated.

It extends lessons that managers have learned in the past few decades in a striking new direction. As in industry, one of the core concepts is focus on the customer. But who is the customer of the U.S. military? It's reasonable to answer, "the American public." However, the American public can't provide the kind of feedback to the American military that the customers of Teradyne or the Ritz-Carlton provide to those companies, or even that the schools in the Kenmore–Town of Tonawanda school district arranged to receive from their stakeholders. Clearly, excellence in the military depends to a large extent on the sense of purpose of its senior people, and external feedback has to play a quite different role in the military from the role it plays in organizations that are closer to their stakeholders. But although just who is the external customer is generally unclear in the military, it is also striking how the concept of *internal customer* held considerable power. Some of the best work on improving management in the Navy has focused first on removing impediments to a good life for the Navy's sailors— and then has built on successes to achieve greater readiness and cost-effectiveness.

The experience of military commanders like Scott Jones can tell all kinds of managers a great deal about how to manage when customers or other key stakeholders either are far from a process or can't give clear feedback about what they want.[1]

U.S.S. *Kinkaid*

Jones was people-focused and pragmatic, and his management system reflected that. Total Quality Leadership as he practiced it included:

- Gathering and using data to discover and eliminate weaknesses
- Focusing on continuous improvement with a simple, standardized approach to change
- Disciplined approaches to delegation and empowerment

Jones was initially skeptical that W. Edwards Deming's ideas could help in the chaos of a ship. The enthusiasm of his senior enlisted man, Master Chief Petty Officer Joel Braun, helped persuade him to take

Deming's ideas seriously, and ultimately, Jones was profoundly influenced by them. With these ways of working, Jones created a less hierarchical and at the same time uncommonly disciplined culture. When he entered a room, there was no snapping to attention. Indeed, it often seemed that he was not even noticed, even though it was clear he was in command. The *Kinkaid*'s crew was constantly working to meet quantitative measures of proficiency in the key skills that defined fighting readiness and capability.

QUICK ACTION TO BUILD A SYSTEM

Of all the managers we visited in different sectors, Jones was the one who most clearly proved that an individual manager could make a difference quickly, dealing with time constraints and yet supporting the long-term goals of his or her organization. "A commanding officer's tour on this ship is 20 months," Jones said. "That means I have 20 months to make a difference. And I cannot afford to do anything that I cannot get benefit out of."

When we met him, Cmdr. Jones had commanded the *Kinkaid* for 15 months. The management system he had in place had begun with a single program that, like many of Jones's initiatives, was intended to immediately benefit his sailors, but had the added benefit of creating a more efficient and effective system aboard the *Kinkaid*.

Jones's first improvement project started two months after his arrival on the ship. He set out to change duty assignments in a way that would increase by about 20 percent the number of days each sailor spent on shore with his family.

When a Navy ship is in port, a portion of the crew must remain on board 24 hours a day to tend essential systems. Most Navy ships are on three-section duty or four-section duty. This means that the crew is divided into either three or four groups, which take turns keeping a 24-hour watch while the others go home to their families. The *Kinkaid* had been on four-section duty; thus, while the ship was in port, 90 of the 360 crew had to remain aboard.

Jones declared he wanted to switch to five-section duty and designated a small group of key people from the crew as a process-action team to study the feasibility of such an action. The team reported that the *Kinkaid* didn't have enough sailors trained in damage control—the containment of fires, flooding, toxic chemical spills, and the like—to make up five separate damage-control staffs. Damage control is a key to combat readiness and the Navy mandates that everyone on its ships be trained in its procedures. But in reality, moderate-sized vessels like the *Kinkaid* will have turnover of a third to half its sailors each year. The result is that at any given time, a good percentage of those aboard will not have been trained in the vessel's particular procedures.

At the time, the *Kinkaid* was preparing for a call at Mazatlán, Mexico, and Jones saw an opportunity. He announced that anyone who had not completed damage control training within six weeks would receive no shore leave in Mazatlán. Naturally, every member of the crew found ways to complete the training. When the ship returned to San Diego, some two months after Jones had taken command, it was able to go on five-section duty with a crew noticeably better trained—and getting more shore leave—than it had been when Jones arrived. Not only was the crew happier, but it was much better prepared to deal with damage that might occur in combat.

Jones's improvement programs snowballed: The project that put the *Kinkaid* on five-section duty exposed the broader weaknesses in the indoctrination process. Jones extended the initial training sailors receive when they come on board the ship from one week to two, adding in the damage control training that sailors had been expected to find time to take after beginning their regular duties. He also added eight hours of instruction in problem-solving tools and streamlined the bureaucracy of the registration process. This hastened the adaptation of both the sailors and their families to the new environment.

"I want wives and parents to support the sailors. Therefore, I spend a lot of time solving housing problems and such," says Jones. Affordable housing for enlisted people in San Diego is an enormous problem, and Jones realizes that helping to arrange a place to live is essential to commanding an excellent ship today. "If the sailor's family is not settled," Jones comments, "the sailor doesn't concentrate on the job."

In every case, Jones's improvements that made life better for the crew also made the ship's operations better.

A Simple Methodology

Jones's philosophy is expressed and implemented in clear, straightforward methodologies.

An Infrastructure of Empowerment

A Navy destroyer is an organization with an unusual hierarchy. The Navy, of course, is divided into officers and enlisted personnel. Enlisted personnel usually join right out of high school and few ever become officers. Most officers either attend the Naval Academy at Annapolis or join after completing college; they take their first key positions on smaller ships. As a result, most officers on ships like the *Kinkaid* are far younger than the chief petty officers, the career enlisted personnel who typically stay on the ship in a single job (e.g., running the engine room or the food service) for tours of four or five years.

Jones, who had himself joined the Navy directly out of high school, had been selected for a program under which the Navy sent him to college, and only after graduation, had become an officer, felt it was critical to involve and empower everyone on his ship in its management system. "The leader's job is of course to set priorities," he says. "But next, it is very important to communicate and make everyone understand."

"I knew there were lots of good ideas out there," Jones adds. "I saw my role as a commanding officer was to provide a forum for those ideas to be considered."

Jones's efforts to empower his crew started with middle managers, the senior enlisted personnel. By training them and giving them responsibility, soliciting and applying their suggestions, Jones made his middle managers his change agents. "More important than applying the suggestions is always to listen," he says.

The personnel of the ship had previously been divided into four departments: engineering, combat systems, operations, and supply. Jones added a fifth, a quality department. He appointed the *Kinkaid*'s most senior enlisted man, Master Chief Petty Officer Joel Braun, who had 20 years' service, to head the Total Quality Leadership department. He sent Braun and his four other best noncommissioned officers to four weeks of training at the Navy's TQL school in San

Diego. Another chief petty officer was made head of the damage control division, a key position on the ship that normally would have gone to a college-graduate officer with the rank of lieutenant.

Actions like these reflected Jones's belief that a commanding officer has "a moral obligation to look out for the personal and professional well-being of the people entrusted to him. We have to face each one not only as a professional, but as an individual."

As the *Kinkaid* evolved an infrastructure to support its management system, the senior noncommissioned officers who had received quality training served as Jones's board of quality advisors. The ship's officers and senior enlisted personnel worked out mission and vision statements with the help of a facilitator from the Pacific Fleet's Total Quality Office. Everyone received training, with the training for ordinary crew members focused on flowcharting.

Jones required all sailors to create flowcharts describing their own work process and to show their commanding officer one opportunity for improvement. In this kind of charting, the person who receives the work is the *internal customer*. Division officers have authority to accept or reject the proposed improvement. But if they reject it, they must tell why and try to help the individual to think about the issue in a more constructive way that will lead to an improvement that *can* be accepted.

Process Orientation

With an infrastructure of empowerment beginning to take root, Jones began to focus on larger processes. Jones saw every task and function aboard the *Kinkaid* as a process that can be disassembled, analyzed, improved, and reassembled. "There are thousands of processes in the ship," he says. "We can improve all the processes through this kind of procedure. It just takes one or two people with profound knowledge to know how to break up the process into component pieces that you can put back together."

The way the *Kinkaid*'s crew learned to load a missile and make radar contact with a target was an example. The crew created metrics—how many minutes for loading, how many seconds for target acquisition—and Jones trained the sailors in each small segment of the process. Then they integrated them and made the sailors understand the whole system.

Similarly, in preparation for battle group deployment, Jones had his sailors first practice shooting the destroyer's large guns, then landing the helicopter, then shooting missiles. He got them proficient at each, then had them do them all together: shoot the gun and land a helicopter, then shoot the gun, land a helicopter, and fight a fire all at the same time.

Data-Oriented Focus on Weaknesses

A third element Jones has imprinted on the *Kinkaid*'s culture is an orientation toward gathering data to reveal weaknesses in the system. For instance, the new noncommissioned head of the damage control division, Chief Robert Morey, did a study and found that 50 percent of the watertight doors on the ship weren't receiving proper planned maintenance. He presented Jones with a Pareto chart showing the percentage of each type of door that was inadequately maintained.[2]

Watertight integrity is a critical component of a ship's ability to sustain attack and keep on functioning. Jones found it difficult to hear the news without anger. Yet, the chief's analytical work represented exactly the kind of effort he wanted to encourage. He recalls that it was a struggle for him to say, "Great, Chief. Good job."

"If the commanding officer goes around yelling and screaming when he hears about a problem with watertight doors, then no other chief will ever come back with a problem," says Jones. "The commanding officer must reward people who bring problems forward."

Well-Managed Phase-In

Jones improvement methodology, though effective, is fairly standard. Indeed, its simplicity seemed to be a key reason why it worked.

But the way Jones phased in the new approach to management was remarkable. His first move was to try for a quick, clear, and visible success that would create awareness of TQL and give sailors a reason to support it. He achieved that with the conversion to five-section duty. That became the lever for other people-oriented systemic improvements designed to elicit enthusiasm, not apprehension, from those who feared change. Thereafter, he continually added improvement methods built on the principles of empowerment, process orientation, and data-driven analysis.

Within ten months of Jones's arrival, Chief of Naval Operations Adm. Frank Kelso II visited the *Kinkaid*. Several sailors made presentations, in their own words, about the improvements they had initiated and the analysis that had contributed to them. Jones recalled, "I had to brief Adm. Kelso and tell him, 'Look how great we are. We found 50 percent of our preventive maintenance checks on doors indicated the required maintenance actions hadn't been completed.' "

This was, of course, said tongue-in-cheek. Jones adds that it is a credit to Admiral Kelso that "a relatively junior officer felt comfortable enough to stand in front of him and admit that his maintenance program was all screwed up." In addition, Jones was able to describe the process that Chief Morey and others had led that fixed the problem and produced a dramatic increase in overall readiness. Kelso responded with profound appreciation. He declared the *Kinkaid*'s efficiency, its morale, and its ability to continually analyze and improve processes would be a new model for the Navy.

ADAPTING NEW MANAGEMENT TO THE MILITARY

Using new management methods in the military involves unique challenges. Primary among them is the fact that everyone in the military submits to a discipline that differs from the practice in other kinds of government agencies or in private industry. No "empowerment" can be allowed to undermine the obedience that soldiers must be ready to display under fire.

Moreover, most postings in the military, like those on the *Kinkaid*, experience rapid turnover of leaders and enlisted personnel. Though the absence of leadership continuity is a problem in civilian organizations too, it is far more acute in the military.

Finally, as on the *Kinkaid*, the management of the quality of life is a crucial problem throughout the military. The military is not just a workplace, but also a home and a family for its people. This is a burden the average business does not have to bear.

Despite the enormous differences between the military and the civilian world, however, we can see in the progress on the *Kinkaid* the same systems view and creation of an integrated management system that we see in other sectors. The same five key principles apply: continuous improvement through a common language, integrating information from outside the organization, integrating information from inside the organization by eliciting feedback and the engagement of the stakeholders, creating an infrastructure that supports the vision, and participation in mutual learning and societal learning.

Jones's integrated system made little use of the word (and the concept of) *customer*. But others in the Navy are making good use of that idea as well.

U.S.S. McKee

The size of an organization has a great deal to do with the type of integrated system it adopts. This is especially true in the military. Another ship we visited, the submarine tender U.S.S. *McKee*, had about four times as many sailors as the *Kinkaid* and, as a result, it clearly needed a more sophisticated infrastructure.

A Larger Ship, a Different System

The *McKee* had 1,500 crew members. It usually remained docked in San Diego, providing submarines and surface ships with repairs, supplies, and personal services such as medical and dental treatment. But it had dramatically proved its importance during Operation Desert Storm in 1990 by sailing to the Persian Gulf and providing the same services for ships in the theater of war. It was generally a more stable place to work than the *Kinkaid*, however: personnel turnover was "only" 30 percent a year.

In 1992, under Capt. Wynn Harding, the *McKee* took its first steps toward evolving a new management system. Under Harding, for instance, the *McKee*'s sailors compiled a clear, step-by-step guide to producing ammunition transaction reports, and as a result, they reduced the number of errors from as many as 24 per month to one or two. (More recently, the number has consistently been zero.)

When Capt. Tom Etter relieved Harding as commanding officer in 1993, Executive Officer Tom Gehring, second in command on the ship, and the ship's other top leaders explained the McKee's process-oriented improvement work to him. He was impressed and set out to do his own study, critically reading five books on Total Quality Management. Ultimately, he was able to build on what his predecessor had initiated and, in the process, to show that a transition between commanding officers can be carried out effectively within the context of an evolving management system.

When we visited, the quality program on the McKee, like the Kinkaid's, involved pragmatic but results-oriented commitment to PDCA improvement cycles. It involved integrating information from outside, integrating information from within, an infrastructure that supported change, and a well-managed program of diffusion. Like Cmdr. Jones, Capt. Etter has made the crew's welfare a priority, with the creation of a crew's lounge having been a key part of the quality program.

On the other hand, the size of the McKee meant that it needed a far broader mobilization infrastructure than did the Kinkaid. Although Etter did not think of himself as having created a "mobilization infrastructure," he actually introduced institutions that had the same kinds of effects as mobilization infrastructures in private industry.

First, he insisted that the ship's Executive Committee become a goal-setting organization for the Total Quality effort. "Capt. Etter refocused us from an organization primarily doing Total Quality because we wanted to do Total Quality, to an organization doing Total Quality to get results," says Lt. John Krause, the ship's communications officer and its Total Quality coordinator. "The captain said, 'Quit telling me what wonderful meetings you are attending, and tell me what you are doing for people.'"

Etter also created a prize called the Harding Award, named after the captain who preceded him as commanding officer. It is given to crew members who achieve particularly impressive improvements, and is a powerful way of taking the quality program in a new, more powerful direction.

A third key part of the McKee's quality infrastructure is weekly sessions that Etter calls Show-Me's. Both shipwide and at the department level, these are meetings where crew are encouraged to display their latest quality improvement work. Everyone aboard knows the top officers of the ship want to see real evidence of improvement work during these hours.

The McKee's infrastructure seemed to be leading to improvement on a wide scale. When we visited, we found flowcharts of key processes posted in key locations such as the ship's combat information center. On a few minutes' notice, Capt. Etter called together a Show-Me for us, at which six groups presented successful improvement efforts. Some groups referred to submarines and their crews as their "customers."

During Etter's tenure, the McKee completed 71 percent more submarine repair work with only a 33 percent increase in work hours. Rework was reduced by 50 percent. The ship reduced hazardous waste streams by 75 percent and workforce back injuries by 90 percent.

The McKee had taught a broader array of analytical tools to its people than the Kinkaid—not just flow-charting, but also brainstorming, cause-and-effect diagrams, and several others. But the McKee did not seem to have developed a common language of improvement to the extent that the Kinkaid had. Enlisted people in the Show-Me that was presented for us had clearly identified and solved real problems. But they sometimes couldn't explain the tool they displayed and it wasn't clear whether the tools had actually contributed to the solutions.

When we visited, the crew had produced many small improvements, but a complete management transformation was not yet visible. The ship had just started to look at what its top officers call its "global processes": communication, training, qualification of crew members for jobs, and time management.

Important Progress in the Navy as a Whole

The experiences of the Kinkaid, the McKee, and several other ships suggest that carefully developed integrated management methods can make a dramatic difference and have already done so in some places. At the lowest level in the Navy, new management thinking has shown it can work just as it does in industry.

Many Navy officers are thinking in more effective and systemic ways. The Atlantic and Pacific fleets recently produced a joint "Troubled Systems Process Report," a careful analysis of each item the Navy uses that has been causing problems, together with a report of what seems to be wrong and what's being done to address it. "In the past, people would just say, 'Oh, these gun mounts are pieces of crap,'" said one supply officer. "Now, they're not only analyzing them, but keeping careful track about what's being done."

Adm. Kelso stressed the similarities between the Navy and private industry, where customer-driven management systems have made such a difference. He noted that the majority of Navy people have well-defined internal customers they must serve, and vision-driven, process-oriented management can help serve them just as well as it helps people serve customers in factories. "If you get down to a sailor in an engine room, his customer is pretty clear," said Kelso. "Internal customer relations on a ship are clean."

Moreover, like Jones and Etter, many passionate officers see Total Quality Leadership as an important opportunity to improve the quality of work life in the Navy. The first TQL project Adm. Kelso directed was an effort to reduce the number of deaths of young service men and women off-duty.

Navy civilians had been some of Deming's most important followers in the 1980s, and probably were first to coin the term Total Quality Management.[3] They had begun teaching Deming's ideas to managers at the Navy's aviation repair facilities in 1985 and had considerable success.

Navy officers were hungry for a methodology of improvement in the 1990s. They recognized the waste that was common in the Navy; they knew they were failing to use good ideas from enlisted people and younger officers. "I'd always had a feeling that we could do things better in the Navy," Adm. Kelso told us in an interview just days before his retirement. "The sort of thing that irritated me was that we kept repeating the same errors. You inspect an organization, and six months later, you find many of the same errors are there again. You go through a career of 30 years like mine, and you wonder, 'Why do they do that?'"

Kelso saw that the Navy was teaching hundreds of courses every year to officers rising through the ranks. Somehow, many of them were developing into excellent leaders. But the Navy's training organizations had few well-defined principles of leadership to offer them. "I wanted to have a management style for the Navy, that we taught in our schools," Kelso recalled.

Therefore, though admirals weren't sure how to apply some parts of Deming's teachings, such as his opposition to performance evaluation systems, the Navy began a serious effort to introduce Total Quality. In the uniformed service, Kelso changed the name of the program from Total Quality Management to Total Quality Leadership. "If you tell a naval officer that he's a manager, he'll reject it. They think of themselves as 'leaders.' A guy who goes to sea or flies an airplane sees a 'manager' as a guy who sits behind a desk."

Why Isn't the Impact Greater?

On the whole, however, the Navy's TQL program hasn't delivered a comprehensive integrated management system. Though it has shown it can dramatically improve how Navy ships operate, everyone associated with it agrees that the Navy remains far from transformation.

Kelso and other Navy leaders acknowledged that when they launched the TQL program, they had no clear methodology for using Total Quality on a ship. Naturally, given this lack of clarity, there have been serious problems in implementation.

W. Edwards Deming played a powerful role in the evolution of the Navy's effort to reform itself. Kelso liked a book he read on Deming, attended one of Deming's four-day seminars, and invited Deming home for dinner. "What most impressed me was his dedication to what he was doing," Kelso told us. "He was 90. He really didn't have to work any more. But he was so dedicated to changing the work ethic in this country."

But Deming's ideas about goal setting and organization seem to have caused significant difficulties. They were incompatible with deeply ingrained—and useful—military tradition. Deming's 14 points include the statements: "Eliminate slogans, exhortations, and targets for the work force asking for zero defects and new levels of productivity. Such exhortations only create adversarial relationships, as the bulk of the causes of low quality and low productivity belong to the system and thus lie beyond the power of the work force. . . . Eliminate work standards (quotas) on the factory floor. Substitute leadership. . . . Eliminate management by objective. Substitute leadership."[4] Deming also referred to "evaluation of performance, merit rating, or annual review" as one of the "seven deadly diseases" of management.

The admirals, however, weren't ready to eliminate slogans, targets, and performance evaluation in the Navy. It is important to note that this is an environment where the entire management system has been overhauled in the past 20 years. "We have a very big organization," said Kelso. "I don't know how you can manage it without some kind of performance review." But they never developed an approach to goal setting and measurement that would lend weight to a review program. In fact, at least in the first three years of TQL, the Navy never clearly defined what it was trying to do and when it hoped to do it.

Also, Kelso rejected the idea of naming a lower-ranking admiral to be "in charge of TQL." As a result, the Navy as a whole got no senior person to perform the duties that "qualify directors" performed in organizations like Teradyne and the Ritz-Carlton.

Kelso's reasons for avoiding the appointment of someone in charge of TQL were good. "If I get a one-star officer to teach Total Quality Leadership, then more senior people will not take it seriously," Kelso told us. But as a result, the Navy had no senior person to organize and monitor training programs, advise executives on quality techniques, and guide the development of a mobilization infrastructure. These tasks fell instead to the Department of the Navy Total Quality Leadership Office. Dominated by civilians, this office had played a key role in the early implementation of Deming's ideas in civilian Navy organizations such as Navy hospitals. But the maintenance and logistics office never developed much clout with top uniformed officers.

The training staff deeply believed in Deming's teachings, and they insisted on standardization in quality leadership training. In principle, that's good. But in practice, the quest for standardization meant that professional trainers, often with little experience on ships, did all the training. We asked one leader of the training effort whether she

Table 6.1 Transformation and Attempted Transformation in the Navy

Elements That Produced Transformation in Manufacturing	U.S.S. *Kinkaid*	U.S.S. McKee	Navy as a Whole
Commitment to continuous improvement throughout the organization.	Cmdr. Jones experienced conversion, and shows deep commitment.	Capt. Harding, then Capt. Edder each showed real commitment.	Leadership demonstrated real commitment.
A new *common language* enables management and ultimately all kinds of employees to become a tight-knit team.	Flowcharting is center of common language.	Less clarity of common language than the *Kinkaid*.	Little common language gains universal acceptance.
Integrating information from outside the organization and inside the organization.	*Customers* not clearly defined; Jones puts priority on listening to crew.	*Customers* are submarine crews. Method of listening to them not yet well defined.	Many units clearly defining their *customers*; standard methods of listening not yet adopted.
	Communicating priorities: new roles for senior enlisted personnel help to mobilize ship.	*Communicating priorities*: "Show-Me's" communicate importance of improvement; Executive Committee starting to focus on "global processes."	*Communicating priorities*: no clear new methods.
	Solving process problems: Flowcharting is emphasized.	*Solving process problems*: numerous new methods.	*Solving process problems*: numerous new methods.
	Learning better: Emphasis on rewarding people for reporting weaknesses.	*Learning better*: Pareto analysis helps to focus learning.	*Learning better*: no standard new methods.

A well-designed infrastructure supporting change:	Simple infrastructure suitable to small organization.	Appropriate infrastructure for larger ship seems to be developing.	Top officers weren't deeply involved until recently in creating infrastructure.
-organizational setting for planning and support of new management, -goal-setting system, -training and education, -promotion, -diffusion of success stories, -awards and recognition, -diagnosis and monitoring.	*Organizational setting:* quality council.	*Organizational setting:* executive committee, quality director.	*Organizational setting:* just being established.
	Goal-setting: limited development (Jones and Quality Council discuss goals).	*Goal setting:* executive committee has improved, but isn't yet systematic.	*Goal setting:* just being established.
	Training: program includes everyone.	*Training:* built own system with examples from own successes.	*Training:* weaknesses widely acknowledged.
	Promotion: simple promotion by Jones and department heads.	*Promotion, diffusion of success stories:* Weekly "Show-Me's."	*Promotion, diffusion of success stories:* Kelso, Bourda involved.
	Diffusion of success stories: simple.	*Awards and recognition:* Harding award, "Show-Me's."	*Awards and recognition:* little connection between TQL effort and existing recognition programs.
	Awards and recognition: recognition by Adm. Kelso had considerable impact on crew.	*Diagnosis:* diagnosis in weekly "Show-Me's."	*Diagnosis and monitoring:* very little.
	Diagnosis: analysis of flowcharts by Jones and department heads.		*Measurement and reward:* instituted entry in each officer's performance appraisal regarding use of TQL practices.

(continued)

Table 6.1 (Continued)

Elements That Produced Transformation in Manufacturing	U.S.S. *Kinkaid*	U.S.S. *McKee*	Navy as a Whole
Participation in mutual learning and societal networking.	Cmdr. Jones worked hard to learn from outsiders.	Capt. Edder was an avid communicator.	Considerable effort to learn from outside—more from a guru than from close work with practitioners.
Results.	Exceptional performance on several indicators.	Numerous individual successes, not yet a genuine transformation of management system.	Isolated successes do not yet add up to a radical improvement.

invited commanders who had led successful transformations to speak in her courses. Her answer: "No, because then we can't control what they say."

In short, there was a rigidity that was fundamentally at odds with the passionate engagement and somewhat trial-and-error approach necessary to evolve a truly integrated management system.

Although the Navy had believing leadership and most of the new methods needed to support a transformation, the new methods hadn't come together into a powerful common language that all Navy people could use to work together on improvements. The Navy had no standard, well-defined *process* through which improvement can be carried out, comparable to the seven-step method used in Teradyne or the DDAE cycle used in Kenmore-Tonawanda.

People in the Navy learned no clear way of selecting what should be improved, and few parts of the Navy rigorously encouraged comparing the situation before and after an improvement effort. Finally, the Navy taught its commanders no clear methodology they could used to phase in new methods, and it lacked a system to sustain TQL in the face of changes of commanding officers.

Table 6.1 summarizes the extent to which the *Kinkaid*, the *McKee*, and the Navy as a whole have key elements of transformation that we found crucial in other sectors. Where all the elements are in place, as on the *Kinkaid*, a transformation has occurred; the *McKee* also has made great progress. But the Navy as a whole lacks many of the elements other leaders have found necessary for true organizational transformation.

CHAPTER 7

The Challenge of Intransigent Organizations

Integrated Systems in Government Agencies

Mayor Joseph Sensenbrenner was filled with skepticism when he walked into an auditorium at the University of Wisconsin's Madison campus in the spring of 1983. He knew that a few of the university's professors had invited him, as Madison's newly elected chief executive, to hear W. Edwards Deming, and that Deming was credited with a key role in the revival of Japanese business after World War II. But he wondered what relevance that could have to city government. However, when Deming began to speak about the flaws in American management, declaring that managers didn't understand the systems they were supposed to run and the contributions their people wanted to make, Sensenbrenner was fascinated. He says it was "the common sense and the humanity" of what Deming was saying that inspired him. Deming's approach seemed to be working in companies around the world. Why, Sensenbrenner thought, couldn't it be applied to making government work better?

Deming himself declared that he didn't know if his ideas would work in the public sector, but Sensenbrenner and several friends in his administration were undeterred. They asked themselves what aspect of city government was most similar to a private-sector operation. The answer was the city's motor equipment division, which maintained and repaired city cars and trucks. Everyone in Madison seemed to agree that it performed poorly. It would be the perfect target for an experiment.

With the assistance of the professors and considerable attention from Sensenbrenner and aides, the garage staff learned problem-solving methods, teamwork, and Deming's 14 points. Performance improved dramatically, and so did morale. It was the first of a significant number of successes in Madison city government. For that matter, it was the first of many public-sector successes throughout the United States.

But Deming's concerns were not entirely unfounded. Outside of successes in education and the military, documented earlier in this book, we have encountered no large public-sector organization that has created the kinds of powerful integrated management systems we've seen in other sectors. Anxious to find some, we talked to staff of the Baldrige committee and the U.S. government's Federal Quality Institute, to numerous university experts, to leaders of state quality organizations and local quality councils. We also investigated winners of the U.S. government's President's Quality Award, which is given for outstanding quality achievement in the federal government. Although we found varying degrees of success, we found nothing that matches the success seen in the private sector.

In this chapter, we examine four public-sector attempts to design integrated management systems.

The first two, the Madison police department and the Ogden IRS Center in Utah, can be described as qualified successes. In the language of the Center for Quality of Management's Services Industries Committee (see Chapter 3), the Madison Police Department mainly manages *moment-of-truth* processes, and the Ogden IRS Center manages mostly *operational* processes. Both programs began with strong leadership, both adopted some new methods that changed the way work was done, and both tried to change their way of thinking from a traditional hierarchical model to something like the social systems model. However, each failed to follow up by developing those methods into standard methodologies through which all parts of the organization could continue to improve predictably. Each developed only a few elements of the infrastructures we saw in the most successful organizations we examined. And, probably as a result, each achieved less radical change than the most successful organizations.

The other organizations—the Environmental Protection Agency and the state government of Massachusetts—although not complete failures, stand as object lessons of the special difficulties presented by public-sector organizations.

The Madison Police Department

The quality improvement system of Madison's government, which has operated continuously since Mayor Sensenbrenner encountered Deming in 1983, is one of the oldest in the nation. It is even older than most in the private sector. But these efforts almost ended with Sensenbrenner's administration. In 1989, his successor, Paul Soglin, took a skeptical look at the program and considered eliminating it to save money. Those who tried to make a case for continuing the program had insufficient ammunition, however, because few measures of success had been identified, quantified, and tracked.

"I wanted to know how much had been spent, and what were the returns," Soglin says now. Sensenbrenner and Police Chief David Couper arranged a session at a Madison hotel where Soglin met Deming and some of Deming's supporters. It didn't go well. Soglin felt Deming and his supporters were "almost insulted that I didn't understand the magnitude of what was being done in Madison. It was as if I was some sort of a barbarian."

Most of Sensenbrenner's close aides left city government, but at least one leader of the quality program found a way to address Soglin's concerns. Tom Mosgaller, a former Catholic seminarian and community organizer, had been hired by the city as quality and productivity administrator. His job had been made a civil person position, so he couldn't be fired easily. When Soglin ordered an audit to determine whether the quality program was a waste of money, Mosgaller worked closely with the auditors. Together, they were able to put together an estimate that Sensenbrenner's quality initiatives had created benefits worth at least five times their costs. Meanwhile, Soglin was reading the

writings of Deming and others in the quality movement. He was talking to program participants, such as the mechanics in the city garage
whom the quality program had encouraged to describe the problems
they saw and work on solving them. "I was beginning to feel, 'If this is
done right, this has fantastic possibilities,'" Soglin says. Soglin decided
to keep the program and build on it.

Sensenbrenner and others had formed the Madison Area Quality
Improvement Network with the goal of bringing Deming's methods to
all organizations in the Madison area. MAQIN had influenced the
executives of Meriter Hospital, introducing them, and others, to Deming's 14 points and the Joiner Triangle's three principles: *quality, scientific approach,* and *all one team.*

But not everyone could easily see the ideas' relevance to government agencies. Police Chief Couper, in fact, had walked out of the
first quality training session for all agency heads, saying politely that
what the trainer was advocating was "very nice," but couldn't work in
the command-and-control environment of the police force.

Madison, like most cities, operated its police department in a centralized, top-down style derived from 1920s efforts to depoliticize the
police by clearly defining lines of authority. Though the city was divided into several districts, the entire department operated from the
municipal building downtown.

After seeing successes in other areas of the city government, however, Couper gradually became a convert. On one hand, the department
began taking a more scientific and "customer"-centered approach to its
work by carefully surveying all the people it "served" to learn how they
felt about the department. For each case it handled, it defined its customers as the victim, the complainant, and even the arrested person, if
an arrest had taken place. The surveys asked everyone how happy they
were with the department's performance. (Interestingly, the majority of
people arrested reported that the department had done fine.)

As Couper focused on imparting principles and values to the organization, authoring 12 principles of quality leadership, the department
worked to decentralize authority toward districts, improve communication, and build teamwork. A visionary slogan was adopted: "Closer to
the People; Quality from the Inside Out." The department's top officers
decided to give the rank and file a chance to take the lead in creating

an experimental police district, where officers could practice a more participative style and a more scientific approach. Top officers including Capt. Ted Balistreri formed a guidance/steering team, but the bulk of the work was done by and the majority of the key decisions were made by an organizing committee consisting of lower-ranking people. No one on the organizing committee held a rank higher than sergeant.

First, members of the organizing committee met with each member of the department, in small groups of 15 or fewer, and asked what they would suggest changing about the department's current management system. They received 179 suggestions in 24 categories.

This marked perhaps the most radical turnabout in the department's style. "Up to that point, I can never remember superiors going to the rank and file and saying 'What can we do to help you do a better job?'" notes Capt. Mike Masterson, former head of the experimental police district who is now in charge of the police department's personnel and training team.

For public input, the organizing committee called eight meetings in four aldermen's districts to seek suggestions from the public. It asked the aldermen whom they should invite, and mailed invitations to each. (The committee also held meetings open to the general public, but found they were not as well attended as those where invitations were sent out.)

Balistreri, who today as assistant chief ranks second in the department, notes that in many ways, the interviewing of police department members and the public was not well handled. The organizing committee asked officers to make suggestions for improvement without first asking them what were the problems that should be addressed. "At some of these meetings, there was a lot of hostility," Balistreri notes. Simply asking for suggestions didn't do much to uncover the real problems that drove the frustration many officers felt.

Nonetheless, the committee developed a new, decentralized approach to running a police district. The objective was to implement what was becoming known as community policing or sometimes problem-oriented policing, under which the police would be decentralized in the community, would hear what the community considered to be its problems, and would figure out ways to solve them.

The organizing committee chose as an experimental district a diverse area on the city's south side. It included a high-crime neighborhood, a wealthy neighborhood, a neighborhood full of college students, and a high school. The district office was placed in a new, tiny, three-room house-like brick building in one of the district's less-desirable neighborhoods.

Of necessity, interaction between detectives and patrol officers increased tremendously, and they became partners in solving problems. "Down there," says Noble Wray, who served as a rank-and-file officer in the district and is now a captain, "my work went to the [detectives], and then they would come back and contact me. The private sector calls it 'market-focused teams.'" Instead of wasting time and resources, officers and detectives worked closely with the community and other government agencies to consider alternative ways of eradicating problems, especially minor infractions, that might minimize or eliminate traditional police involvement. "We had more of a systems approach to what we were doing," says Wray.

Chief Couper also set up the Quality Leadership Council to make improvements in the running of police operations at headquarters. A key area where officers had suggested improvements was in the department's process of promoting officers to higher ranks. To address that, the Quality Leadership Council, which had no member ranked higher than lieutenant, took initiative in setting up a leadership-training program. The Council also took the lead in trying to transfer successful ideas from the experimental district to the whole department.

Capt. Masterson suggests that the quality program in the police department is part of the "long-term reengineering of city government and other services into a neighborhood-based integrated community system that involves the cops." That's an excellent statement of the goal, and such a reengineered system would certainly be desirable, but at least when we visited, there did not seem to be a great deal of evidence to indicate that the dream would come true.

The creation of the experimental police district represented a significant and at least partially successful attempt to adopt new thinking and to redesign the system of managing interactions, making radical changes where necessary. But didn't develop any quantitative way of evaluating the experimental police district's success. And it can't be said to have designed a coherent new management *system* like those in the more dramatically successful organizations we reviewed in earlier chapters. It has adopted some important new

common language (*processes, values,* and *customers*), but it has not
adopted any well-developed set of new methods that can be used to
pursue truly improvement in a continuously scientific way. It introduced a process of surveying its "customers," for instance, but it
hasn't developed any consistent way of using the data.

Because the processes in the Madison Police Department represent
moment-of-truth service processes more than operational processes,
finding or creating dependable new methods to pursue customer focus,
continuous improvement, total involvement, and better learning might
be difficult. The department would be in a better position to do this if
it had developed an adequate infrastructure to support its system. But
in the Madison Police Department, we found only a few effective elements of infrastructure. The department has no consistent goal-setting
system, for instance, and the Quality Leadership Council has so far not
functioned dependably to provide improvement planning and support.

Madison is a wonderful city and its police department deserves
credit for the noble efforts it is making to better serve all its stakeholders. But thus far, it is an example of an integrated management
system still waiting to happen. The same can be said about another
government agency we studied, the Ogden IRS Center in Utah.

Ogden Internal Revenue
Service Center

As mentioned before, the Madison Police Department is defined by
how it responds to its customers' unpredictable moment-of-truth
needs. By contrast, the measure of success at the Ogden IRS Center is
how well it performs enormous but relatively predictable operational
processes.

The Ogden Center handles collections in a 14-state area that extends to the tip of Alaska. More than 3,000 full-time employees and
nearly an equal number of seasonal workers process returns, look for
noncompliance, and handle taxpayer inquiries and complaints. The
largest share of the Ogden Center's people work in "the pipeline," a series of enormous rooms where employees, using some sophisticated

high-tech machinery, some cleverly designed manual systems, and a great deal of simple, laborious effort, sort envelopes with taxpayers' returns in them.

As the returns move through the pipeline, they are opened, sorted, and examined to be sure all schedules are included. The data is transcribed into computers and checked for accuracy and completeness. (Ogden has a 1,000-person staff that does nothing but data conversion on the pipeline, taking paper returns and entering data from them into computers.) Payment checks are banked and notices are sent to taxpayers that seem to have made obvious errors. The data is then transferred electronically to an IRS computer center and further checked for validity. Then the U.S. Treasury issues refunds.

In addition to running the pipeline, units at the Center respond to taxpayer inquiries, conduct computer analyses to identify fraud and underreporting, and provide support for people in smaller IRS offices who conduct tax audits and collect delinquent taxes.

In 1985, executives at the Ogden Center acknowledged what was a developing IRS-wide problem. A key indicator of performance at the IRS had traditionally been "cost per thousand returns processed," a measure that led managers to emphasize—perhaps overemphasize—cost cutting. In 1985, the agency's aggressive efforts, which had included dramatic cuts in training budgets, led to a noticeable decrease in quality of pipeline operations.

In 1986, a new director of the Ogden Center, Robert Wenzel, decided to make quality improvement his top priority and to benchmark the quality initiatives of Florida Power & Light, an electric utility that later won the Deming Prize of the Union of Japanese Scientists and Engineers. The Center also began to use techniques taught by the consulting firm Juran Institute, which had also worked with Ritz-Carlton.

Employees at the Ogden IRS Center strongly supported the quality improvement effort. The Center's suggestion program garnered high participation, paying bonuses to 148 employees for suggested improvements in a single year.

Wenzel named Deborah Egan to head the Quality Improvement Division within the Ogden Service Center. Egan managed an extensive program of promotion through newsletters, posters, and displays throughout the Center. It was designed to disseminate and reinforce a culture of quality that included:

- The concept that the IRS has *customers:* "anyone who receives a service or a product as a result of action we have taken"
- The adoption of *core values,* such as respect for the individual and service to the customer
- The principle of *teamwork*
- The concept of *eliminating barriers to quality*

The Center adopted a team-driven, project-by-project approach to quality. Using an eight-step PDCA-type improvement methodology, the Center's divisions completed 32 improvement projects over five years.

Each division of the Ogden Service Center we visited had its own innovations that made life better for taxpayers. The most impressive department was the Data Conversion Division, where employees convert data from paper to computer files by entering the data on computer terminals. The division had reduced its error rate every year for five years. There was strong evidence of widespread involvement of many employees in improvement activities, with handwritten slogans on a number of cubicles. Director Dick Nelson gave his reserved parking space, close to the building entrance, to the employee who came up with the best suggestion each month.

Teams in other parts of the Ogden Center could cite additional important successes. A team in the Communications and Customer Service Branch within the Information and Accounting Systems Division reduced by 80 percent the portion of computer runs that had to be redone. The Problem Resolution Office had reduced the percentage of unresolved taxpayer problems more than 30 days old from 9.2 percent in 1992 to 2.9 percent in 1993.

The organization also made a host of small but important changes in how it related to employees, for instance by adding a day care center. Some surveys showed significant improvement in employee satisfaction.

The Ogden Service Center won the President's Quality Award in 1992, just as Wenzel was being promoted from director there to a higher-ranking job in Washington. Wenzel's successor, Michael Bigelow, continued the program with modifications.

But it's fair to say that no powerful integrated management system—no system that enables the organization to apply the scientific method to the organization's key challenges—has yet emerged in Ogden. Indeed, Ogden, like the Madison Police Department, lacked many of the elements that our research showed to be necessary to a self-perpetuating integrated management system. Three gaps seem particularly significant in Ogden: common language, consistently used problem-solving methods, and a goal-setting system.

The only element of new common language of improvement that we encountered was the introduction of the idea that people to whom the IRS provides services or products are *customers*. The promotion of the customer concept is an important start. But in more successful organizations, a more fully developed common language becomes a way of encouraging the utilization of an array of new methods throughout the organization.

And, although top management and the managers of individual divisions *had* developed useful methods to work toward improvement, few if any were integrated throughout the organization. Those that were integrated (e.g., the eight-step improvement process) were understood by only a small fraction of the employees. Managers studied courses on eight-step improvement, but none of the promotional material developed by the Quality Improvement Division provided further explanation or advice in the implementation of the method or any other improvement methodology.

The 32 eight-step improvement projects completed between 1987 and 1991 are a strikingly modest number compared to similarly large organizations in private industry. The number of problem-solving teams seems to have declined as the organization tried to turn system-wide issues over to systems analysis professionals after 1991. None of the managers we met were routinely using the eight-step process to solve problems. And the systems analysts do not appear to have achieved dramatic improvement either. With the possible exception of the Data Conversion Division, total involvement in improvement remained only a dream when we visited.

Finally, when we visited, the Center had no defined goal-setting system. The people at Ogden were proud of their successes and very willing to acknowledge that they had many weaknesses. But there was remarkably little evidence of effort to determine *which* weaknesses were important and start problem-solving that would eliminate them.

It is perhaps too early to judge the Ogden Center's effort. Today, the Ogden IRS Center is struggling to address its problems. A new director has reinvigorated the process and introduced a rigorous planning system that sets goals more clearly. Indeed, the IRS will always have a few problems, not the least of which is trying to serve a customer that can never be truly satisfied. (After all, it's a bit far-fetched to imagine the IRS will ever produce truly happy taxpayers.)

The programs we observed at the IRS and in Madison fell short of what we would have liked to see. But their achievements were clear. By contrast, many efforts to bring change in government—perhaps even more than in other sectors—have accomplished little. We've observed two cases that seemed to have produced no lasting benefit: change efforts at the federal government's Environmental Protection Agency and in the government of the state of Massachusetts. Both of these cases illustrate some of the key reasons governmental organizations have a harder time developing integrated systems.

The Environmental Protection Agency

In September 1988, the governing board of the National Research Council (NRC) approved a project called the "State of the Art Study of Statistical Quality Control Procedures."[1] It was to be carried out by the Committee on Applied and Theoretical Statistics, Board on Mathematical Sciences. The project was intended to serve the needs of several government agencies, but ultimately focused only on the Environmental Protection Agency.

In fact, the study was narrowed even further to focus only on a group within the EPA called the Quality Assurance Management Staff. QAMS had developed several potentially effective methodologies known as data quality objectives, which were formulated to ensure the accuracy and relevance of the data gathered for EPA cleanup projects.

Going into the study, the NRC team expected that QAMS had played a leading role in the organizationwide quality effort at the EPA, yet, inexplicably, that had not been the case. QAMS reported to an assistant administrator in charge of R&D. Neither the methodology of the QAMS nor any other methodology for data quality assurance was brought into the agencywide TQM program.

Nevertheless, the team organized by the NRC felt that it was wrong to address the statistical quality assurance issue narrowly focused on QAMS, so it broadened its study to include agencywide TQM efforts. The final report was highly critical of the overall EPA approach to TQM, and the NRC decided not to issue the report.

The experience at the EPA provides an example of a well-intentioned effort to evolve an integrated management system that fell short. It did so, we believe, for a number of reasons common to many organizations. Perhaps chief among them, the fact that QAMS was not part of the overall TQM program betrays a lack of understanding of the top management in EPA of what TQM was all about.

Before the TQM program, everyone at the EPA agreed that the organization suffered from numerous process problems. Regional officials made decisions that frequently cost both the government and private industry billions of dollars, and sometimes disrupted communities for years. Yet, regional project managers, the people in charge of actually carrying out projects to improve the environment, had so little training in scientific methods that they couldn't understand basic concepts in data quality used by QAMS. Quality assurance managers were low-grade civil servants who also did not receive adequate training, especially in the statistical quality methods.

The TQM program did nothing to address these problems and may actually have made them worse. The entire program was initiated by an outside consulting company, and there is no evidence that the consultant tried to lead the EPA toward looking at the quality issue in a systemic way. Each region was charged with designing its own TQM program using training provided by the consultant. Executives from different regions rarely talked to each other about their TQM programs, despite the fact that they were coping with very similar problems.

The EPA never created a coherent set of new methods for improvement work, and many TQM practices that could have helped the agency to improve were never used. (The consultant's standard methods had little relevance to statistical quality methods and thus had little application to the EPA's core functions.) No benchmarking was done, the PDCA approach was practiced only sporadically, and there was no process to summarize lessons learned at the end of a project.

Our experience indicates many of the people at the EPA were skilled and intelligent. And they cared about doing a good job. But the EPA misunderstood the process of improvement and faced barriers tougher than those outside of government.

The EPA dramatically illustrates how the environment of a political agency makes it hard for managers to do what's needed to change an organization. Defensiveness continually limited communication. People in the EPA feared the political costs of acknowledging that someone else might perform a job better than they. They couldn't conceive of visiting another region to learn what that region might be doing more effectively. As one said, "We cannot possibly admit that another region is better." Given such competitiveness and lack of cooperation among divisions, the idea of integrating best practices was foreign to the culture.

Budget, time, and political pressures strongly discouraged EPA regional administrators from placing a high priority on the collection of the kind of data that would be appropriate for making big environmental remediation decisions. The kind of data collection and analysis that should guide an effective cleanup of the environment takes time, expertise, and money. While these are being conducted, officials have no impressive results to show either politicians or public. Because of this, frontline EPA administrators felt they could not afford the upfront costs of data quality assurance, even though costs would almost certainly be lower and the quality of cleanup higher in the long run if data were effectively gathered and applied.

A difference in structure between the IRS and the EPA seems to have hurt the EPA quality program. Whereas, the IRS has only one political appointee, the commissioner of Internal Revenue, the EPA has political appointees in charge of each region. They are extremely sensitive to pressure from "customers."

But customer focus, though clearly a meaningful concept for the EPA, may have far less inherent power for this agency than the concept has in private industry or even on Navy ships. When the EPA thinks of customers, it tends to emphasize its *intermediate* customers, which include lawmakers, other regulatory agencies, industries being monitored, and the scientific community. The agency works with them to benefit its *ultimate* customers, the general public, in the same sense that auto manufacturers work with auto dealers and rental car companies to benefit drivers.

But these intermediate customers and the general public rarely provide feedback to the EPA and its regions that is as beneficial as that provided by the customers of private companies. If an auto company produces mediocre cars, consumers complain and stop buying the product; auto dealers and rental companies push for improvements, too. Even in the Navy, where a sailor handling ammunition is trained to consider the gunner who will use it as the customer, feedback from the customer is likely to provide exactly the kind of information that the sailor needs.

Communications from customers don't have nearly as beneficial an effect on the EPA, however. The EPA feels little fear that it will go bankrupt if short-sighted action fails to provide real solutions for end users in the long run. In fact, part of the problem at the EPA may be too much focus on communications from intermediate customers such as politicians, regulated industries, and activist groups who push for immediate actions without understanding or reflecting final customers' (i.e., the public's) real needs.

Thus, although the people at the EPA are, in general, genuinely concerned with improvement, the EPA, like many government organizations, seems inherently biased—by its purposes, processes, and structures—against some of the basic tenets of integrated management systems. Those biases are not insurmountable, but they are more stubborn than barriers we have seen in other sectors.

The State of Massachusetts

The effort to introduce Total Quality Management to the state of Massachusetts had many more of the elements of successful programs than the EPA's. But in the end, it was equally unsuccessful. It demonstrated not only the weaknesses in the approach of Gov. William Weld, but also the difficulties of any effort to introduce new management top-down in an environment where employees have considerable job security and expect top leaders to be gone in a few years.

When Weld was elected in 1990, he showed strong interest in the Total Quality ideas that were then at a peak of popularity in private companies. He declared his administration to be "government in the service of its *customers.*" Weld asked his key executives to set up a Quality Improvement Council, including leaders of the state's top executive agencies and also top officials of the court system and the state's education and health care agencies. The council also included representatives of unions and the private sector. Thomas H. Lee, one of the authors of this book, served as a private-sector representative.

Priscilla Douglas, assistant secretary of the Office of Public Safety and deputy chair of the Governor's Council, championed the effort to change management. Another key advocate was Susan Tierney, secretary of environmental affairs. Douglas and Tierney took the six-day course at our Center for Quality of Management, in a class where most of the participants were senior managers of private companies.

During the course, Tierney recalls, she was struck by "the importance of an organization's leader in championing quality" and "continuing to put pressure on senior managers to make it happen." But she felt that getting this kind of leadership would be difficult in the public sector. Tierney couldn't see how she could be the champion in the sense that the private-sector executives discussed champions.

"In any agency like mine, the ability to make a change very much depended on the action of the budget agency, the administration and finance agency, the procurement czars," she comments. But Weld didn't seem to be the champion, either. She felt that the governor, despite his genuine belief in quality improvement, wasn't willing to put in the time to promote change in agencies whose leaders weren't interested. Tierney's early concerns about leadership proved well founded.

The first attempt to create an integrated management system for state government was a series of pilot projects, cross-functional team efforts in numerous agencies. State agencies created approximately 15 improvement teams in 1992. That's a small number for an organization that has 60,000 employees in a hierarchical bureaucracy famed for its lack of responsiveness. To achieve dramatic improvement in such an environment, a leader would have to provide strong guidance for several years at least.

But elected and appointed leaders have difficulty providing that kind of long-term leadership. Tierney noted in an interview, "In the life cycle of organizations, if you're a four-year governor or a four-year president, you have at best an 18- to 24-month period in which you can get people to start tough change. It starts about six months into the job, and it ends, at best, 24 months later. You can't start in the first six months, because you don't have your appointees in place. You can't start after that, because the people in middle management positions have a strong reason to believe you won't be there at the end of another two years. I've observed this at both the state and the federal levels, and it's worse at the federal."

Tierney's description clearly indicates some limits of change driven by political leaders. The Weld administration TQM program never acquired the strength in the first half of his term that could have enabled it to become an important cause of change in state government. At end of the first year, the private-sector members of the state's Quality Improvement Council found the reports on the achievements of that year quite vague. The governor was playing little part in developing the phase-in strategy, and had little visibility in the TQM program.

What Will It Take to Create Dramatic Improvement in Government?

The experiences of the governmental institutions we examined seem collectively to indicate that designing integrated management systems in this sector is especially difficult. Yet, there is reason to believe that government organizations *can* achieve radical improvement *if* they adhere to the basic practices outlined in Chapter 1 and employed by successful organizations in other sectors.

The military and public schools are, of course, part of government, and in the Kenmore-Tonawanda public schools and on the U.S.S. *Kinkaid*, we saw great success proportionate to the extent to which each followed the best practices of integrated management. The same was true for the Ogden IRS Center and the Madison Police Department; and their success was proportionate to the extent that they followed integrated management principles. Even in the Environmental Protection Agency and the state of Massachusetts, tools used to manage interactions in other sectors had similar results where they were applied.

If they hope to achieve dramatic improvement, however, government leaders need to work at evolving true integrated management systems. Several problems make this extraordinarily difficult in government:

- Few government organizations have the continuity of leadership needed to manage real change.
- Few government organizations get the kind of feedback from customers or clients that effectively drives improvement in the private sector and sometimes contributes to it in education, health care, and the military.
- Many government organizations are culturally and structurally predisposed toward making decisions and taking actions for political and bureaucratic reasons. This tends to preclude continuous improvement as a priority.
- Although many people in the public sector are anxious to do a good job, we rarely found a sense of urgency for change. In fact, perhaps because government organizations are so intransigent, many of the leaders seemed overly impressed and contented with modest and nonsystemic improvements.

The lack of continuity of leadership presents an especially enormous barrier to positive change in government. As we've seen in previous chapters, each successful leader must design a new management system suitable for managing the unique set of processes and dealing with the unique set of customer, client, and employee needs that the particular organization faces. Often, politicians and political appointees know the organization's customers, but are less than familiar with its processes and employees.

Further, a new management system must be diffused through the organization so that it can change the purposes and routines of the people in it. But politicians and their appointees usually don't have time to manage such a process. Career government officials, on the other hand, do have continuity in the organization, but frequently can't make the needed changes because of continual alterations in personnel and priorities among the political appointees they serve.

Another key impediment to governmental change lies in the public sector's most striking difference from the private sector. In the former, there are no free market forces at work. Both HP MPG and Teradyne knew that unless their products and services quickly became much better, customers would go elsewhere, and the companies would disappear. But few government agencies will go out of business because they can't satisfy their customers. If Superintendent John Helfrich in Kenmore-Tonawanda or his Board of Education had tried to pretend that their school system faced that kind of crisis, it's unlikely they would have been believed.

As our research has shown, each type of organization must evolve its own, customized integrated management system. Specific methods and tactics that work well in the private sector may—often do—fall flat when applied in government organizations. But the essential broad-based practices that create integrated management systems should have equal applicability across all sectors. There's good reason to believe that the design of integrated management systems can improve government, albeit at a slower pace than it is affecting other sectors. Many government service organizations have an incipient capacity to do things much better. In almost every organization in every large state, there is a nucleus of people who have glimpsed what can be done. What is lacking is a continuity of leadership and purpose along with a sense of urgency for improvement. To a great extent, both can be accomplished with greater emphasis on and accountability to the needs of customers.

CHAPTER 8

Act Locally

What We Have Learned,
What You Can Do

No one can blueprint your integrated management system for you. But our case studies do show how effective integrated management systems have evolved. They demonstrate tactics you can employ to create a system through which the people of your organization can consistently put the scientific method to work.

Thus, we can glean from these cases a framework for creating an integrated management system and a handful of necessary elements without which, it seems, it's unlikely that an organization or a management team will be able to effectively adopt the practices introduced in Chapter 1. In this chapter, we distill those critical elements. We try to answer the most practical question: How can *you* begin to create an integrated system for your organization?

The evidence suggests that organizations evolve a new system through a two-part path. The elements are intertwined, but it helps to think of them separately. First, successful organizations address beliefs, spirit, and vision at the top of the organization. The kinds of changes described in this chapter have the effect of creating appropriate management of the purposes of the people in the organization, creating a situation where people's purposes still differ, but they are aligned well enough so that everyone's purposes can be pursued together.

As leaders work on their own beliefs, spirit, and vision, they also launch the process of making effective use of the scientific method by promoting the creation of social systems model structures and processes throughout the organization.

Table 8.1 on pages 190–193 lists some key elements of how the organizations we studied changed purposes, structures, and processes.

Beliefs, Spirit, and Vision of the Leader

Any organizational transformation must begin with a catalyst, a person—often, but not necessarily, the CEO—who deeply believes in the need for change and is willing to champion that belief. That leader's desire for change most often derives from recognition of a crisis, perhaps an obvious crisis, perhaps a latent one. Teradyne's Alex d'Arbeloff was shocked by a drop in market share. At Eastman Chemical, leaders faced the potential of losing one of their most important customers. On the U.S.S. *Kinkaid,* Cmdr. Scott Jones shared with other top Navy officers a sense that the end of the cold war meant the Navy had to do a better job or sink into mediocrity.

In some cases, however, the leader can galvanize an organization without a crisis, by communicating a basic sense of what the organization is capable of being. Horst Schulze at Ritz-Carlton and John Helfrich at Kenmore-Tonawanda simply saw that life could be much better than it had traditionally been in the hotel industry and in K–12 education, and communicated that understanding to their people.

Having recognized the urgency of change, the leader focuses on leading it. There is no single method for doing this. Some leaders, Deavenport and Schulze, for instance, relied on charismatic force to infuse their organizations with powerful visions. Schulze would personally meet with staff at all levels and help them develop mission statements consistent with the Ritz's motto, "We are ladies and gentlemen serving ladies and gentlemen." But most of the successful leaders weren't quite so charismatic. In many situations (in the health care and education sectors, especially), personal charisma could have created problems because it would have alienated people in the organization.

Regardless of personal style, however, the successful leaders we met all shared similar beliefs, took similar steps, and developed a spirit

Table 8.1 Purposes, Structures, and Processes in Organizations That Created Integrated Management Systems

	Teradyne	HP MPG	Eastman Chemical	Ritz-Carlton	Synetics
Leadership for Aligned Purposes					
Leaders' source of role models.	CQM.	CQM.	Japanese, MIT CAES.	Juran Institute, Baldrige Committee.	CQM.
How vision developed.	Top-down but participative approach.	2nd-tier managers developed parts of new vision first; Kawakita method used to clarify.	Largely top-down process.	Strongly top-down process.	Reward, recognition, vision, values transmitted mainly top-down.
Small Changes in Structure					
Unit that supported change.	Two Total Quality managers.	Quality department.	VP of Quality and Environmental Affairs.	Quality department.	Quality department.
Team management system.	Extensive, built around sponsorship system and guidebook.	Guidebook; many processes from HP corporate.	Developed, taught own standard improvement methodology.	Hotel quality directors taught to use improvement methodology.	Senior executives teach improvement workshop when needed.
Revolutions in Processes					
Methodology for reactive improvement.	7-step process.	11-step process.	PECI.	Standard book developed largely from Juran ideas.	Adaptation of CQM 7-step process.
Proactive improvement.	Annual cycle of asking customers what they want to see improved.	Hoshin kanri system picks key improvement areas for year.	Specific execs "own" core competencies and companywide processes.	Individual hotels asked to experiment with major redesign of key processes.	Large-scale redesign of big companywide processes.

KenTon Schools	Intermountain Health Care	Meriter Health Services	U.S.S. *Kinkaid*	U.S.S. *McKee*
IDEA.	Deming-influenced businesses.	Joiner Assoc., area businesses.	W. E. Deming.	Navy quality specialists.
Bottom-up process: individual schools create vision before headquarters.	Upper middle managers create vision, sell it.	Personal quality improvement projects by top executives showed change worth-while.	Top-down: addressing big problems showed new ways could work.	Top-down, then upper managers sold program to new com-mander.
Administrative assistant to the superintendent.	Clinical prac-tice improve-ment group.	Quality department.	Total Quality Leadership department.	Total Quality coordinator.
IDEA facilitation training was standard.	Standard seminar, but doctors are allowed to improvise.	Quality depart-ment arranges training, tracks team progress.	TQL depart-ment oversees flow-charting.	"Show-Me's" allow officers to guide im-provement teams.
DDAE cycle.	Doctors are allowed to choose meth-odology.	Joiner meth-odology used.	Flowcharting required as improvement process.	Many methods; weaknesses seen in im-provement process.
DDAE cycle used both reactively and proactively.	Clinical prac-tice improve-ment group identifies key processes to improve.	Focus on cre-ating centers of excellence.	Captain selected key improvement areas.	Executive officer team selects key improvement areas.

(continued)

Table 8.1 (Continued)

	Teradyne	HP MPG	Eastman Chemical	Ritz-Carlton	Synetics
Revolutions in Processes					
Customer focus processes.	Customer teams unite account managers, application, and service engineers.	Focus on customer-oriented culture change.	Executive visits and carefully conducted survey.	Core motto is "Move heaven and earth to create a happy customer."	"Customer days," values, focus on customer-oriented culture.
Nonfinancial goal-setting.	Annual defining of key goals desired by customers.	Hoshin process includes nonfinancial goals.	Seeks to be preferred supplier on 44 measures.	Tracks share of customers with "memorable experience."	Executive committee sets goals for key processes.
Total involvement.	"Crusade" leads to involvement cascading from top down; widespread team participation.	Hoshin kanri, displays on wall take involvement to all levels.	Extensive promotion reaches all employees.	Schulze's charismatic leadership, hotel-level quality officers, "line up" each day.	Processes defined, then promoted through traveling officers, "fairs."

that shared much in common with the spirit of all the other successful chiefs. Consider these beliefs:

- Each leader believed in a vision of how his or her organization should contribute better to society. Each could articulate that vision to others and stimulate a desire to change. This didn't mean all the leaders spent a lot of time with "vision statements" (though some did). Each, however, could talk easily and persuasively about what his or her organization should be trying to do.
- Each felt that all, or almost all, employees could develop more and contribute more than they had in the past.
- Each believed deeply in process-oriented management, that the various processes of the organization had to be analyzed and improved.

KenTon Schools	Intermountain Health Care	Meriter Health Services	U.S.S. *Kinkaid*	U.S.S. *McKee*
School improvement teams reach out to all stakeholders.	Long history of community focus.	Surveys identify key customer concerns for first time.	Limited use of customer or stakeholder concepts.	Treats submarines it serves as customers.
School improvement teams set goals each year.	Goals for clinical practice improvement.	Tough competition causes focus on financial goals.	Big shipwide improvement goals.	Limited large-scale goal setting.
Diffusion of success stories through monthly meetings, speeches, posters, pins.	Seminars, speeches, etc. promote methodologies of improvement.	Newsletter, etc., promote improvement, interorganizational core team involves doctors.	Responsibility given to non-commissioned officer.	"Show-Me's," award system promote widespread participation.

Based on those foundation beliefs, the leaders also took the same basic series of steps toward transforming their organizations:

- First, leaders went through a period of study. They thought about new ways of managing. They learned about these from senior executives outside their own organization, from benchmarking visits to organizations they admired, and from reading. Many also turned to nonprofit organizations such as the Malcolm Baldrige National Quality Award Committee, Massachusetts Institute of Technology's Center for Advanced Engineering Studies (MIT CAES), and the Institute for Development of Educational Activities (IDEA) in Dayton, Ohio. Generally speaking, one might say that the prerequisite for change is the leader's willingness to learn.

- Once leaders were persuaded they had something to say, they had to direct the process of change. Small initial changes produced hope in the organization.

- In addition to demonstrating their new spirit in speeches, new programs, or both, leaders introduced new, participatory, process-oriented methods that addressed key problems whose importance everyone in the organization recognized. They made people change their actions.

- The change process led to a new, shared vision of the organization. Sometimes, the leader played the key role in developing it, but in some organizations, the leader created conditions where people other than the leader could be first to articulate a clear picture. In either case, what was important was that a vision emerged from a participatory process in which many of the organization's people contributed what they knew about the needs of the organization and its customers.

The result was a vision that deserved widespread acceptance. It produced the alignment of purposes within the organization, enough shared or at least mutually consistent purposes among the organization's people that they could work extraordinarily well together.

Eastman Chemical's Earnie Deavenport suggests that a leader who takes this approach brings to an organization what he calls "the Moses Factor." Moses, of course, was the son of a common Hebrew slave, born at a time when the Egyptian Pharaoh sought to kill all male Hebrew babies. Moses' mother abandoned him in a spot carefully chosen so that Pharaoh's daughter would discover him. Raised in Pharaoh's household, Moses fled to the desert after killing an Egyptian slave overseer, then returned to lead his people years later. Moses led people who didn't *have* to follow him. But, impressed by Moses and his message, the enslaved Hebrews accepted him despite enormous risk.

Moses' success as a leader can be viewed in light of the theory of psychologist G. Clotaire Rapaille.[1] Rapaille believes that each of us carries imprints or archetypes from our upbringing—basic ideas, emotions, and associations about things in our lives—in the limbic part of the brain. When we encounter something that corresponds to the archetype, we respond viscerally. Rapaille contends that the fundamental archetype for leadership is *hope*, that we feel leadership is present when we feel hopeful. Unlike most other leaders in ancient history, Moses neither inherited leadership nor seized it by force, but achieved it by offering a vision of hope.

The successful leaders we have met in this book derived the power of their leadership in much the same way. They began by offering their people a vision of the future. They then initiated small changes that addressed key problems in the organization, thereby creating hope that the vision was achievable. And that, in turn, began to change the organization's behavior in significant ways.

At HP MPG, for example, a seemingly small process change like putting quality first in meetings led to an important structural change, and cascaded into many more dramatic process changes. Similarly, the first quality initiative of Cmdr. Scott Jones of the U.S.S. *Kinkaid* was to commission a small group of crew members as a process action team to reduce the size of crews that had to remain on the ship when it was in port. Within six weeks, the team identified the additional skills that would be needed so the ship could be staffed with smaller crews. Jones then focused the ship's training program on providing those skills, specifically in areas of damage control: the ability to fight fires, flooding, toxic chemical spills, and the like. The additional training not only gave the ship skills it would need in any battle, it allowed sailors to spend more time at home with their families. The entire process demonstrated that new, participative techniques like the process action team's study could improve the ship's ability to do its job while also improving life for the crew.

To achieve a real transformation, however, leaders needed more than just a few focused projects. They needed a vision of what the organization should look like after its change, and they needed to help the people of the organization to share that vision. In the majority of the organizations, the pattern of dissemination was top-down. The leader and a small group of senior executives cultivated a new spirit in themselves, then used the success of their focused projects to sell a comprehensive picture of what the organization should become, cascading the message down though the levels of the organization.

For example, after developing a new vision of Teradyne with his top executives, d'Arbeloff conducted a CEO crusade to sell it to the rest of the organization. In six sessions held at Teradyne facilities around the world, d'Arbeloff met with many of Teradyne's 180 key middle managers. He asked each to do homework before the sessions, and he charged each with carrying the message of the new Teradyne to the people who reported to him or her. In delivering a message that called for a new focus on teamwork, d'Arbeloff demonstrated concretely that he himself would act as a team member. He carefully solicited and acted on feedback from the members of his audience each time he spoke. As we have said, this kind of willingness to listen and respect for the diverse purposes of all employees is a hallmark of the kind of leadership necessary to transform an organization into an integrated management system.

Not all the organizations we observed used a top-down model, however. John Helfrich, superintendent of the Kenmore–Town of Tonawanda schools, used a bottom-up process. He didn't define any vision; he merely required that each school set up a process for defining its own vision. Then the individual school visions played a key role in development of the vision and spirit of the district as a whole. Like Helfrich, Brent James at Intermountain Health Care also adopted subtle and decentralized tactics necessitated by the nature of his organization.

Other organizations followed what Ikujiro Nonaka and Hirotaka Takeuchi call a middle-up-down process.[2] Managers other than the CEO were the first to clearly articulate much of the new vision and spirit. Then together, the leader and the middle-level people sold their picture to the rest of the organization. That happened at Hewlett-Packard Medical Products Group; it also happened when David Langford, a teacher of music, business, and computer skills, began an effort to practice mutual learning with his students in Sitka, Alaska.

Most of the integrated management systems we studied neglected one important element: contingency planning. Few of the managers made a careful effort to write down the assumptions underlying their basic vision. Therefore, they had no way to track whether changes in the environment called the vision or the basic design of their change processes into question. Eastman Chemical, for example, paid a high price for this.

When a basic vision of the future was evolved, it's wise to write down key assumptions about the environment that, if wrong, would make large parts of the business design questionable. Then, the environment needs to be reviewed at well-defined intervals—perhaps every three months—to determine whether the assumptions are still valid and, if not, what changes are needed.

Of course, it is not enough to create and disseminate a vision and check it against the environment. An organization must figure out a way to actually *do* what is envisioned. These processes are actually intertwined and concurrent, but must be addressed separately. Creating vision is a matter of building shared *purposes;* doing involves creating and continuously applying new *structures and processes* that enable everyone in the organization to pursue their purposes together.

Doing It: Changing Your Organization's Structure

In an effort to support their vision of the future, each successful organization we observed made similar small but significant changes in their structures designed to nurture the dramatic process changes that would follow. We observed three main categories of structural adjustment.

ADOPTING THE CONCEPT OF THE INTERNAL CUSTOMER

Most companies give employees one key measure of success: pleasing the boss. This fundamentally hierarchical approach subordinates people to authority without effectively coordinating their work or engaging their intelligence. A shift in thinking toward pleasing your internal customer—defined as whoever receives or is affected by your work—effectively redefines the entire organizational structure to be more oriented toward real results. This was perhaps the most universal change we observed in the companies we studied.

CREATING A PLANNING AND SUPPORT UNIT

Each successful organization established a small unit to provide planning, coordination, and support for change. This unit went by different names in different organizations, but was, in essence, a central department in charge of managing key aspects of the integrated management system. The majority of organizations gave it a name with the word *quality* in it. At Intermountain Health Care, it was called the Clinical Practice Improvement Group and in KenTon an individual with the title administrative assistant to the superintendent largely filled the role. Most of the successful organizations chose an experienced, admired manager from within the organization as the head of this group. None hired an outside "expert" to head it. Progress in improving operations was faster when the quality director's staff was so small that it could only take on the role of teachers and coaches, not dictators of the change process. In fact, larger quality units seemed less effective. Their size may have undercut the important notion that quality and other improvements are everyone's job, not just the quality department's.

On the other hand, all the successful organizations but one (Intermountain Health Care System) seemed to give their planning and support unit considerable power to control the language that would be used for improvement work. Each supervised widespread training. In several less successful organizations, employees utilized several different sources of training with little coordination among them. Thus, different people were using different versions of the scientific method, and no comprehensive common language developed.

Where organizations were too large for two or three people in a planning and support unit to coordinate change, successful organizations designated employees in each of the various divisions to be quality leaders in their group, to work with and be coordinated by the central unit. For instance, each of the business units at HP MPG—the Clinical Systems Business Unit, the Imaging Systems Business Unit, and others—had its own quality director. These were not quality professionals, but people with other business experience who took the lead on quality issues in their particular unit. At HP

MPG, for instance, Quality Director Brad Harrington coordinated these executives and helped them plan for and manage change.

Often, larger organizations would also name executives outside the central quality unit—effectively *deputize* them—to coordinate particular aspects of companywide change. We saw examples of that at HP MPG and Eastman Chemical, where members of the senior management took charge of different parts of the change effort.

Giving people responsibility for running an important part of the organization *and* coordinating an important aspect of change seems to encourage everyone throughout the organization to take both operations and effective change seriously. This is an excellent example of the management of interactions in the organization through organizational design. This illustrates a critical aspect of systems theory: The structure of the system must be designed to facilitate interactions among all the elements and reduce functional compartmentalization.

A Team Management System

The use of teams—permanent, cross-functional, ad hoc, or project-driven—seems to be an essential characteristic of successful integrated management systems. In each successful organization we studied, some fairly well designed group of teams played the key role in actually implementing the organization's version of the scientific method. Each successful organization we encountered not only employed teams, but created a special mechanism for managing and improving them. Typically, they created a system through which teams were registered with a central planning and support unit and "sponsored" by particular senior managers. The team management systems seemed to be significant elements of organizations' efforts to teach their people to use the scientific method in groups. Team-oriented work produces two important outcomes crucial to integrated management systems: it forces creative and knowledge-sharing interactions among people and groups, and it fosters the dispersion of a common language of improvement throughout the organization.

Each of these types of structural changes—adopting the concept of internal customers, creating a central unit with responsibility for planning and supporting the new management, and using various types of teams—illustrates a crucial principle of integrated systems at work. That is, to be effective, a system must be structured to facilitate, even force, the beneficial interaction of all its elements. The central task of managing an integrated system, then, is managing those interactions.

Doing It: Revolutionizing Your Processes

Structural changes can *facilitate* beneficial interactions, but the processes within a system *define* those interactions. Though most of the successful organizations we looked at made relatively few and modest structural modifications, their process changes were more numerous and more radical. The processes differed significantly from one organization to the next, and from one sector to the next. But beyond the specific applications, we found improvement methods to be, in most cases, largely similar. They followed the pattern of the PDCA cycle, described in Chapter 1. The methods that doctors used to improve cardiac and orthopedic surgery in hospitals, for instance, bore a striking resemblance to the methods that manufacturers used to improve work on the shop floor.

We concluded that the many processes adopted by the successful organizations we studied could be grouped into several broad categories, described below. It is safe to say that creating an integrated management system at your organization will involve employing some processes in each of these categories.

CONTINUOUS IMPROVEMENT PROCESSES

To achieve continuous improvement, each successful organization taught its people a well-defined, standard methodology strikingly resembling that of scientists solving a scientific problem. Each could be considered a variant of the plan-do-check act problem-solving process. Some organizations taught a four-step, some a seven-step, and some an eleven-step improvement method. Most worked to standardize the language of their particular approach.

Organization members learned how to choose a problem, then collect data, create hypotheses about the solution, choose the most plausible hypothesis, and test that hypothesis to learn whether it was correct. Finally, if evidence supported the hypothesis, they created a new standard procedure that would solve that problem for the organization.

As we showed in Chapter 3, organizations whose key functions did not repeat predictably, such as service companies and education providers, had a more difficult time using the scientific method to improve. In manufacturing or the military, the youngest, lowest-ranking people were able to apply the scientific method and improve the organization's systems. Applying the scientific method to moment-of-truth or innovation processes was more difficult. Synetics, for example, learned to apply improvement processes in a just-in-time fashion to accommodate its moment-of-truth orientation. It launched a problem-solving project mainly when it faced a major problem. The Kenmore-Tonawanda school system, in trying to address complex goals and multiple stakeholders, put a little twist on PDCA. Its dialogue-decision-action-evaluation started out by collecting not hard data, but stakeholders' opinions about what should be done. From those, it created and enacted potential solutions, measuring the results against each school's overall mission.

In each of the organizations, the standard improvement process utilized a set of standard, relatively straightforward improvement tools such as flowcharting, Pareto analysis, and cause-and-effect diagrams. These allowed people with or without scientific training to work together on real, scientific analysis, often quantitatively based. A key to success was limiting the number of tools used and using them companywide to avoid confusion and reinforce a common language of analysis.

Reactive Improvement Processes

When the problem-solving processes were introduced, leaders often gave people little guidance on *what* they should improve. In most

202 ■ ACT LOCALLY

organizations, leaders simply encouraged people to find and correct weaknesses. This kind of *reactive* problem solving is most effective when cause and effect are clearly identifiable, manageable, and isolated from other processes. If groups try to solve one problem that involves extensive interaction with another problem, the solution is likely to be difficult to implement and may make the other problem worse. But every organization found many problems that reactive problem solving could improve.

Teradyne and Intermountain Health Care, for instance, relied overwhelmingly on relatively small-scale, reactive group problem solving. Teradyne launched over one thousand quality improvement teams, each focused on a single problem, "like so many chisels chipping away at a block of marble to see what kind of company there is inside," wrote CEO d'Arbeloff. Similarly, Intermountain Health Care initiated a series of focused reactive problem-solving processes in the 1980s that lowered its prices to nearly 15 percent, on average, less than local competitors.

Organizations with processes that didn't predictably repeat couldn't unleash as many problem-solving groups, but they still achieved significant improvement through reactive problem-solving teams.

Proactive Improvement Processes

In most of the successful organizations, improvement eventually went far beyond reactive problem solving. Executives also struggled to seek out and anticipate problems in their organizations, to be *proactive* problem solvers. They benchmarked their organization's capabilities against those of other organizations. They evaluated what organizational capabilities they would need to serve customers in the future, and then they developed programs to create those capabilities.

A typical example is Synetics, the information systems consulting company, which employed a facilitator from Bose Corp. to lead top management in a discussion of what barriers stood in the way of growth. The group concluded that the company needed to better define its processes of marketing, bid preparation, and personnel development. Synetics then created clear, flowcharted processes for each.

CUSTOMER FOCUS PROCESSES

One of us remembers a visit to a group of customers of General Electric in the 1970s during which they offered a number of seemingly good ideas about how GE could improve. When the ideas were presented to the boss back at GE, however, his response was a surprisingly dismissive "What do they know?" For many organizations in American industry, that has been the traditional posture. The idea of listening to and taking care of customers has been almost foreign.

By contrast, one of the distinguishing characteristics of each of the successful organizations we have examined is an unwavering focus on the needs and desires of its *customers* and other key stakeholders. Each of these organizations, in fact, has gone to extraordinary lengths to integrate the customer viewpoint into the heart of both its strategy and operations. In every case, improvement could be correlated with a vast increase in the contact between the organization's people and its customers.

These organizations found new ways to help customers to not only ask and answer explicit questions about current products or services, but also to articulate images of what they desired in the future. In this regard, Teradyne, HP MPG, and Synetics used the Language-Processing (LP) method to create powerful images that helped employees throughout the company understand customers' current and future desires.

In addition to creating new ways of hearing customers, each organization introduced new, standardized language for gathering and communicating customer data, and added new ways of disseminating that data more widely. Each reviewed its regularly scheduled market research and reworked it to elicit more accurate views. Eastman Chemical, for example, developed categories on which customers could be asked to rate the performance of any chemical business: conformance to specifications, product mix, price, responsiveness, on-time delivery, and so forth.

Once gathered, the better information was also better disseminated through the organization. Smart companies realize that to harness the intelligence and energy of all employees, they have to put information in everyone's hands. Companies that in the past had considered customer information to be for top management alone began distributing it widely, through newsletters, shared databases, and training seminars.

The for-profit organizations we studied focused primarily on their true customers, the people who provided the resources on which the organization depended and whose approval was a legitimate measure of how well it was doing. For nonprofit organizations, the task was larger and more complicated. The idea of having customers was largely foreign to them. The hospitals knew they had to serve doctors, patients, and insurance companies. The Navy knew it must satisfy the U.S. taxpayer as well as other branches of the service. Public schools were aware of many constituencies, including students, their teachers, parents, and future employers. But in every case, the interests of these various groups often conflicted, and none exercised the kind of direct economic influence on the organization that an automobile buyer exerts on Ford or Chrysler.

Though they often used the word customer to describe those they served, nonprofits found the concept limiting and problematic. Navy ships, for example, found it effective to teach young sailors to serve anyone who would receive their work as an internal customer, but had to acknowledge that the idea that the general public is the military's customer is largely meaningless from an improvement point of view.

Public schools also found the customer concept problematic. Inarguably, a school's most central focus should be on students, but students aren't real customers. They don't provide the resources for the organization, and the schools shouldn't always cater to their desires. There are others that require recognition, some of whom do have economic leverage.

The most successful organizations were able to expand their vision, their lexicon, and their processes to encompass a wider range of *stakeholders*. The hospitals we examined, for instance, were able to adopt processes that accommodated the unique needs of the medical community while still listening to patients and insurers. Mt. Edgecumbe's Langford decided to call his students *colleagues* to emphasize that the school system is a learning community composed of staff, teachers, and students.

In the final analysis, successful organizations, even in the private sector, must consider what groups other than customers deserve their attention. Eastman Chemical, for example, included government regulators and the people affected by pollution from its plants as key stakeholders. To truly transform itself, an organization must create not only customer-focus processes, but also stakeholder-focus processes that perform a parallel function.

TOTAL INVOLVEMENT PROCESSES

Customer-focus processes raise critical issues, and continuous improvement processes create dependable ways of acting on them. But that is not enough. To make improvement occur, individuals and groups throughout the organization must take independent initiative guided by the organization's spirit and vision. For that to happen, the organization has to carry out four ongoing involvement processes.

Leaders must continually communicate the spirit and vision to the organization's people.

Eastman Chemical's Deavenport puts it best: "If you say, 'OK, now we've communicated everything we have to communicate,' it's time to do it all over again." An organization is never the same from one moment to the next, but continually changes its roiling mixture of elements: people, ideas, circumstances, structures, processes. Because the interaction among elements of the system is continual, its spirit, vision, and purpose must be constantly reimprinted. And that is the job of leadership.

Once again, we think it's interesting to view this in a social psychological framework. Chris Argyris has suggested that all people operate from two theories: the espoused theory and the theory in use. The espoused theory reflects what they believe is the right thing to do; the theory in use, which usually dictates behavior, reflects what they feel they need to do to "survive." How do you make it possible for people to believe that what they need to do to survive can be aligned with what they (and you) believe they *should* do? The answer isn't simple, but one point is clear. If you continually communicate the spirit and vision, then you create a context in which people can find ways to build on it in their daily work lives. Rapaille eventually concluded that a leader created hope by finding and repairing the breach between what people envision and what they actually do. Leadership, then, is the art of continually and vigilantly finding ways to align what is being done with what has been envisioned. (See Appendix D for more on these topics.)

The organization must develop and implement a system that helps people on teams manage interactions among themselves and with the rest of the organization.

All the successful organizations we have seen created a well-defined mechanism for management of improvement teams and, equally important, did so in a participatory way. This often led to dramatic, but nonhierarchical change.

Teradyne's experience illustrates this especially well. After Teradyne introduced organizationwide training in team problem solving in early 1991, employees quickly formed nearly 200 teams and met with a good deal of success. But managers had seen team programs lose momentum in dozens of other companies when easy-to-solve problems gave way to more difficult ones. To forestall stagnation, Teradyne decided to apply its seven-step improvement process to the management of teams. Afterwards, statistics showed that the rate of progress of Quality Improvement Teams increased and the number of QIT report completions rose rapidly.

Although no other organization followed exactly the same process as Teradyne's, each found some way of developing team management methods such that people throughout the organization felt ownership of the improvement process.

The organization must promote its standard methodology of improvement by recognizing important gains and publicizing achievements.

Each successful organization continually provided people with concrete examples of how others in the organization had achieved real improvement. Promotion systems typically included newsletters, bulletin boards, and displays on the building's lawn or outside walls. Displays on the walls of Teradyne were perhaps typical, presenting summaries of a team's achievements accompanied by color photos of its members.

Line managers were typically expected to nominate people and groups who'd achieved real improvements using the new techniques. At sessions such as the "Show-Me's" aboard the U.S.S. *McKee*, people described what they had done and were honored for it. Top executives used the events to make their visions more concrete.

The organization must demonstrate genuine concern for its employees' quality of life as an essential element of building community.

In each of the successful organizations, leaders balanced their effort to serve stakeholders outside the organization with real, and widely appreciated, efforts to create a good life for employees. Taking care of the quality of employees' lives wasn't an "add-on." Scott Jones on the U.S.S. *Kinkaid* spent almost as much time helping his enlisted people find housing in the absurdly tight San Diego rental market as he spent promoting quality improvement. Eastman Chemical, Teradyne, and Hewlett-Packard Medical Products Group all struggled to minimize layoffs in bad times.

In these complex social systems, the structures and processes that made life better for employees were tightly interwoven with those that made life better for customers. The serious consideration of employee needs paid off in the long run in measurable organizational improvement and customer satisfaction. The proudest boast of the executives of Ritz-Carlton is that, whereas average employee turnover in their industry exceeds 100 percent per year, it is less than 35 percent at their hotels.

GOAL-SETTING PROCESSES

Successful organizations tend to develop goal-setting processes that go beyond traditional measures such as profitability or market share (in for-profit companies) or number of people served (in nonprofit organizations).

The KenTon public schools, for example, had teams in each school that created long-term visions and each year chose steps and annual goals that would bring the schools closer to those visions. The Hewlett-Packard Medical Products Group borrowed the goal-setting system hoshin kanri from Japanese organizations, a system for establishing a small number of breakthrough priorities each year and pushing the organization to achieve them.

Goal-setting processes tie all the continuous improvement process activities together. The actual work of improvement can remain highly decentralized, often with thousands of people working on hundreds of improvement teams whose individual goals may have been chosen by the team members. But in setting goals and ensuring that at least some of the organization's improvement efforts are tied to those goals, leaders integrate the system and guide it to better performance.

EFFECTIVE LEARNING PROCESSES

Traditionally, training is associated with those new to an organization or new to a job. Most companies haven't looked to training programs to achieve dramatic change in the performance of experienced employees. Successful organizations, however, consider learning an essential and *ongoing* part of everyone's job. They realize that what an employee needs to know changes continually and dramatically over time. And they use training as a tactic to promote continuous improvement and support the overarching vision. In a fully evolved integrated management system, effective learning processes underlie and support all others.

All the successful organizations integrated training into many aspects of planning and operations. They delivered it in brief, modular units targeted to support specific improvement goals. These modular events might be organizationwide, to introduce a standard problem-solving methodology, for instance, or just-in-time, to offer specific tools for solving real and present problems.

The most effective organizations evaluate their training with PDCA-type analysis, too. Training that works—that improves processes and outcomes—is retained. Otherwise, it is discontinued.

MONITORING AND ASSESSMENT PROCESSES

An essential aspect of continuous improvement is continual monitoring and assessment of management systems. Many of the most effective organizations regularly invite thoughtful outsiders to evaluate the effectiveness of their systems. The most sophisticated monitoring and assessment process we saw was the Quality Maturity System review that Hewlett-Packard carried out for all its business units, including the Medical Products Group. The system, which is based on a grading scale, gives HP a way to unify its management standards throughout the company without incurring the costs of centralization. Eastman Chemical and the Ritz-Carlton used Malcolm Baldrige National Quality Award reviews to provide similar guidance. Kenmore–Town of Tonawanda schools used School of Excellence programs administered by state and national authorities.

Fruitful Management Science

All integrated management systems evolve from the application of the existing body of management knowledge to a specific set of circumstances using the scientific method. Although there is no formula for transforming an organization, there are a number of common approaches and considerations that will help you create your own unique system. As we have shown in this chapter, the development of that system will likely follow some variation of the following sequence:

1. A clear assertion of vision by a champion (or champions) within the organization
2. Dissemination of that vision and alignment of purposes throughout the organization
3. A recasting of structures and processes to support continuous improvement based on that vision

The organizations presented in this book each followed a similar sequence and each improved greatly, though to varying degrees. But, as we said in Chapter 1, most of them viewed themselves as pursuing Total Quality initiatives and not consciously building an integrated management system. As a result, these organizations may not have taken an optimal systemic view, and most did not attempt to integrate everything that the body of management science had to offer.

In the next and final chapter, we take a look at the state of the art, what's possible when an organization *consciously* seeks to design an integrated system that *concurrently* incorporates a number of cutting-edge methodologies. We then turn our attention to what is missing from the state of the art. How must the established body of management knowledge be improved to deal with ever more challenging organizational and societal problems?

CHAPTER 9

Think Globally

The State of Management Today:
What Still Must Be Done

Recently the president of the newly formed Academy of Engineering in the People's Republic of China invited one of the authors of this book, Tom Lee, to discuss future trends in management. In preparing his remarks, Tom asked himself the same question each of us would ask if invited to assess an organization: "What are the weaknesses in the system?"

In this case, however, the organization—the system—was society itself. At CQM, we have given a good deal of thought to the future trends that ought to occur in management. And we have always approached them from the same perspective that CQM has taken since its founding—the "weakness orientation" encouraged by TQM philosophy.

In China, Tom pointed out that there are three major weaknesses in the American management community today and that, to some degree, they reflect American cultural and societal biases. The power of the American economy and America's culture has allowed these weaknesses to influence management throughout the world.

First, we in America are drawn to fads and panaceas—the "silver-bullet" theory of management. Second, we tend not to think systemically and we settle for an inadequate or non-existent understanding of the science of systems. And third, we focus inadequately in the idea that our organizations are *human* systems and we fail to develop management thinking that builds on social sciences and humanities.

The Faddish Culture

Soon after CQM was founded in 1989, we invited Frank Voehl of Florida Power & Light, the first U.S. company to win the Deming Prize, to speak to us. What he said made an indelible impression. He talked about the dangers of the "Lone Ranger mentality" in American companies. He was referring, of course, to the icon of the old movie and television Westerns who rode into town, masked and anonymous, and righted all wrongs with a gun that shot silver bullets.

Voehl suggested that the popularity of the Lone Ranger was very much a culture issue. We all—even the immigrants among us—want to believe that all problems are not only fixable, but can be obliterated with a single magical action from a sufficiently virtuous hero. This uniquely American myth goes hand in hand with our famous can-do attitude. It carries over into all American institutions and is especially prevalent among business managers. "If it ain't broke, don't fix it" is the mantra; but if it *is* broke, the boss will ride in on a white horse and offer the silver bullet solution. It's no wonder that the biological model, with its emphasis on the brain providing centralized control, is the easiest one for Americans to accept. The CEO, the boss, the division manager, they are all the Lone Rangers of their particular realms.

This mentality is not limited to corporations, however. Every institution that affects the body of management knowledge is guilty of searching for silver bullets. The faddish culture is driven partly by the consulting industry's perception that fads are what the market will buy. It's caused partly by the media's desire for sensational news. How often have you heard that TQM, strategic planning, or reengineering is the answer, only to be told quite soon thereafter that TQM, strategic planning, or reengineering is dead?

Unfortunately, the Lone Ranger only rarely practiced the scientific method. He couldn't. If you have to ride into town to solve its problems almost entirely by yourself within the time span of a single half-hour television episode, you've got to act on brilliant hunches and awe people with your charisma.

Managers, too, often need to rely on hunches and charisma. But usually a group of people can accomplish a great deal more if they can clearly define the question they face, collect data, develop answers, test them, and then apply the answers that pass the tests.

We have tried in this book to describe how organizations can overcome the silver-bullet fixation and apply the scientific method to their problems. But until a significant share of the management community rises up against the silver-bullet fixation, both the body of management knowledge and the performance in our organizations will suffer.

Inadequate Understanding and Application of Systems Science

You hear the word *system* bandied about quite a bit in our society. The notion of a variety of elements and forces working in sometimes complex harmony is powerfully appealing to most people and strikes them as an intuitively correct way to view the world around them. They quite rightly see their workplaces, their communities, their government, even their favorite football team as systems.

But few have an adequate understanding of how systems actually work. When it comes to organizations, even fewer have any idea of how systems science can be applied.

Before integrated management can have a truly transforming effect on our organizations, we believe there are three aspects of systems that must be *far* better understood and applied: how their performance can be *measured,* how they should be *designed,* and how they can anticipate *contingencies.* The successful organizations we've seen in this book have achieved progress in some of these areas. But none has really addressed them adequately.

THE IMPORTANCE OF DESIGN

In lecturing on the importance of interactions among the elements of a system, Russell Ackoff sometimes uses the following example. If you decided you wanted to create the best automobile in the world, you might begin by finding out which manufacturer makes the best engine and acquire one of those. Then you might research fuel pumps, carburetors, chassis, electrical systems, brakes, and so on until you had purchased the best of each. The problem is you could never assemble all those elements to make a car. They just wouldn't fit. None of the excellence of the individual elements could be transferred to the system as a whole. If a car won't run, it can't even be called a system.

Our CQM associate Dave Walden pointed out problems with this example. "This is not the way real life works," he noted. Automobile designers study all the best-made parts, decide what features they want, and then *design* their own elements to *make sure they fit* into a coherent whole."

This, of course, is absolutely correct. And it points to a simple but powerful lesson about management systems. Many American organizations evolve through an ill-assorted collection of programs whose relationships to each other are not much better thought through than the relationships among the parts of Ackoff's hypothetical car. There has been a bit of marketing, a bit of industrial engineering, a bit of humanistic "organization development," and a bit of strategic planning that attempts to predict the future and plan for it. When performance is disappointing, managers have added a bit of TQM or reengineering.

But it's just as important for an organization to be designed as it is for a car. To truly create the future of an organization you must design it. The designer may be the CEO or it may be a team, but whoever it is must consider all the system's stakeholders, its entire transactional environment, and its core mission and vision. Those in turn have to lead to a coherent point of view about the system's functions, structures, and processes. This is not designed as some in the strategic planning school present it, where a committee decides what the organization must be and forces the rest to come along. But organizations need design of the kind that good engineers and artists practice it—a process of experimentation leading in what will emerge as a coherent direction. The kind of process we've presented in Chapter 8 is an example and TQM or Reengineering or Strategic Planning are "enablers"—parts of the overall design that allow the system to function as intended. Like the car designer, the management system designer must thoroughly understand the features and the *limitations* of the enabling elements before any can be usefully integrated into the system. This is closely related to what Ackoff calls "Idealized Design."

Most systems literature, indeed most systems thinking, virtually ignores the importance of design. It presents systems as if they just happened. And this results in a serious weakness in our management community. We don't think carefully about our roles as designers. We need to make design and redesign more prevalent. Rectifying the situation calls for increased awareness through a kind of education that is not currently available in the United States.

THE NEED FOR COMPREHENSIVE MEASUREMENT

In Chapter 1 and Appendix A, we have discussed the ideas of Russ Ackoff and his associate Jamshid Gharajedaghi, who have defined two types of properties of systems. Type 1 properties can be deduced directly from the properties of the elements of the system. In a system such as an automobile, an example of a Type 1 property is its weight. Type 2 properties can be seen only in the system as a whole. They are derived not from the elements but from the *interaction* among the elements.

Gharajedaghi points out that Type 2 properties are difficult if not impossible to measure directly. One can only measure their manifestations. Love, for instance, is a Type 2 property of a marriage. You cannot measure it directly. A Valentine's Day present may or may not demonstrate it. Add in romantic vacations, coming home early for dinner, watching the children . . . the number of manifestations begins to prove the existence of love. The point is that if you measure enough manifestations, your confidence in the Type 2 property you are measuring can be greatly strengthened.

In an organizational system, managers must operate, plan, and manage change. The overall performance of the management team is a Type 2 property of the system and is therefore, like love, difficult to measure directly. Instead we must evaluate that performance by looking to its manifestations. Rising sales and profits are important (in a for-profit company). But they represent only part of what performance is. Is the organization managing its internal processes effectively? Is it learning to do things better? How well are managers listening to and satisfying key stakeholder groups? Evaluating management performance by any single manifestation is not only misleading, it inevitably causes faddishness because you'll eventually have to look at other measures, which will push you in different directions.

It is the job of managers to identify what particular set of manifestations is sufficient to prove the efficacy of their integrated system. And that, of course, varies from case to case. But once a set of appropriate manifestations has been identified, it must be continually monitored and measured (with new measures added and old ones occasionally deleted as circumstances change).

Efforts to advance the state of the art in this regard have been mostly disappointing. Methods like activity-based accounting or balanced scorecarding are often promoted as comprehensive ways to measure corporate performance. A true "balance scorecard" certainly has that potential. But often the "balanced" scorecard is brought in just as a set of metrics for a particular strategic initiative.

Measuring an operating system is like squeezing a balloon. If you focus pressure at one point or just a few points, other areas of the balloon become overstressed, stretch and perhaps break, destroying the integrity of the system. Good measurement is comprehensive, focusing on all areas of the system at once. It is only under such even pressure that the weak parts of the structure will become evident.[1]

THE NECESSITY OF CONTINGENCY THINKING

Without an "early warning system," even the best planning and operations processes can be blindsided by external shocks to the system. Ackoff suggests that any plan inherently has a set of critical assumptions and that the best systems create plans that anticipate any subset of those assumptions going awry.

Some of the most sophisticated systems actually integrate early-warning practices into their continuous improvement planning. General Electric, for example, regularly identifies important contingencies and identifies trigger points at which action should be taken to adjust to them. In one business unit, for instance, GE requires that managers in charge of each business venture to identify the four most important assumptions that underlie their business planning and state them in quantitative terms. Then the managers must state how the real world might diverge from the underlying assumptions in ways that would call the business plan into question. Finally, they must track on a monthly basis the actual performance of indicators that tell whether the assumptions are being fulfilled. They must graph that performance on charts with lines showing the values of the indicators they had forecasted and the values that they had said would indicate the plans needed to be revised. When the real-world indicators cross the lines, the managers must respond by re-evaluating their plans.

Royal Dutch Shell addresses contingency thinking in another way by encouraging managers to imaging different scenarios, some representing radically different views of the world, and formulating plans to deal with each.

But, up to now, the vast majority of systems thinking has ignored or given short shrift to contingency planning at great peril.

Eastman Chemical could have avoided its disastrous experience with PET resin if it had followed a process like General Electric's. This is obviously an area that needs a great deal more attention and refinement as a part of integrated management system design. The Naval Inventory Control Point (NAVICP) case discussed later in this chapter gives an indication of how contingency thinking may evolve.

Inadequate Integration of Management with the Social Sciences and Humanities

In one of the first classes Tom Lee ever gave on TQM in China, one of the students, a graduate of the Sloan Fellows program at MIT, made a telling comment. "At MIT," she said, "we studied the theory behind some of the TQM practices in humanities courses. But, we never heard about them in our management classes."

It is unfortunately all too true that the study of the human element in systems has been mostly neglected in the teaching and literature of systems dynamics. Yet, that human element is the distinguishing characteristic of social model systems, indeed of all human organizations. This is certainly true of Ackoff's thinking. He has often said, in fact, that systems sciences are so intertwined with the humanities that we should call it systems *scianities.*

It is only logical, then, that the study of human motivations, responses, and purposes be central to the study of management. At CQM, we have worked diligently to make it so, integrating conversation competence (which includes semantics), action science, and ontology into the CQM management education portfolio. (We have already mentioned our efforts in integrating Rapaille's work into our activities. See Appendix D for a fuller discussion of our efforts in this area.)

Although the social sciences and humanities are beginning to take a stronger role in management *thinking,* they are still largely absent in management *practice.* Few organizations actively consider the human element in their planning, structures, and processes. That, of course, must change. Again, the NAVICP case offers a glimpse at how an organization can achieve breakthrough improvement by directly incorporating a social science–humanities viewpoint into the design of its integrated management system.

Where Do We Go from Here?

We believe there are two keys to advancing management science to address the weaknesses we've just discussed:

- First, we need a national educational effort.
- Second, we need mutual, continual learning among all sectors of the management community.

MEETING THE EDUCATIONAL NEEDS OF ORGANIZATIONS

Education in management science needs to go far beyond academic institutions and include the participation of all parties in the management community: "gurus," consultants, media, practicing managers, and industrial leaders. We need a broad effort to help people understand what it means to take a systems view of organizations and the processes involved in creating integrated management systems that can apply the scientific method.

Management education in American academia has unfortunately often emphasized the *what* rather than the *how*. It has instructed students in shareholder value, told them to pursue continuous improvement, and urged them to create challenging, fulfilling work for employees. But it has given remarkably little sense of how practitioners actually deliver these things. To become as useful as they need to be, universities must begin to align their programs with practitioners in the field. In some places, this is already being done. MIT's Leaders for Manufacturing program, for instance, has deviated from the school's long tradition that a graduate thesis should be done on the campus. It now encourages students to spend seven months in a company to work on a real-life project. Babson College offers course credit for group work in the Management Consulting Field Experience (MCFE) program; students consult with companies in teams of three to five.

Some universities have aggressively linked their research projects to the "real world." The use of companies as field-testing laboratories is still a rather unusual practice, but one that can yield big dividends and should be encouraged.

Even with the introduction of such innovative practices, however, we believe three educational needs of corporations and other organizations need further attention:

- Lifelong education
- Modular education
- Just-in-time education

Academia has been talking about lifelong education for some time, but has yet to provide it in a form that will genuinely help people perform better in organizations. And the current competitive environment means that what we need to learn today was probably not being taught a year ago and may not be useful in the near future. This is why modular approaches and just-in-time courses are attractive. They are particularly important when one must learn how to integrate different practices into a management system. Because, as we have seen, there is no one system that fits all, the training one needs obviously varies from one organization to another.

Although academia can still improve its ability to teach the fundamentals of interdisciplinary systems science as a foundation, it does not seem reasonable to expect those same institutions to efficiently provide the ongoing, just-in-time modular learning that will build on the foundation. For that, we believe, corporate universities may be a natural answer. There are now more than 1,000 corporate universities in the United States; at Motorola, General Motors, The Disney Company, and General Electric, among others, employees at all levels are learning exactly what they need to know, when they need to know it. This is an important and encouraging trend, but it is still not sufficient. Academic and corporate education must be complemented by a widely accepted and practiced ethic of mutual learning.

APPLYING THE ETHIC OF MUTUAL LEARNING

In 1989, two of the authors of this book, Tom Lee and Shoji Shiba, participated in a new education program at MIT called Leaders for Manufacturing. There they began a seminal discussion with Ray Stata, the founder and chief executive of Analog Devices, about ways to strengthen American business. Shiba was definitive: "In Japan," he said, "we believe in mutual learning or societal learning. Companies learn from other companies." He felt that U.S. companies at that time did not and were not acculturated to doing so. He suggested the formation of an American version of the Union of Japanese Scientists and Engineers (JUSE).

JUSE is an organization that promotes mutual learning as a key process to improve the performance of manufacturing organizations. It had been a topic of much admiration and discussion on the Reagan administration's Council for Competitiveness in the 1980s. Shiba suggested that an American JUSE would be a good way to begin to provide a framework for mutual learning among U.S. companies.

Stata's appetite was whetted, and he asked if Shiba would conduct a workshop for his managers. It went so well that Stata asked if

Shiba might be interested in spending more time helping other American companies. That was the beginning of the Center for Quality of Management.

In the first few years after CQM was founded, we imitated JUSE as closely as we could. Our mutual learning revolved mostly around the practice of Total Quality Management, which was prevalent in Japan. But, true to our weakness-orientation philosophy, we began to continually probe the flaws in the TQM approach. Through our experiences with Bolt Beranek/Newman, Hewlett-Packard, and other member companies, we came to the conclusion that there are at least five weaknesses in TQM as practiced in the United States. In a presentation to the Japan Techo-Economic Society (JATES), Tom Lee articulated those weaknesses:

- There is a general lack of understanding of TQM as a major shift in the management paradigm.
- Strategic planning is not part of TQM.
- There is little application of organization theory in TQM.
- TQM does not treat time as an independent variable.
- TQM has good analytic methods for processes and structures, but no equivalent methods and practices for the human behavior aspects of management.

Perhaps the greatest of these weaknesses was TQM's dissociation from the planning process. Most Japanese companies used hoshin planning to implement their TQM initiatives, but those efforts were usually decoupled from strategic planning.

We wanted to address this and decided to conduct a few experiments with Russ Ackoff's associate Jamshid Gharajedaghi to see if a combination of TQM and idealized design could yield a better-integrated system. We chose Ackoff's system for many reasons, but one of the most important was that it has a built-in weakness orientation. No planning system we know of deals with the weakness in an organization in such a comprehensive way. (Indeed, Tom Lee had wanted to integrate idealized design with TQM from the start of the Center for Quality of Management, but some of our member companies convinced us that we must go step-by-step. So we postponed the integration of Ackoff's method until 1992.)

After 1992, we turned our attention to incorporating methods that focused on conversation competence, the study of effective communication (see Appendix D). We subsequently integrated several schools of thought on the subject of conversation competence, including concept engineering, the semantics taught by S. I. Hayakawa, the dialogue taught by David Bohm, the action science developed by Chris Argyris and Don Schon, and ontology developed by Fernando Flores.

More recently, we have chosen to shift our focus to exploring new methods of planning, leadership, and cycle time reduction. Our approach remains the same. Team members from CQM companies listen to experts, do research, and in the end, draw conclusions about how to integrate what they have learned.

When we did the research for this book, we found that many organizations were following the same learning curve as we were at CQM. Not too long ago, "crisis management" was the prevailing paradigm in American organizations. This, of course, allowed no time for systemic thinking and precious little time for planning. The adoption of Total Quality methods has gone a long way toward supplanting that approach. Once organizations began to introduce process-oriented management, managers were able to see beyond their individual problems to the underlying pattern of events. The resulting process improvements led to tremendous incremental increases in productivity.

We began the research for this book seeking to study organizations benefiting from TQM, but soon discovered that the best achieved greatly enhanced benefits by going beyond TQM and integrating other enablers, too. Looking for a more powerful tool set, these companies had begun to create—often without knowing it—comprehensive integrated management systems. Yet, though these systems proved vastly more successful than TQM alone, they still reflected many of the weaknesses we discussed earlier in this chapter. Most evolved through trial and error from more narrow management approaches and, as a result, were not designed with a complete understanding or even awareness of systems science. Many lacked comprehensive measurement systems, had no contingency planning mechanisms and failed to fully integrate human purposes and behaviors into their overall approach.

We became more and more convinced that the idea of integrated management systems is still in its infancy. Nevertheless, we have begun to see examples in the field of integrated management moving into a second—more sophisticated, more comprehensive, more intentional—phase of its development.

One such example is the work done by Gary Burchill (currently president of the Center for Quality of Management) when he was a commander in the Navy and director of Planning and Operations Research at the Naval Inventory Control Point (NAVICP). There he developed an approach called *Structural Process Improvement* that was designed to find methodological solutions for many of the areas of management weakness cited earlier in this chapter.

STRUCTURAL PROCESS IMPROVEMENT AT THE NAVICP

From the outset, Burchill sought to draw on a wide range of available management knowledge. He combined some of Russell Ackoff's Idealized Design framework (see Appendix A) with concepts and methodologies from TQM, systems dynamics, and other areas, each of them well thought out methodologies that had been studied by academics. Thus, Burchill created a comprehensive approach to getting below the pattern of events and revealing the underlying structures. In doing so, his approach seems to have enabled the NAVICP to address improvement in a more integrated and comprehensive way than even most of the successful organizations discussed earlier in this book.

We offer here a brief synopsis of the NAVICP case as an example of what can be done when mutual learning is actively and widely pursued and its results are very deliberately integrated to address weaknesses in organizations. We do not offer this as the ultimate example of integration; there is still a long road ahead. But we do believe it shows a clearer picture of where that road is leading.

The Naval Inventory Control Point manages spare parts for all of the submarines, ships, and airplanes of the U.S. Navy. In 1994, when it was known as the Ships Parts and Control Center, it was one of the largest logistics operations in the U.S. military and therefore one of the largest managed systems in the world. It carried an inventory of almost a half million line items valued in excess of $16 billion. Its annual "sales" approached $4.5 billion.

At the time, Gary Burchill was working on integrating the Aviation Supply Office with the Ships Parts Control Center to create what would become the NAVICP. A rapid reduction in the Department of Defense infrastructure due to federal budget constraints made his job that much harder and created potentially devastating effects. The Navy not only had to find ways to spend less on inventory parts, it had to do so with a third fewer people. Inventory control managers needed timely and actionable information more than ever.

NAVICP needed a breakthrough improvement in performance to maintain fleet operational readiness. "I needed a step function improvement in a core business process," Burchill remembers. "Having no real knowledge of what the number could be, I set a target of 25 percent."

The Structural Process Improvement methodology that Burchill created consisted of three broad phases: structural mapping, environmental assessment, and structural alignment. Because they were taking a radically different approach from what the Navy was used to, Burchill and six cohorts began to approach the project as a "skunk works." They put in approximately 15 hours per week for three months in structural mapping assessment and alignment. Once they had a coherent plan, they'd try to sell it to the higher-ups.

STRUCTURAL MAPPING

Two-thirds of the effort in structural process improvement goes into structural mapping, a time-consuming process that allows one to find the pathway to structural alignment.

As many other organizations in this book have done, the NAVICP team began with Language Processing. The Language-Processing Method (see Chapter 2) is an excellent way to develop grounded data and to abstract those to higher-level concepts. The team elicited employees' images of how the organization worked, and then identified, in a common language, the major obstructions to its optimal functioning. They focused on potential obstructions in Ackoff's five crucial structural dimensions of the operating environment (see Appendix A) and their humanistic components (in parentheses below):

- Authority (power): obstructions resulting from difficulties executing authority
- Emotion (beauty): obstructions arising when emotions inhibit job performance
- Physical processes or methods (knowledge): obstructions attributable to flawed operational processes
- Measurement systems (wealth): obstructions caused by poor or nonexistent measurement methods
- Conflict resolution (values): obstructions existing in known and identifiable conflicts[2]

Having created an LP diagram for each structural dimension that showed perceived obstructions and the variables associated with them, the team incorporated this into a summary diagram. The headings identified key problem areas in the operating environment, such as "Inventory managers' decision aids are not adequate" and "Process performance measures are not comprehensive."

However, the LP diagrams did not—and are not designed to—show the dynamic relationships that exist between the operating variables. So Burchill's group introduced *causal loop diagrams*[3] to help overcome this limitation.

Causal loop diagrams are a technique from systems dynamics designed to show the principal feedback loops in a system. Essentially, the operational variables identified in Language Processing are combined in cause-and-effect pairs. An arc is drawn from one variable to the other, indicating which causes which, and is labeled with an S ("same") or an O ("opposite"). Evaluation of these feedback loops helps explain the dynamics of complex situations.[4] S indicates two variables moving up or down in tandem, promoting movement—either growth or decay—by compounding the change in one direction. O indicates an inverse relationship between the variables; that is, they tend to move in opposite directions, generating a balancing influence on the system, tending toward equilibrium.

As a final step, the pairwise arcs are combined in a single diagram creating a comprehensive, closed-loop schematic that represents the function of the system. The NAVICP team took many iterations to reach this point. It found that different people in the organization saw the relationships between variables somewhat differently. Ultimately, though, they created one main story line and connected the various subplots into one main causal loop diagram, shown in Figure 9.1.

Structural mapping, like the archetyping from Peter Senge's work,[5] allows one to encapsulate behavior at the highest level. "We didn't need to build a computer model because the causal loop diagrams obviously showed what had to be done," says Burchill.

The main story line involves the middle two loops. It begins when a problem or symptom is identified in some specific component of inventory management/supply support. The response to such a problem is that a special inventory management project addressing that specific issue is sent to the production floor. As the special project is completed, the specific symptom, which triggered the project, decreases. Typically, then, a "special projects to the rescue" loop serves as a short-term solution to each problem symptom.

An alternative to instituting a special project each time is to conduct a complete stock number diagnosis, which is a time-consuming

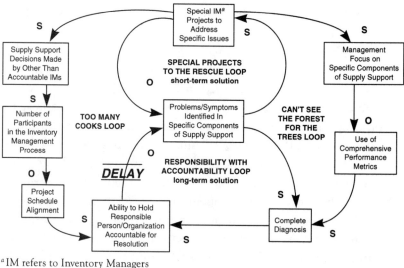

[a] IM refers to Inventory Managers
"S" indicates that two factors move in the *same* direction
"O" indicates that two factors move in the *opposite* direction

Figure 9.1 NAVICP Causal Loop Diagram: Obstruction Analysis

but long-term solution. A complete diagnosis would increase management's ability to locate the root cause of any given symptom and thus better assign responsibility and accountability for corrective action. This long-term approach would build a fundamental solution and eliminate the recurring pattern of special projects, which were preventing the inventory managers from conducting a complete stock number diagnosis. However, with the long-term approach, there would be a delay before the specific problem symptoms decreased.

The overall causal loop diagram identified a couple of key problems in the operation. The "too many cooks" loop showed that as the number of special projects increased, so did the number of players, and this reduced management's ability to properly align the various project schedules.

The "can't see the forest for the trees" loop indicated that as the number of special projects increased, so did management's focus on specific components of inventory management/supply support. The more managers focused on specific components of supply support, the more attention they paid to specific versus comprehensive performance indicators (metrics). Ultimately, as the use of comprehensive performance indicators decreased, the ability to do complete diagnosis also decreased.

This structural map shows how the well-intended action ("special projects to the rescue") actually undermines the organization's fundamental capability to identify and resolve the root causes of problems.

"The big epiphany I had," says Burchill, "was when I saw that causal loop diagrams revealed an unintended organizational structure that caused people to act in ways that deviated from the ideal. It wasn't deviant behavior; it was perfectly natural behavior on their part given the circumstances."

Environmental Assessment

The second phase of structural process improvement focuses on three related lines of inquiry: stakeholders, market trends, and business opportunities. This assessment is conducted in an iterative fashion and usually requires three or more cycles through all three areas before coherence is achieved.

Stakeholders

The organization's internal and external stakeholders are evaluated to determine the amount of influence each can exert on the organization's policies and practices, and the amount of leverage the organization has on its stakeholders. This is plotted on x and y axes (Figure 9.2).

The environmental assessment done by Burchill's group concluded that the NAVICP had a wide variety of stakeholders. Those with the most influence, but with whom the NAVICP had almost no leverage, were the higher-ups within the Navy. "Hardware Commands" made the big, centralized decisions about which airplanes, ships, and subs to buy. On a localized basis around the world, "Type Commands" set requirements for ships and aircraft, and their "Supply System Commands" instituted policies and procedures. In the aggregate, these three groups set the parameters within which the NAVICP had to live while still meeting its objectives.

A second level of stakeholders was composed of Navy groups that controlled the distribution and maintenance of parts and equipment in the field. These included groups that performed local maintenance activities at each base or port; those that maintained highly technical

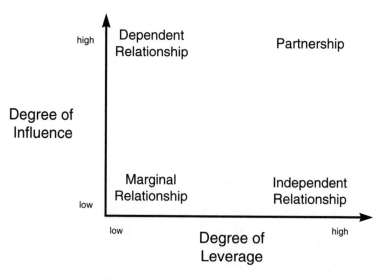

Figure 9.2 Stakeholder Analysis

equipment, such as sonar and missile hardware; those that did major overhaul, repair, and rebuilding; and those that ran the major inventory stock points around the world. Each of these groups was becoming an increasingly more important player in the downsized Navy and presented far greater opportunities for the NAVICP to leverage change.

A third level of stakeholders was, of course, the 4,500 or so employees of the NAVICP.

Each of these stakeholder groups had to be served by the NAVICP with a coherent and coordinated strategy that reduced costs, increased reliability, and, most important, maintained a high level of service to the Naval forces underway in the world's hot spots.

Market Trends

The next step in environmental assessment is a trend analysis of the market, competitors, and technology associated with the operating environment. Market trends influence customer requirements and expectations. Competitor trends affect the customer's ability to find suitable substitutes. Finally, technology trends affect the organization's ability to deliver its product or service.

Each trend is analyzed to determine both the expected impact on the current rules of the game and the rate at which the change is happening over an appropriate planning horizon. An xy plot is prepared similar to the one shown in Figure 9.2 with "Degree of Impact" on the vertical axis and "Rate of Change" on the horizontal.

The trend analyses done by Burchill's group revealed that they were operating in an intricate, rapidly changing environment. Each ship and each base around the world had a different set of inventory requirements, and each had to be monitored for potential failure of existing equipment. The task of what to stock, where, when, and for whom was being complicated by a number of factors.

First, the downsizing of the military that had been going on since the early 1990s had reduced the number of ships in the Navy to about one-third of what it had been in the 1980s. With fewer vessels available to accomplish the same number of, or more, objectives, the Navy was encouraging the development of *multiuse platforms*. Each ship, weapon, and piece of equipment had to serve a variety of purposes in a variety of situations. This meant fewer types of inventory had to be stocked, but it increased the risk factor if the estimated need for any given part was too low.

Second, all types of equipment were becoming more and more technology-intensive, and the technology changed rapidly. This dramatically increased pressure to utilize commercial, off-the-shelf equipment that was not designed for the harsh environment of ships at sea. To make things even more complicated, the Navy was increasingly trying to globalize, to move toward using technologies that had equivalent application among its allies. In that kind of environment, figuring out whether a piece of equipment would need repair, overhaul, or replacement—or just become obsolete—was becoming one of the NAVICP's biggest challenges. This was especially true when you consider that acquisition regulations added months if not years to the process of acquiring a piece of inventory, making it necessary to anticipate needs years down the road.

Third, the defense industry was undergoing a major consolidation that had a huge impact on the staffing, service, and products of the Navy's major vendors. The Navy was also doing some ongoing consolidating of its own as the Base Realignment and Closure Committee tried to downsize strategically. Both factors made it difficult for the NAVICP to anticipate whom it would be working with, in the public or private sector, and what it could count on in terms of quality, service, and delivery.

All of these challenges, of course, existed within the parameters of a shrinking budget, necessitating some pretty nimble tactics in which repair and replacement resources were continually traded off from areas of low probability of deployment to areas of high probability.

Business Opportunities and Key Success Factors

The third area of environmental assessment attempts to identify the key factors of a successful business operation given the conditions revealed by the stakeholder and trend analyses. Specific emphasis is focused on those stakeholder groups with high influence and those trends with both a high degree of impact and a high rate of change. The analysis attempts to answer three related questions:

What conditions must be met for the organization to be viable in the environment?

What problems or needs should the organization try to meet? What capabilities does the organization have to be good at to deliver the necessary products or services?

An extensive list of factors can be developed, but a focus on the vital few is essential. The NAVICP settled on two overarching strategies that would govern its integrated management system:

- *Maintain weapon systems, not line items:* The old view of maintaining inventory focused on individual parts. Burchill's group wanted to move toward a system that evaluated inventory needs based on changing technology, obsolescence, multiuse platforms, and so on. The NAVICP goal would no longer be viewed as maintaining stock of individual line items, but as maintaining the integrity of weapon systems.
- *Manage repairables, not consumables:* Burchill's team decided that, given its limited resources, the NAVICP should focus its business on acquiring, distributing, and maintaining big-ticket durable, or repairable, items. Responsibility for stocking smaller-ticket, one-time-use consumables would, wherever possible, be transferred to the Defense Logistics Agency.

STRUCTURAL ALIGNMENT

With the structural map and environmental analysis complete, Burchill's group began trying to bring the system into structural alignment through *obstruction analysis,* to find the high-leverage intervention points; *gap analysis,* to develop an improvement target; and *hoshin management,* to deploy the implementation.

Obstruction Analysis

The purpose of obstruction analysis is to reveal the high-leverage points for structural alignment within each of the major loops of the structural map (the causal loops diagrams). A high-leverage point is a variable that can be altered easily to drive the system behavior in the desired direction. High-leverage points are usually associated with tangible (mechanical or "physical") processes and seldom involve the behavior of individuals or organizations. For that reason, Burchill focused first on the *use of comprehensive performance metrics,* a physical process, as an area of intervention likely to have a strong payoff.

An inventory manager has essentially five courses of action regarding any decision: Do I buy something? Do I repair something? Do I engage in some combination of procurement and repair? Do I dispose of something? Do I do nothing? There can be a huge time delay between making a decision and seeing the results of it. In most cases, we're talking about highly specialized, extremely expensive parts, nothing that can just be pulled off the shelf at a contractor's facility.

For example, from the day a decision to procure is made, it can take six to 18 months to negotiate a contract with the vendor, then another 12 to 24 months before delivery. Then it can take another year before you know whether the decision was prudent in the first place. With the Navy's old system, procurement personnel had weak early-warning systems to forecast where and when parts and supplies would be needed. "If someone made the wrong decision three years ago," says Burchill, "some young sailors off the coast of some battle area are going to find themselves without radar."

Burchill's group identified a key obstruction in this scenario. There were three computer programs that inventory managers used to make decisions: one for procurement, one for repair, and one for disposal. Each program had a good mathematical model and was well coded, but there were interdependencies that were not accounted for. So, for any given decision, the answer you got could depend on which sequence you ran the programs. Clearly, this was another high-leverage intervention point.

Gap Analysis

Once the high-leverage points have been identified, gap analysis can be used to develop performance improvement targets for each point. Gap analysis begins by establishing the "ideal" state of the selected variables, either through formal benchmarking or creative thought experiments. The only constraint placed on the ideal state is that it must exist somewhere today (though not necessarily in your company or industry). Once you have determined the ideal and current states at the desired intervention point, you can describe the gap between them. Next, propose a solution that reduces the gap.

The NAVICP group determined that the gap between the ideal and the current state of comprehensive performance metrics was that a process showing linkages from different contributors did not exist. They developed a method of collecting data at each process point that would link functional specialists' contributions to overall readiness and performance. This would allow the NAVICP to predict problems up to two years away.

The Burchill group was almost through with its analysis—and still operating as a skunk works—when Adm. Ralph Mitchell, who was the CEO, began to get curious about what was going on.

"I was missing a lot of regular meetings," remembers Burchill, "and Admiral Mitchell was somewhat mystified. One day, he wandered by my office and it just happened that our team was in session. We had LP and causal loop diagrams all over the walls. He looked around and asked 'What on earth is this?'

"When we gave him our presentation, he left really excited. He put a lot of stock in the expertise of the team, and he was an extremely people-centered person to begin with. What we were doing resonated with him."

That afternoon, another bunch of senior officers showed up, and over the next few days, Burchill and his group gave a lot of briefings. Their plan for a bottom-up dissemination process quickly turned top-down.

The process of getting the analysis ratified by senior managers across the organization took nearly two months and culminated at a strategic planning retreat in which 10 of 11 recommendations were incorporated into NAVICPs strategic plan. "You've got to give a lot of credit to the Navy Captains who recognized the need to go somewhere new," says Burchill.

Once this approximate solution was agreed upon and ratified by senior management, it was then deployed using the hoshin management process.

Hoshin Management

Given the current and target state for each intervention point, traditional hoshin management practices are used to deploy the improvement goals. That is, each part of the plan is described with specific steps. Each step involves a statement of desired outcome, a metric, a target value, a deadline date, and a means statement with a designated owner.[6] Figure 9.3 shows the hoshin template Burchill's group devised for the implementation of the weapon system performance indicators.

This highlights the ability of structural process improvement to incorporate TQM tools. The group identified 30 process-result performance measures, ensuring that anyone can see what is going to be measured, where it is going to be measured, and from where the very specific data elements are to be retrieved. This system is now developed and deployed on a client-server network in which any member of a weapon system team can pull up on his or her computer the exact status of weapon systems across a whole spectrum of process performance indicators. In short, the NAVICP now has a comprehensive and

STRATEGIC PLAN TACTICAL GOALS	TACTICAL/SUB-GOAL: 1.0 Organizational Rightsizing 1.1 Implement Weapon System Teams in 059 G/D/O OWNER: Gary Burchill REPORT DATE:				
Statement of Desired Outcome (May show different owner than basic tactical goal.)	Focused Means/Sub-Goal Owner (if different from Goal)	Metrics to Measure Progress	Target Value Actual Value	Deadline Date Actual Date if Different	Status
1.1.3 Develop Weapon System Team Performance Indicators	1. Identify Metric Team members—owner Div. Heads	# of people	8	1AUG94	
	2. Identify 6 process input metrics for each functional area—owner PI Team	# of metrics	24	8AUG94	
	3. Create Tree Diagram of metrics—owner PI Team	Tree Diagram	1	15AUG94	
	4. Operationally define selected metrics—owner PI Team	# of Op. Defs.	12–24	29AUG94	
	5. Prototype metric operational definitions—owner PI Team	# of proto-types	12–24	1OCT94	
	6. OP Review and select process performance indicator ser.—owner Div. Heads	Process Perf. indicator set	1	1OCT94	
STATUS LEGEND: <<<=SLIPPED A LOT <<=SLIPPED A LITTLE @=ON TRACK >=A LITTLE AHEAD >>>=A LOT AHEAD V=COMPLETED					

Figure 9.3 NAVICP Hoshin Template

predictive process-result performance measurement system, linking the contributions of different functional specialists online.

A RADICALLY BETTER SOLUTION

The creation of a comprehensive performance measurement system changed the focus of management attention in the NAVICP. As a result, the number of special projects decreased. The implementation of the Burchill group's recommendations for various processes took three to 18 months, depending on the complexity of the individual process. The longest lead times were those required for the development and implementation of new computer systems. The combined impact of all the interventions set the stage for breakthrough improvements in a core business process and helped NAVICP support fleet readiness despite budgetary cutbacks.

The advantages of structural process improvement over traditional TQM and over all the other integrated approaches chronicled in this book are threefold:

- TQM traditionally tends to concentrate on "physical" processes and data-driven measurement systems, but structural process improvement incorporates *crucial work-life variables* that create obstructions, such as problems arising in connection with authority, emotion, and/or the handling of conflicts. These variables, often swept under the rug, can ultimately determine whether process improvement really takes hold in an organization.
- Causal loop analysis makes it possible to integrate these variables in the structural map; this lets people see how well-intended actions in one area may show up as unintended and undesirable consequences somewhere else. Causal loop diagrams allow you to map out a change, the constraints surrounding it, and areas of potential resistance by the change process.
- Feedback loops indicate areas of integration and interrelation. They often show that intervention is required in more than one area within the structure for the overall effect of change to be positive.

Structural process improvement as applied to the NAVICP represents the state of the art in *designing* (as opposed to evolving) integrated management systems for several key reasons discussed in this chapter:

- It was a very deliberate approach to transcend an incremental or faddish approach and link Total Quality discipline and system science and system dynamics tools to structural analysis.
- It systematically incorporated intangible human performance factors into its considerations.
- It developed comprehensive measurement techniques.
- It developed comprehensive environmental assessment techniques that gave it an ongoing mechanism for contingency planning.

By going below the many layers of unintended organizational structure imposed by a succession of leaders with well-intentioned agendas, structural process improvement shows how a designed integrated management system can foster breakthrough improvement. For that reason, we believe, the work at the NAVICP defines an important step in the journey toward truly transformed organizations.

The Continuing Struggle

At CQM over the years, we have seen that both the theories and the practices of management have to evolve. We seek to incorporate better, more comprehensive methods into our integrated system thinking.

We believe management is a true science and compare its growth to that of the natural sciences in the early part of the twentieth century. At that time, physics, chemistry, and biology were considered more or less mutually exclusive disciplines. But years of experimentation and shared information have demonstrated that they were all simply different languages describing the same phenomena. Integrating those languages has led, and continues to lead, to an ever more unified and effective approach to seeing and explaining the natural world.

We believe mutual learning will evolve the state and efficacy of management thinking in much the same way. CQM was founded on that principle and has been practicing it for years, bringing together some of the best minds in industry, academia, and the consulting community. The methods we have used to build CQM are the same we espouse for companies.

But the work is just beginning. We continue to learn as a team, and we try to reach conclusions that make sense for all types of organizations. The appendices to this book include tools we believe many people will find useful in the next stages of this journey. You have read about the results of many outstanding managers' efforts throughout this book, and we hope we have inspired you to join us in the journey of mutual learning.

INTRODUCTION
TO THE
APPENDICES

In laying out the dominant themes of this book—systemic thinking, integration, and the social model of organizations—we have referenced and built on a good deal of pioneering thinking about management and human behavior. Obviously, much of that thinking is too rich and vast to have been included fully in the course of our own narrative, but there are several areas that we felt should be expanded on to provide enriching context and to further illuminate and bolster our arguments. Four of those areas are discussed in the following appendices.

Appendix A more fully explores the often-referenced work of Russell Ackoff that has been crucial to integrated management systems thinking for decades. Ackoff's careful analysis of the concept of systems, his advocacy of the social model of organizations, and his notion of idealized design of systems all underpin much of the thinking advanced at CQM and in this book.

The key to successfully managing a system, we have argued, is managing the interactions among its elements. In a social model system, that means aligning the purposes, processes, and structures of the organization with those of the individuals that compose it. Although the cases in this book repeatedly demonstrate the critical link between leadership and the successful transformation of organizations, we did not fully define and explore the nature of leadership required to build an integrated management system. In Appendix B, we do so, presenting Shoji Shiba's in-depth thinking on the subject. We feel his focus on the multidimensionality of skill needed by leaders is a perspective that strengthens and deepens the conclusions we reached in the body of this book regarding human interactions.

Once purposes, processes, and structures have been aligned, the advantage of the social model—over the biological model and certainly over the mechanical model—is in its promotion of individuals acting collectively. Appendix C discusses the power of collective action—and the relevance of chaos—in responding to rapid environmental change.

Of course, the key to collective action in the social model is the effective, powerful use of a common language. People must understand one another accurately, completely, and without bias to set and implement goals, coordinate actions, and build trust. In Appendix D, we explore the notion of conversation competence that underpins several of the methods mentioned in this book, such as Language Processing and Concept Engineering, as well as the work of Fernando Flores, Chris Argyris, David Bohm, and others. We also report on one set of specific methods that several CQM member companies have been experimenting with and using.

The Systems Theories of Russell Ackoff

Elements crucial to integrated management systems have been visible at least since the 1970s. The work of Russell Ackoff and his associates is among the most central. Ackoff recommends the social model (sometimes called the social systems model or the sociocultural model) of organizations.[1]

Understanding "Systems"

More than most thinkers, Ackoff's work is based on careful analysis of the concept of the *system* and on *systems thinking*. To understand his work, therefore, we have to start by carefully defining what we mean by the word system. Ackoff defines a system as a set of two or more elements that satisfies the following conditions:

1. The behavior of each element has an effect on the behavior of the whole.
2. The behavior of the elements and their effects on the whole are interdependent.
3. However subgroups of the elements are formed, *each* has an effect on the behavior of the whole and *none* has an independent effect on it.

To put it another way, a system is a group of elements that can't be divided into independent parts without loss of some important properties of the whole.[2]

Managing Interactions: A Big Challenge in Systems of All Kinds

Systems obviously vary enormously. A tiny electric motor is a simple system; a large human organization like the KenTon school district is an extraordinarily complex system. Yet, we can make some statements that apply to all kinds of systems.

1. THREE KINDS OF VARIABLES DEFINE ANY SYSTEM.

These variables are:

- The system's *functions* in some larger system—that is, the role the system plays in a larger environment
- The system's *structure*—its elements and how they are put together
- The *processes* that take place within it—what happens to and among the elements when the system operates

An automobile, for instance, is a system. It may have many functions, but we can say that its primary function is to transport people. Its structure is simply how its parts are arranged physically. Its processes are the ways in which the parts interact as it operates.

A small business such as a restaurant is also a system, one composed of human beings and some physical things that the people interact with (a building, tables, chairs, plates, a kitchen, food). Like a car, a restaurant also has many functions. We can perhaps summarize them by saying that the restaurant's function is to provide good meals in an enjoyable atmosphere. The cooks, the waiters, and the owner, together with the kitchen equipment, dining room tables, and so on, are elements in the system. The system's structure includes those elements and the relationships that exist among them: the cooks work with the kitchen equipment, the waiters work in the dining room, some means of communication connects the two, and someone (usually the owner or a manager) has authority to coordinate the actions of both groups.

The processes include taking orders, communicating them to the cooks, cooking the food, and serving it.

2. Every system has properties that its parts don't possess individually.

The properties of a particular automobile may include a "smooth ride" or "responsive handling." None of the parts of the automobile really possesses those properties, although certain parts may contribute importantly to creating them. If we examine the shock absorbers, for example, we won't find "smooth ride," and if we look at the steering column, we won't find "responsive handling." We have to look at the whole car (or the interaction of subsets of its parts).

The properties (or "qualities") of a restaurant may include "excellent service." Clearly, this implies that some of the individual employees care deeply about good service and work hard to provide it. But having employees who care and work hard is not, by itself, "good service." Good service is something that all the people in the system produce together. Similarly, the properties of a school district may include "collegial atmosphere," but no individual element, not even the superintendent, can really be said to be the source of "collegial atmosphere."

The properties of any system can be divided into two categories. One type of property, which Ackoff and his associate Jamshid Gharajedaghi call a *Type 1 property,* can be deduced directly from the properties of the elements. A Type 1 property of a car is its weight. A Type 1 property of a restaurant is the number of square feet it occupies. You can measure a Type 1 property in a straightforward way.

The other type of property is a *Type 2 property.* It can't be deduced in any simple way from the elements. In addition to such properties as "smooth ride" in cars and "good service" in restaurants, examples of properties of the whole include *intelligence* in human beings, *performance* of an electric motor, *love* in a human relationship, and *beauty* in a work of art.

Many Type 2 properties can't be measured directly, and none can be measured by simply looking at the elements of the system. How can you tell whether a restaurant has "good service," a school district has "collegial atmosphere," or a couple is "in love"? Any simple measure will mislead you. To gauge Type 2 properties such as intelligence or performance, we often have to examine some Type 1 properties that the Type 2 properties have created. We judge the performance of a motor by measuring speed, torque, and so on. We might even evaluate whether a husband loves his wife by noting how often he mentions her, how frequently he manages to meet her for dinner, and other such evidence.

The Type 2 properties of a system often matter far more to people than the Type 1 properties.

3. INTERACTIONS AMONG THE ELEMENTS PRODUCE THE TYPE 2 PROPERTIES IN ALL SYSTEMS.

Therefore, managing interactions is always a central task for people in charge of systems. Interactions in any system create something new and important, and sometimes something quite unexpected. Whether you're an engineer working on the design of a new light switch or the CEO of a Fortune 500 company, you'll do best if you focus on the interactions of the elements in your system at least as much as on the elements themselves.

Artists and designers, who create systems of inanimate objects, are almost universally taught the importance of focusing on interactions. Artists seek out high-quality materials, and the designers of automobiles choose excellent suppliers of components. Both recognize that the quality of their final products depends as much on complex, subtle relationships *among* the components as on the quality of the components themselves.

But somehow, many of the most influential management thinkers have failed to recognize the centrality of managing interactions. Until recently, many how-to books for managers (even managers of schools) would prescribe simple, hierarchical structures to link the elements in organizations. When they discussed improvement, they would recommend sending employees to courses where they would learn new techniques in isolation from their fellow employees. They didn't encourage leaders to create and manage the same kinds of complex, subtle interactions among the elements of organizations that teachers of art and design regularly promoted in the creation of works of art or well-engineered machines.

A fundamental element of Ackoff's social systems model thinking is an emphasis on managing *interactions* of people in organizations.

The Social Model and the Pursuit of Human Purposes

Designers and managers of all kinds of systems need to focus on interactions; however, managers of systems composed of people obviously face challenges that differ sharply from those facing artists working on paintings or engineers designing machines. A theory of management has to include a coherent way of thinking about what is unique about human systems.

Ackoff suggests that what is unique about managing human systems derives fundamentally from the fact that human beings (unlike the elements of a painting or the parts of a machine) have the ability to pursue *purposes.*

A purpose is an aim, often a long-term aim, that people (and perhaps other animals as well) seek by making and implementing choices over time. Prosperity, for instance, is a purpose. A person pursuing prosperity will often follow one approach for a time and then, recognizing the limits of the first approach, adopt an entirely different course. We may seek prosperity by endeavoring to maximize our salaries at our current employer this year. Next year, we may pursue prosperity by going back to school.

A person may have as one of his or her purposes the performance of some important function for an organization or for society as a whole. Such a purpose may be driven by the pursuit of prosperity. (We seek to maximize the wealth of corporate stockholders because that course will maximize our own.) Or our purposes may contain an element of altruism. Frequently, there is a mixture of both. Henry Ford, for instance, articulated altruistic purposes when he said, "I hold that it is better to sell a large number of cars at a reasonably small profit. . . . I hold this because it enables a larger number of people to buy and enjoy the use of a car and because it gives a larger number of men employment at good wages. Those are the two aims I have in life."[3]

In pursuit of their purposes, humans can show great creativity. Thus, when a person's purposes include doing something important for an organization or for society, the individual's creative abilities can create great benefits.

How Old-Style Thinking Misuses People's Talents

Unfortunately, many traditional ways of thinking about organizations have discouraged managers from taking full advantage of this human capability. Lacking a strong set of valid theories of management, people have tended to think about organizations using analogies. Sometimes, they thought of the organization as a machine: an owner owns a company the way a person owns a machine, and the parts are supposed to do as they are told as parts of a machine follow an engineer's blueprint. Sometimes, they thought of the organization as a biological organism: top management was the "brain" and the rest of the organization was the "arms and legs."

These analogies had powerful effects on how people behaved. Henry Ford, for instance, thought of his company as a machine. In Ackoff's terms, this means he followed the *mechanical model of management.*

To a machine, the owner is god. Machines are not supposed to have ideas of their own. As the previous quotation shows, Ford himself had some genuinely noble purposes. His biographers demonstrate that he made real sacrifices in pursuit of them, continually refusing the financial backing of investors who insisted he focus on high-priced cars.

But because of his concept of the organization, Ford made no effort to share his purposes with the people who worked for him. In fact, he routinely quashed any initiative his employees took, even if it was entirely supportive of his own long-term aims. While Ford was in Europe in 1912, for example, his engineers began without permission to work on an improved version of the Model T. In doing so, they violated the mechanical model's principles. Ford returned and saw the prototype. He was horrified to find that employees had tried something new without authorization. He did nothing to investigate whether the new car was better than the old. He walked around the prototype, leaped at the door on the driver's side, and pulled it off its hinges. Then he did the same to the door on the passenger's side. He jumped on the hood, kicked in the windshield, then climbed on top and stomped the roof in.[4]

Henry Ford was the god of Ford Motor Co. No one would change his car but he.

That kind of use of the machine analogy seems bizarrely old-fashioned to us today. But many of today's managers make somewhat similar mistakes derived from the application of the analogy of a biological organism, what Ackoff calls the *biological model of management*. And those mistakes can be almost as destructive as the effects of the mechanical model on Henry Ford.

Biological models came to dominate U.S. managers' way of thinking from the mid–twentieth century. Managers thought of companies as "living organisms" and urged that the people in charge of each part be respected and treated as the experts in their own work. In some respects, this represented dramatic progress compared to Ford's approach.

But biological models have profound limitations. The two most important principles used to manage under the biological model were management by objectives (MBO) and management by exception.[5] Under MBO, the boss would establish an objective and then give incentives to encourage the employee to accomplish the objective in whatever way the employee thought best. The boss would try to leave the employee alone unless something unusual happened (an "exception"). This management behavior closely resembled the way the brain of an animal leaves the leg alone to carry out many of the tasks involved in walking, unless nerves send a message reporting some unusual sensation.

This can sound very sophisticated and even empowering. Good MBO managers interfere with their subordinates much less than Henry Ford did.

But like the mechanical model, biological model management is still based on the idea that top executives will make all the key decisions and the rest of the members of the organization will pursue well-defined subordinate goals. The biological model makes no provision for the people of the organization to contribute in ways that the senior manager hadn't thought of when objectives were established. It doesn't allow for anything like the kind of subtle systems of managing interactions that we found in the successful companies we studied.

The mechanical model and the biological model are more hierarchical than real organizations have to be. They make little provision for horizontal couplings among different parts of the organization, or for different people on a team to take leadership on different aspects of the work group's job.

As we see in this book, today's effective organizations know how to break out of hierarchical thinking when that's appropriate. But deeply ingrained MBO ideas, derived from biological model thinking, permeate most of our larger organizations. It's almost instinctive for many executives to pursue goals by dividing the goals into pieces and parceling out the pieces among subordinates. This frequently gives the subordinates, or the team as a whole, little chance to use their own creativity to find genuinely new ways of solving problems.

THE SOCIAL MODEL: A BASIS FOR BETTER METHODS

By recognizing the limitations of the machine and biological organism analogies and describing an organization in terms of functions, purposes, structure, and processes, Ackoff suggests, the social model opens the way to powerful analysis of how organizations really work and how they should work. And it helps us move toward wise management of human interactions.

The social model sees organizations as *purposeful systems.* Just as human beings are capable of pursuing aims that involve intelligence and choice, so are organizations. Individuals pursue personal prosperity for themselves; organizations pursue prosperity for their stakeholders, for instance.

But an organization is a very different kind of purposeful system from an individual human being. The parts of a human being don't have purposes of their own. Your legs and feet don't have intelligence and the ability to make choices. If we decide to go to the kitchen for coffee so that we can stay up late working on a project, for example, our legs and feet simply handle the details of taking us there. They won't come back and say, "We think you should have a dry martini and go to bed, so you'll be well rested in the morning."

When you assign a task to people in an organization, on the other hand, they can come back with exactly that kind of feedback.

This creates both enormous opportunities and profound problems for managers. Employees and the organization as a whole can share purposes aligned to the functions the organization performs for society. If they do, they can think of ever better ways of performing those functions.

But the benefits won't appear unless the organization's structures and processes support the improvements. The organization will have to adopt structures quite different from the simple hierarchical arrangements that the mechanical model and the biological model brought to mind, structures like those of the successful organizations in this book. KenTon's school improvement teams were an example. Another clear example was in LDS Hospital in Salt Lake City, where a highly paid medical doctor served on a problem-solving team headed by a nurse whose knowledge of the problem being attacked was greater than the doctor's.

Hierarchical models are unlikely to inspire these kinds of structures.

Unfortunately, creating the right purposes, structure, and processes in an organization, and coordinating interactions so people do both their routine and their creative work effectively, is a profoundly difficult task. *Under the social model, the leaders' job is to manage purposes, structures, and processes of the organization so that all its people can use their independent intelligence to contribute to the performance of the organization's functions for its stakeholders and the larger society. Leaders communicate purposes, and they design structures and processes.*

The approaches we examined in the preceding chapters make the work of managers consistent with the desires of employees who, as they've grown more educated over the past few decades, have often rebelled against being treated as unthinking parts of a machine or narrowly specialized parts of an organism. The social model recognizes

Table A.1 Models of Management

	Mechanical Model	Biological Model	Social Model
Era of greatest influence.	1800s–1940.	1930s–1990s.	1980s–
Basic understanding of an organization.	The organization is like a *machine*, and designers prescribe all details of what parts should do.	The organization is like a *human body*, with top management ("the brain") giving the parts freedom to handle details on their own.	The organization is like a *society*, a loosely coupled group of people working together to achieve individual and shared purposes.
How managers think about the interactions in the organization.	Interactions among standardized, interchangeable parts.	Interaction among organizational units with different functions, displayed on an organizational chart.	Interactions among purposeful people and organizational units.
What managers consider fundamental in determining properties of the whole system.	The predictable behavior of individual parts.	Division of labor and performance of the functional units; management by objectives and management by exception.	The purposeful interactions among the elements.
Purpose of the organization.	The organization has no purpose of its own; serves the owner's purposes.	Organization has purposes decided by one group: top management.	Organization serves many purposes—the purposes of all its members.
Measurements used by managers.	Inputs, e.g., tons of steel and labor hours required to make a car.	Output, e.g., return on investment.	Interactions and outputs, e.g., customer satisfaction and economic value added.

Table A.1 (Continued)

	Mechanical Model	Biological Model	Social Model
Way of thinking about the future.	Cause-and-effect analysis (deterministic, like classical physics).	Predict and prepare.	Future is not predictable; interaction of purposeful elements will create the future.
Possibilities for change.	Change possible only through redesign by owner and by specialist experts.	Slow change possible as organizational units adapt to changes in environment.	Fast change possible through collective action of system members. But change is difficult to initiate and manage.

that you can't get people to make their full contribution unless they feel respected for their own minds and purposes.

Table A.1 compares the way organizations function under the mechanical model, the biological model, and the social systems model.

LIMITATIONS AND POTENTIAL OF ACKOFF'S SOCIAL MODEL

Social model thinking is inevitably more complex than hierarchical model thinking, and today the social model probably raises more questions than it answers. But it offers a foundation on which we can build a dependable body of management knowledge.

A key strength of the mechanical model and the biological model is that they simplify the task of management. Thinkers influenced by the machine analogy and the biological organism analogy have provided very straightforward advice. "Scientific management" thinkers, influenced by the mechanical model, said: Decide what you want your employees to do and tell them exactly how to do it. MBO thinkers, influenced by the biological model said: Tell your employees what to do in general terms, decide how you'll measure their performance, and leave the details to them until you discover a problem.

The social model doesn't provide such simple prescriptions. Just knowing about the social model and understanding some basic systems concepts does not necessarily enable a manager to run an organization better.

Ackoff offers many important ideas.[6] One is the concept of *idealized design*. Idealized design is a method that helps a cross-section of the people of an organization plan the ideal company system for the company's present circumstances. Typically, the idealized design is a substantial breakthrough in the way of operating compared with the company's prior system.[7] But he doesn't seek to provide the how-to's for a complete management system. He says he wants to present "guidelines" rather than "manuals" for managers.

We agree that guidelines are useful. But we also believe the management profession needs detailed advice—with appropriate cautions as to when the advice can and can't be relied on.

INADEQUATE APPLICATION OF SYSTEMS SCIENCE TODAY

In Chapter 9, we discussed the inadequate understanding and application of systems science as one of the weaknesses of management today. We illustrate this point with Figure A.1, a chart that the systems thinker Jamshid Gharajedaghi often uses.

The chart summarizes the elements of what Ackoff and Gharajedaghi both refer to as *interactive management*. The four blocks in the middle summarize the elements of the idealized design process mentioned above. The left block, "systems dimensions," represents elements we want to discuss here. These five dimensions—power, beauty, wealth, knowledge, and values—illustrate the multidimensionality of purposes of both individuals and the organization. Ackoff has said:

> My principal witness are the philosophers of ancient Greece.
> . . . They divided the pursuits of man into four categories:
> 1. The scientific—the pursuit of truth
> 2. The political-economic—the pursuit of plenty

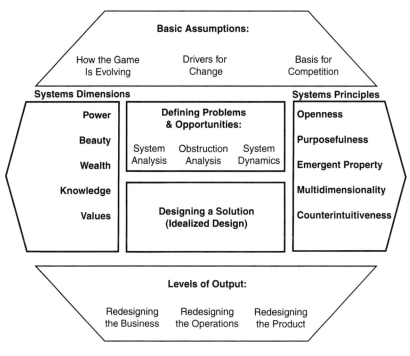

Figure A.1   Interactive Management

3. The ethical-moral—the pursuit of goodness and virtue, and

4. The aesthetic—the pursuit of beauty.

Gharajedaghi's chart adds a fifth, "power," but it can arguably be included in the second pursuit. In a videotape that Ackoff produced jointly with W. Edwards Deming, Ackoff pointed out that in the United States, we have a tendency to consider the pursuits as independent efforts. We pursue the truth in academic institutions, the plenty at work, and beauty when we are outside academia or work.

Life would be much better if we could integrate these pursuits in a holistic way.

The most important point of these dimensions in our view is that these are probably the most important examples of the manifestations of Type 2 properties: the purpose of the people and the organization. Any processes and the associated measurement system one designs needs to take into account all five dimensions.

Today, no one can provide the kind of detailed social model prescription for leading an organization that we believe managers need. The situation was similar when real science supplanted ancient systems as a guide for medical doctors and engineers. The new science didn't immediately produce clear directions for healing people or building great structures. Researchers and practitioners had to develop a body of scientifically valid principles and techniques before powerful improvement could be achieved.

We believe the social model provides a foundation for similar progress in management. It accurately describes real, multipurpose organizations. Working with the social systems model, we can develop methods of dealing with management problems that more fully mobilize the capabilities of all the members of an organization. To do that, however, managers need to work with Ackoff's ideas and those of others to create integrated management systems.

Leadership and Breakthrough

Research for this book has clearly demonstrated the critical link between leadership and the successful transformation of organizations. It is a vast and fertile subject that Shoji Shiba has avidly pursued. With his TQM background, it has been natural for him to think about leadership in terms of both incremental improvement and breakthrough improvement. Over the decades, he has seen an evolution of the skills required by business leaders—from skill at incremental improvement within a business, to skill with breakthrough improvement within the same business, and finally, to skill at breakthrough improvement into a new business area. Based on his studies with a number of organizations, he derived a model for breakthrough that is discussed below. (Another strong influence on Shiba's thinking about leadership has been, consistent with his own leadership principle of seeking new perspectives from novel sources, his hobby of studying paintings. For context, we have also included some of his thinking in that area.)

Shiba has given a series of lectures on leadership that provide the basis for the material in this appendix. We feel his focus on the multidimensionality of skill needed by leaders is a perspective that strengthens and deepens the conclusions we reached in the body of this book regarding human interactions, structure, and processes. For that reason, we present it here.[1]

Companies everywhere are dealing with increased complexity (size of organization and geographical dispersion of organization, as well as increased financial, governmental, legal, and regulatory issues). Companies everywhere are dealing with increased speed of change (shorter times between product introductions, increased demands for response from customers). Companies everywhere are dealing with unforesee-able shocks (such as, in 1998, an Asian financial crisis, the sudden drop of the price of a PC to under $1,000).

With these sorts of challenges, companies need leadership more than ever, to declare needed changes in the organization, to provide a vision that the rest of the organization can align itself around, to ar-ticulate that vision in a way that everyone can understand. But as the need for clear leadership increases, it also becomes increasingly evi-dent that one person can't do everything any more. Organizations are too complex, and the need for the right sort of involvement of people throughout the organization is essential. Highly skilled leadership is needed at all levels of the organization, leadership empowered to make high-quality decisions. Thus, it is necessary to think of leader-ship as a system or process and a set of skills that can be seen and im-proved upon. The rest of this book has addressed the systems and processes leaders use; the emphasis of our discussion here is the skills of leadership.[2]

Three Sets of Skills (and Five Effective Principles) of Leadership

Leaders require three sets of skills: technical, human, and conceptual. Each of these is shown as a region in Figure B.1.

As can be seen by the expanding areas of the regions in the figure, as the management level increases, the requisite amount of each leader-ship skill increases and there is also a change in the type of technical skill needed. The rest of this appendix has a section on each of these areas of skill. In the course of the descriptions of the three types of lead-ership skill, *five principles of effective leadership* are also emphasized.

FIRST LEADERSHIP SKILL: TECHNICAL SKILL

Technical skill has two parts: pure technical knowledge or functional skill, and skill to improve the efficiency of technology, that is, im-provement skill or problem-solving skill.

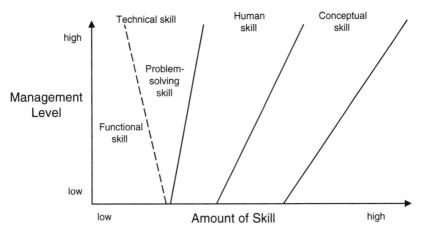

Figure B.1   Skills for Leadership

As a leader gets to be more senior, he or she usually needs less pure technical skill and more improvement skill. Therefore, senior leaders need to focus on developing improvement skill. Because the plan-do-check-act cycle is the engine for improvement, PDCA is something every leader must understand.

However, a leader's concerns change over time, as do the data he or she has access to. For instance, early in one's career, one is typically concerned with doing one's own job as reliably and efficiently as

---

Five Principles of Effective Leadership

1. A leader's future skill for problem solving depends almost completely on skill with language.
2. Nothing can be done alone: create infrastructures to mobilize teams and the organization.
3. Don't be afraid to jump into the fishbowl.
4. Focus on qualitative data rather than quantitative data to achieve breakthrough.
5. Do not stick to surface phenomena; rather, jump out of the fishbowl to capture the structure beneath the surface.

possible (process control). Later, the concern is more with improving existing work process or products (reactive improvement). As a leader becomes still more senior, he or she is seeking to understand future business and customer needs to reengineer processes or products to meet those needs (proactive improvement).

The kinds of data one typically sees in process control, reactive improvement, and proactive improvement are each different.[3] Most important for senior managers, the data one inevitably must deal with when trying to proactively improve something are language or qualitative data (numerical data are typically supplementary). We hear from customers in the qualitative language of subjective likes and dislikes. We hear from investors in the qualitative language of subjective needs. We primarily hear from our employees and suppliers via subjective or qualitative language. This brings us to the first principle for effective leadership:

> *Effective Leadership Principle 1:* A leader's future skill for problem-solving depends almost completely on skill with language.

To make good decisions and take effective action, one must ground opinions in concrete fact and one must abstract from concrete facts to new concepts. A primary tool for grounding is semantics[4] and a primary tool for abstraction is the Language-Processing method.[5]

Here is an example of grounding using semantics.[6] The leader hears an initial statement from someone: "The operations manager would not listen to the engineers." By working to ground the statement, the leader discovers the more concrete fact: "Process engineers analyzed forging deviations and presented the details for a process change, but the manager did not implement the changes." The second statement provides more information and might well help the leader avoid a wrong conclusion or decision.

Now here is an example of abstraction. Suppose the leader hears the following two statements:

> "Last year, top management *postponed a self-assessment workshop* two times, giving the reason that there were higher priorities for the company."

"Top management of X company *did not show up* at the TQM *kick-off meeting* in May."

Both of these statements are quite concrete and factual, but what should the leader make of them taken together? Using his or her skill with the LP method, the "key item" in each statement is noted (indicated by italics). The leader might form the following hypothesis of what the two key items mean together: *"to initiate new activities."*

To recapitulate, the senior leader mostly deals with proactive improvement, which mostly deals with language or qualitative data, which demands language skill on the part of the leader, and the most powerfully useful language skills for the senior leader are grounding and abstraction.

SECOND LEADERSHIP SKILL: HUMAN SKILL

Human skill, the second skill of leadership, is divided into several categories:

Face-to-face human interaction skill
Team communication skill[7]
Skill to communicate with the entire organization[8]

The higher one rises in the leadership of an organization, the more important the third of these becomes. Unfortunately, the CEO cannot successfully communicate directly with all employees. It is difficult for the top leader or manager to actually access and *truly* communicate with more than a few employees in the organization, and then, usually just the few nearest the top. The traditional idea of top-down communication throughout the entire organization doesn't work well. Thus, various infrastructures or systems are needed to effect communication from the top throughout the entire organization. This brings us to the second principle for effective leadership:

Effective Leadership Principle 2: Nothing can be done alone: you must create infrastructures to mobilize teams and the organization.

Three good examples of infrastructures to communicate with and mobilize the entire organization are Shiba's 7 Infrastructures model, Disneyland, and books published external to the organization.

The 7 Infrastructures, which is a central focus of Shiba's teaching, is a strategy for communicating with the entire organization. Its seven components are:

1. goal setting
2. a suborganization that supports mobilization of the entire organization
3. education and training
4. promotion
5. diffusion of success stories
6. awards and incentive
7. diagnosis and monitoring

Two of the seven, goal setting and diagnosis and monitoring, are particularly important for senior leaders. However, all seven are used to communicate with the entire organization.

Disneyland has a superb infrastructure for communicating with the masses. All Disneylands are built on the same plan. There is one entrance so they can control the image people see going in. Once inside the entrance, people pass a happy police officer or a lovely young lady or Disney characters, all of whom are intended to make people happier. As one goes down the main street, there is a very open feeling in the space between the three-storey rows of town buildings on each side; this openness comes from the fact that the first storey of the buildings is built to 9/10 scale, the second storey to 8/10 scale, and the third storey to 6/10 scale. The Disneyland infrastructure is aimed at giving the same image to everyone.

Another tool to communicate to the entire organization it to speak *publicly* (well beyond one's own organization) so that what one says is reflected by the outside world back to the people in the organization. For instance, Andy Grove's book *Only the Paranoid Survive* describes of how a company must deal with listening more to customers. This book was widely read throughout the world; consequently, people inside Grove's company were motivated to read the book and thus know much more about what Grove thinks than they would ever learn from internal memos and presentations (imagine what would have happened had he sent a book-length internal "memo" to all employees).

Dr. Koji Kobayashi at NEC did the same thing when he was trying to promote the convergence of computers and communications some years ago.[9] He wrote three books that were widely read (and translated into English as well), and thus everyone in his own company also read them and knew what he thought needed to happen.

Returning momentarily to the seventh of Shiba's 7 Infrastructures, diagnosis consists of both on-line and off-line diagnosis. The former should follow the 70/30 rule, in which 70 percent of the commentary is positive (the parts of the process that were relatively well done) and no more than 30 percent deals with a selected *few* problem areas.[10] Figure B.2 diagrams this process.

On-line diagnosis presents the tip of the iceberg. Off-line diagnosis addresses the volume below the surface of the water. This can be done using a system such as the 7 Infrastructures to ensure the integrity of alignment activities.

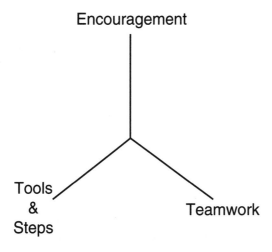

Figure B.2 Components of Diagnosis

THIRD LEADERSHIP SKILL: CONCEPTUAL SKILL

Conceptual skills, which constitute the third leadership skill set, are the source of creative thinking. This is the key skill for leaders seeking breakthrough; hence, our discussion of it is more extensive than that of the other two skills. We divide our description of conceptual skill, into three stages:

1. Exploration and formulation of a new concept
2. Moving from the past business to the new business
3. Recreating organizational integrity

Conceptual Stage 1: Exploration and Formulation of a New Concept

Conceptual skill begins with an exploration process Shiba calls *the fishbowl principle*. It has three parts, as shown in Figure B.3.

First, one needs to "jump into the fishbowl"—for instance, visit users of your product or service in their own work and use environment. Second, one "swims with the fish"—experiences their environment. Third, one "jumps up"—tries to see the user environment in a broader context and analyzes what was going on in the fishbowl and what the essence of the fish was. One uses these three skills to create a new hypothesis.

The fishbowl principle is in contrast to standing outside the fishbowl looking in and measuring how well what is going on in the fishbowl matches a preconceived hypothesis (see Figure B.4).

Shiba says that his fishbowl principle is derived from his hobby of studying the paintings of great artists. Consider these examples from the history of painting:

- Michelangelo used the perspective approach. Looking at the painting *The Last Supper,* one can see it was done using perspective lines. The painter is using objective measurement to draw beauty from an outside perspective (something like standing outside the fishbowl and logically evaluating the hypothesis).[11]
- The impressionists, for instance, Monet, jumped in and swam in nature and industrial society. They left the studio and went

Source: Shoji Shiba et al., *A New American TQM* (Portland, OR: Productivity Press, 1993), 185. Used with permission.

Figure B.3　Jumping into the Fishbowl

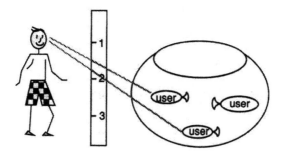

Source: Shoji Shiba et al., *A New American TQM* (Portland, OR: Productivity Press, 1993), 184. Used with permission.

Figure B.4　Looking In from Outside the Fishbowl

outside. Thus, paintings show the steam of locomotives in the background and iron fences and bridges, steam and iron being symbols of modernity at the time.

- The abstractionists, for instance, Picasso, used a jump-out (jump-up) approach: they swam in nature and then jumped out and painted what they saw. The purpose of the painting was not to copy nature, but to show the viewer the sentiment, emotion, and concept the artist saw in nature.

This brings us to the third principle of effective leadership:

Effective Leadership Principle 3: Don't be afraid to jump into the fishbowl.

To benefit from a jump into the fishbowl, one must practice the skill of unlearning: there will be little reason to gain the fishes' perspective if one cannot forget preconceptions, assumptions, and cultural constraints. On the subject of unlearning, Nobel Prize winner Leo Esaki (who won the prize for his work with transistor tunnel effects) offered the following *Five Things Not to Do to Be a Nobel Prize Winner:*

1. Do not allow yourself to be trapped by your past experiences.
2. Do not allow yourself to be overly attached to any authority.
3. Do not hold on to what you don't need.
4. Do not avoid confrontation.[12]
5. Do not lose childhood curiosity in everyday life.[13]

A second requirement for jumping into the fishbowl is learning to take the time to do it. Everyone says they have no time. Alex d'Arbeloff is an example of a CEO who took the necessary time during Teradyne's mobilization of TQM. He says "the top person should spend one-fifth of his time on new tasks." He continues to do this even though he is now spending half his time as chairman of MIT.

As was already mentioned, the fishbowl principle is about creating a new concept rather than about validating an existing concept. Thus, it is not necessary to have large amounts of quantitative data to statistically validate a concept. Rather, one needs to seek inputs from all possible sources, and this means collecting *qualitative* data. This leads us to our next principle of effective leadership (and its corollary):

Effective Leadership Principle 4: Focus on qualitative data rather than quantitative data to achieve breakthrough.

Collection of qualitative data involves seeking real, specific, personal cases. We want people to tell us their actual stories, rather than to give us their (frequently, not well-founded) generalizations. Specific examples are typically rich in detail that can suggest many new possibilities.

In collecting qualitative data, diversity, not quantity, is key. Again, during exploration, we are not seeking statistically valid numbers of samples to verify a hypothesis; rather, we are looking for as many different ideas as we can find that can suggest new concepts to us.[14]

Finally, in collecting qualitative data, seek *symbolic cases*, images of real behavior. When we gather diverse, real, specific cases, we will hear lots of opinions and learn many facts. Focus on that subset of cases that provides the most value in terms of providing graspable input (input images) and input that can be abstracted into useful concepts that can be conveyed to others (output images). Symbolic cases provide this value.

Symbolic cases or examples are those cases that are very specific and real but also represent an important class of situations. Some examples follow.

When Shiba visited one company, someone was already waiting for him at the front door, and when he got to the meeting room, people were on time for the meeting. From these symbolic cases, Shiba created his hypothesis that a core value of the company was that *time matters*. This was *his* way of grasping the invisible culture of the company.

Another situation occurred at MIT's Leaders for Manufacturing (LFM) program, a joint graduate program of MIT's Engineering School and the Sloan School of Management. One day, some executives visited LFM to tell the students about their company. Shiba noted that the most important impression he received came from that fact that the visitors were all dressed in dark blue jackets with a white shirt and a dark red tie. For him, this was the key symbolic case. Standing there in their identical dress, they touted the importance of diversity of products and markets. From this, Shiba hypothesized that the company strongly needed diversity.

Of course, there is no single interpretation of a behavior. Each person selects his or her own examples of symbolic behavior and creates his or her own hypothesis. Leaders must train themselves to be open to what images are telling them. Shiba suggests that potential leaders look at painters to help them understand the use of symbolic images. Painters are geniuses at showing symbolic images, such as in *The Surrender of Breda* by Diego Velazquez (Museo del Prado, Madrid). Nicknamed *The Lances*, the painting depicts one army in disarray surrendering to the other army with their lances standing tall and all in a row. Other notable symbolic images can be seen in Edouard Manet's *The Railway*, showing a Paris scene with white vapor in the background from steam locomotives, invisible in the painting, and an iron fence in the middle ground (National Gallery, Washington, D.C.). For Manet, these images were symbolic of modernity in his age.

After exploration, a leader needs to formulate a new concept, and this leads to our next principle of effective leadership:

Effective Leadership Principle 5: Do not stick to surface phenomena; rather, jump out of the fishbowl to capture the structure beneath the surface.

After jumping out of the fishbowl, from above, one can see many types of fishbowls and many types of fish. The ability to intentionally shift your perspective and way of thinking allows you to conceptualize a coherent hypothesis about what is truly taking place in the overall environment. There are three different dimensions to this kind of thinking: time, space, and point of view (see Figure B.5).

One can change the *time* scale of observation, for instance, by looking month by month or year by year instead of day by day. In this way, one may see longer-term patterns. Alternatively, one might look minute by minute instead of day by day to see details that might otherwise be missed.

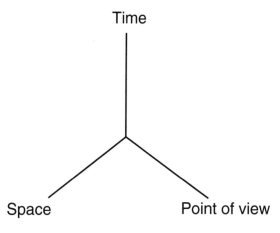

Figure B.5   Three Dimensions of Thinking

One can change the *space* in which or from which one observes, for instance, by doing benchmarking in another country, or getting down on one's knees to see how the product is used by children.

One can change the human *point of view*, for instance, by looking at things from the customer's or market's point of view rather than from the company's point of view.

Comparison is also a useful technique for a leader to use to understand, structure, and create a hypothesis. Again, we look to art as an analogy. If one compares two paintings of a couple dancing—for instance, Pierre-August Renoir's *Dance in the City* and *Dance in the Country* (Le Musée d'Orsay, Paris)—one sees and understands more than either painting shows alone. By comparing the paintings, one is better able to see what is going on (or is not going on) in each.

In another example of comparison, Shiba notes two companies that visited and gave presentations to MIT's LFM program one summer. In each presentation, the company listed its core values. The first company, Intel, listed its core values as "results-oriented, risk taking, great place to work, quality, discipline, and customer orientation." The second company, General Motors, listed as its core values "customer enthusiasm, innovation, team work, integrity, and continuous improvement." Take a moment to think about and compare these two sets of core values. What hypothesis would you draw? Remember, each person needs to create his or her own hypothesis.

The hypothesis Shiba draws from these two different sets of core values is "different frequency of new product introduction." For instance, Intel has no time for continuous improvement: they must "copy exactly!"

As shown in Figure B.6, a graphic summary of what has been said about conceptual thinking, leaders will do well to develop skill in capturing an appropriate symbolic case, creating a hypothesis, proving the hypothesis with data (the hypothesis alone is just a hypothesis—one needs somehow to validate its plausibility), and finally, broadcasting the hypothesis.

Conceptual Stage 2: Moving from the Past Business to the New Business

Once a leader has done the necessary exploration, he or she needs to decide where to go next. Such a juncture is represented graphically by what Shiba calls "Andy Grove's inflection curve" (as illustrated by the portion of Figure B.7 within the dotted box). A company can either stay on the AB arch that rises and then declines, or, at the top of the arc (point E), it can begin a new upward turn into a new business and go on to new heights. (Inflection point F is a good place to begin to notice that something has changed and something has to be

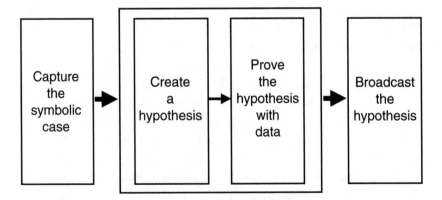

Figure B.6   Elements of Conceptual Skill

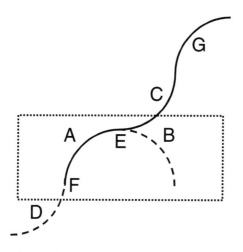

Figure B.7 The Inflection Point for Business

done.) Having chosen the new direction, one needs to focus mobilization on breakthrough in that direction.

For reasons that will become clear later, Shiba likes to think about
these inflection points in terms of the three questions shown in Figure B.8. Shiba provides three examples of companies making a breakthrough transition at this inflection point: Seiko, YHP, and Teradyne.

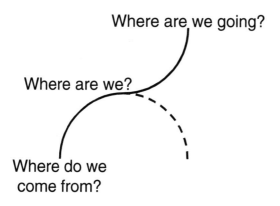

Figure B.8 Breakthrough Transition Questions

Seiko. In 1989, Nobuyoshi Kambe was appointed Head of Seiko's Sports and Leisure Products Division. At the time of his appointment, the division was in dire straits: sales were low ($30 million/year), they were running a deficit ($3 million/year), and they had high inventories and high costs. Kambe was told by Seiko's CEO to recover the division's profitability within three years.

Kambe got permission from the CEO to do something drastic to make the business turn around, even to change the business; in the end, they turned the business around by developing one of the most popular golf clubs in Japan, the "S-Yard." Between 1993 and 1996, they sold half a million of these clubs with sales revenue in 1996 of $120 million.

The division's journey to recovery involved the following three steps: reducing personnel, setting an ideal future, and swimming with the fish.

Kambe began by shaking up the division personnel. Half of the division's people were transferred to other divisions of the company, a quarter were encouraged to take early retirement, and another quarter that were newly recruited into the division (see Figure B.9). When the

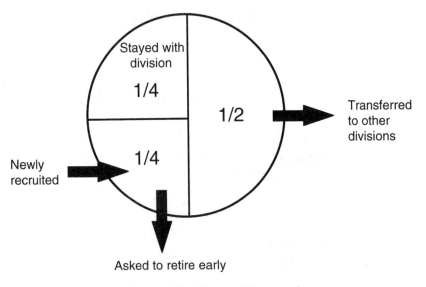

Figure B.9   Change of Personnel

personnel transition was done, there were half as many people in the division overall, and only half of these had previously been employed in the division.

Next, Kambe and his people decided that their ideal future was to develop original and attractive new products, breaking with their traditional business of selling imported sporting goods, particularly sports-related clocks and watches. In other words, they decided that their ideal future involved freedom from traditional Seiko products (see Figure B.10). They looked at high-volume markets, such as fishing, skiing, and golf. They chose golf as their focus.

Finally, they jumped into the fishbowl using voice-of-the-customer methods to invent a special new type of golf driver, from which they obtained the great business success already mentioned (see Figure B.11).

By swimming with the fish, they learned that the market could be divided into two important segments: golfers under 50 years of age and golfers 50 years of age and older. The top three priorities of these

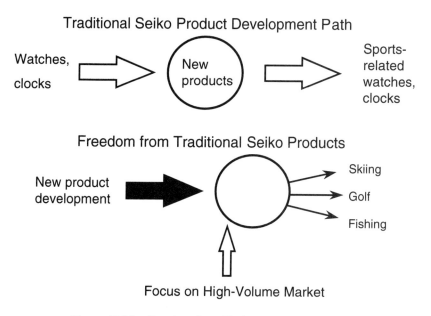

Traditional Seiko Product Development Path

Watches, clocks → New products → Sports-related watches, clocks

Freedom from Traditional Seiko Products

New product development → Skiing / Golf / Fishing

Focus on High-Volume Market

Figure B.10 Freedom from Traditional Seiko Products

Popularity	Younger than 50	50 and older
1st	No hook, no slice!	
2nd	More distance!	No hook, no slice!
3rd	I want to have a golf club with a famous brand name.	I don't care for any brand name.

Figure B.11   Voice of the Customer Using the Fishbowl Principle

two market segments are shown in Figure B.11. Under-50 Japanese golfers cared about straight shots, distance, and having a brand name club; older golfers wanted the distance and accuracy that would let them compete with younger golfers but didn't care about brand name.

This data from the fishbowl provided an opportunity for Kambe's division and a development team without significant golf experience to design a new type of golf club for over-50 golfers. The characteristics of this club are shown in Figure B.12.

The key factors in Seiko's breakthrough to a new business as Shiba sees them are shown in Figure B.13. First, Kambe's group was in dire straits: they had a crisis that required them to make a real change. Next, the group broke free from Seiko's traditional approaches. They then stirred things up with a massive personnel change and envisioned an ideal future involving original and attractive new products. With this motivation and ability to separate from the past (unfreezing of prior conceptions) and a vision of a new future, they had the discipline to use specific voice-of-the-customer methods to discover a route to new business success.

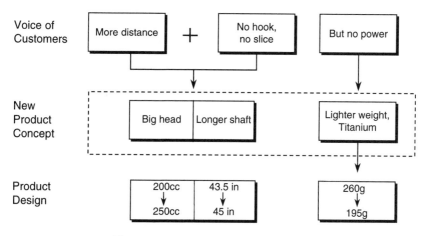

Figure B.12 New Golf Club Concept

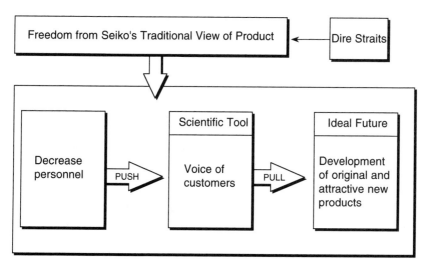

Figure B.13 Key Factors in Seiko's Breakthrough

YHP. In the past, YHP, the Japanese subsidiary of Hewlett-Packard, had had mediocre performance. Then Ken Sasaoka, Japanese manager, said to the parent company, "Why don't you let me run YHP? We really think we can do a better job." Bill Hewlett and Dave Packard agreed.[15] What followed at YHP is illustrated in Figure B.14.

After becoming a self-operated unit, YHP challenged for the Deming Prize. Earlier in his business career, Sasaoka had been involved in a dip-soldering improvement effort, where incomplete soldering was reduced from .4 percent to 3ppm, a greater than 1000 percent improvement. For Sasaoka, this experience with massive improvement of dip soldering was a symbolic case that gave him an image of how much improvement could be achieved.

Knowing that improvement methods worked and with the push and pull and challenge for the Deming prize, YHP had the motivation to use the scientific methods of hoshin management and seven steps to do the improvement. A few years later, YHP won the Deming Prize.

Teradyne. In the late 1980s, Teradyne was in crisis, documented earlier in this book. They had been trying to use TQM and build their own management system. Now CEO Alex d'Arbeloff decided that

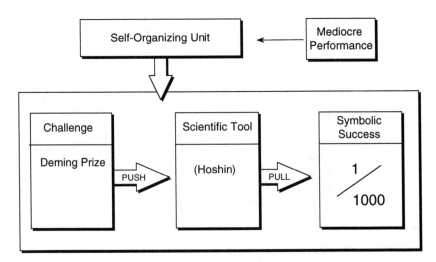

Figure B.14 Key Factors in YHP's Breakthrough

they would break free of the restrictions of TQM. Some might say that Teradyne implemented TQM, but this understates what they did. They did not implement a TQM system that anyone else could have taught them; rather, they implemented their own system, customized to their needs and fully integrated with how they managed the company (see Figure B.15).

As described earlier in the book, d'Arbeloff personally explained to the 60 or so top people in the company why they had to change the way they managed and emphasized that they *were* going to change. He and the other top manager of the company also personally demonstrated the use of PDCA, improving their TQM implementation. Finally, they adopted the scientific methods known as the seven steps and PDCA as their improvement methods.

A Model for Breakthrough.   Shiba sees the same pattern in each of these cases (see Figure B.16). This pattern constitutes his model for breakthrough:[16]

1. Some event brings about a commitment to breakthrough.
2. There is an unlearning of past tradition or practices.

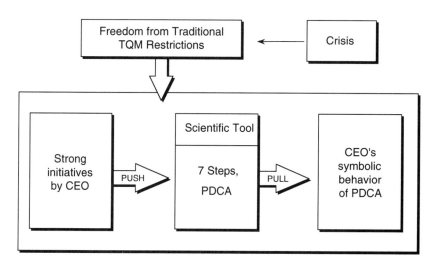

Figure B.15   Key Factors in Teradyne's Breakthrough

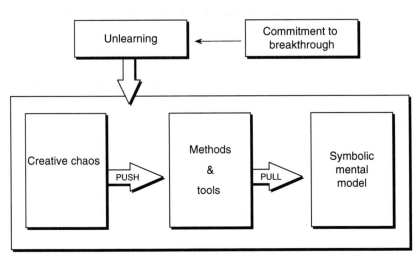

Figure B.16   Steps for Breakthrough

3. Creative chaos is created to push mobilization along.
4. A symbolic mental model (success) is available to pull the mobilization along.
5. The scientific method and tools are used to make the change. The scientific method is capable of great change; it is the most effective and efficient method of understanding what is going on in real life and transforming it—if we can enable ourselves to use it. Steps 1 to 4 of this model provide the motivation and unfreezing of previous methods that enable the discipline of the scientific method.

And then you get the breakthrough.

Figure B.17 is a comparison of the three examples given above with this five-step model for breakthrough.

Shiba sees steps two through five of the above as a new breakthrough cycle, the UCMT cycle: Unlearn, socialize creative Chaos, externalize symbolic mental Model, methods and Tools (see Figure B.18). UCM is about creating a new mental model in yourself; T is about getting a technical breakthrough.

Key Factors	YHP	Seiko	Teradyne
1. Commitment to breakthrough	Mediocre performance and quality problems	Dire straits	Crisis
2. Unlearning	More autonomy for YHP	Freedom from traditional brand	Freedom from TQM restrictions
3. Create creative chaos	Challenge for Deming Prize	Decrease personnel	CEO's strong initiative
4. Symbolic success	1000x improvement (by 7 steps)	Ideal future of original and attractive new products	CEO's demonstration of PDCA
5. Scientific method and tools	Hoshin management	Voice of the customer	PDCA; 7 steps

Figure B.17   Key Factors in Breakthrough

Breakthrough takes place in two phases: a *mental breakthrough* and a *technical breakthrough* (see Figure B.19). The U, C, and M quadrants of the cycle are about mental breakthrough; the T quadrant of the cycle is about technical breakthrough. Mental breakthrough precedes technical breakthrough; you can't use the methodology of breakthrough if you are hung up in a nonbreakthrough mentality. For instance, Teradyne's division in Nashua, New Hampshire, is world class

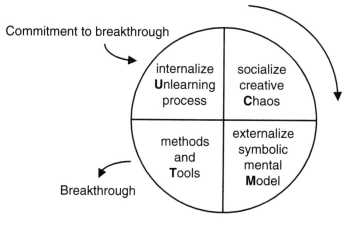

Figure B.18   The UCMT Cycle

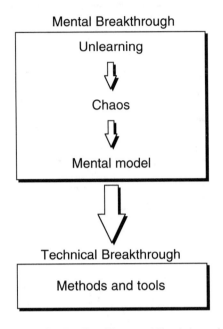

Figure B.19   Two Phases of Breakthrough

in applying the seven steps to typical processes. However, because of their focus on typical processes, they have a hard time seeing how to apply the seven steps to big problems in the organization.

Shiba sees the UCMT cycle as taking its place alongside the Standardize, Do, Check, Act, and PDCA cycles in an evolution from control through incremental improvement to breakthrough, as shown in Figures B.20 and B.21.

In the 1930s, the business need was for control (SDCA). In the 1960s and 1970s, the business need was for continuous improvement (PDCA), which began with ongoing incremental improvement (using the seven steps), and in 1970s expanded to include ongoing breakthrough improvements of the existing business (using hoshin management). In the 1990s, the business need in a number of cases was for *breakthrough into a new business area.*

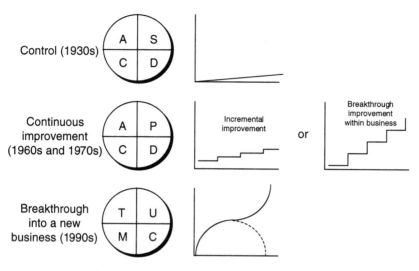

Figure B.20 From Control to Breakthrough

Three Theories of Human Behavior. A word about the "human aspect" referenced in Figure B.21: Leadership is about people, so a leader needs a theory about how people behave—their human nature. Theories X, Y, and W are each a kind of hypothesis about human behavior that is necessary to design an integrated management system.

	Control in the 1930s	Continuous improvement in the 1960s and 1970s	Breakthrough to new business in the 1990s
Cycle:	SDCA	PDCA	UCMT
To create:	Product	Function	Competence
Fitness:	Standard	Use; cost	Latent requirements; changing paradigm
To serve:	Supplier/buyer	Customer	Stakeholder
New concept:	Variance/deviation	Process improvement	Unlearning
Human aspect:	Theory X	Theory Y	Theory W
Societal change:	Mass production	Consumer revolution	Continuous change of society

Figure B.21 Evolution of the Business Improvement Paradigm

Theory X says that people want stability and to be led. It suggests the power of standardization and control of workers in the pursuit of mass production. Theory Y says that people seek self-determination and innovation. It suggests the accrual of knowledge, continuous improvement, and worker development and empowerment in pursuit of creating something new.

Shiba's Theory W embraces the duality of the nature of people: people want both a stable, controlled environment and to create something new (in many ways, these two are in conflict). We want strong clear leadership that tells us what to do and makes us secure; however, we also want to contribute to something new that changes our present existence and makes us feel uncomfortable.

The new Theory W was suggested to Shiba by his study of the painting by Paul Gauguin entitled *Where do we come from? What are we? Where are we going?* (Museum of Fine Arts, Boston). This masterpiece symbolically represents the questions all leaders must answer to successfully lead their organizations to sustained ("eternal") existence.

The painting is divided into three parts, with an arc of representative narrative flowing from right to left.[17] The right side of the painting illustrates a baby and its growing up; this represents the question *Where do we come from?* The middle of the painting illustrates adults in the fullness of life; this represents the question *What are we?* The left side of the painting illustrates the decline of old age; this represents the question *Where are we going?*[18]

The top right and top left corners of the painting are in a lighter color and a shape that indicates a cycle from the top left back to the top right of the painting, as if the left side of the painting was connected to the right side in a cylinder. This cycle represents the possibility of eternal life of the human species: as the old generation passes, the possibility of a new generation exists.

Parallel to the theme of Gauguin's painting, business also seeks "eternal life." The three questions of Gauguin are similar to the questions we must ask as we move along Grove's inflection curve (see Figure B.9). We came from somewhere (Where did we come from?), we must decide what we want to do next (What are we?), and we must then figure out how to get there (Where are we going?).

We are all faced with the duality depicted in this painting. We know we cannot sustain ourselves if we allow no change, but we like working on clear goals and we are uncomfortable with change. We recognize that if we are to continue to survive, our identity must evolve, but denying our existing identity temporarily leaves us without identity. Breakthrough requires unlearning and chaos before we settle into our new, improved situation. Thus, to continue its existence, each organization and each individual in the organization (in their professional and personal lives) must grapple with the eternal questions: Where do we come from? What are we? Where are we going? Successfully answering these questions can bring enlightenment and transformation, and move both a corporation and the people within it through a threshold to a place where all kinds of masterpieces can be created. Leaders who can demonstrate and catalyze this will not only achieve breakthroughs, but also enable people to understand and become *who they are.*

All three theories, X, Y, and W, must be present in different situations in a real company: Theory X is for control, Theory Y is for continuous improvement, and Theory W is for breakthrough.

Conceptual Stage 3: Recreating Organizational Integrity

Once a leader has explored the situation broadly and formed a hypothesis of what must be done, once a leader has found the commitment to break with the past and has generated the creative chaos and symbolic example that push and pull the discipline to apply scientific improvement methods, once the organization has undergone breakthrough change and broken into the new business area, then the leader must see that a *new organizational integrity* is created. It is as important for an organization as it is for a person to *be what you are.*

Shiba tells the story of Mitsutake Teratoto, an executive with a Japanese tire manufacturer who was asked to create a new business. He was sick with anxiety about what new business to choose. Then one day, he listened to his emotions. What he really cared about was golf. Without golf, life would not be complete for him. Therefore, he chose golf as his new business. Success was not easy. This new division of the tire company didn't have the technology for making golf equipment nor marketing relating to golf. However, Teratoto kept working, and after 10 years, he eventually achieved great success.

This is a fundamental principle of business, leadership, and life. Each organization and each person must find their unique place. We must listen carefully and respond honestly to what our emotions tell us. Throughout our lives, we become no one else but who we are. You might say the sixth and overarching principle of effective leadership is: *We only live once; let us be who we are.*

APPENDIX C
The Power of
Collective Action

In Chapter 1, we discussed the important difference between the biological model and the social model in responding to environmental changes. In this appendix, we elaborate on that discussion.

Collective Actions in the Physical Sciences

We are all familiar with how water flows down a bathtub drain. What we are seeing is a phenomenon called turbulence, which, familiar as it is, still defies detailed scientific description by experts on fluid mechanics. Like many natural phenomena, it comes under the heading of *collective action*, outcomes so complex and interrelated that direct causal chains cannot be deciphered.

In the 1950s, when there was great concern that energy sources were becoming depleted, some looked to thermonuclear fusion as an answer. Many prominent scientists made very convincing proposals. The idea was to confine a high-temperature plasma for a long enough time to create a fusion reaction. It was generally agreed that this could be done with magnetic fields. But when the experiment was tried, the plasma could not be contained. The collective action of the plasma did not respond to the magnetic fields as predicted.

Today, we know that there are different kinds of collective phenomena in the physical world; some we can understand and predict, and some still defy our understanding. More recently, the study of collective action has become linked with chaos theory and, more generally, the idea that the physical world as we see it is simply a collection of surface manifestations of infinite numbers of random occurrences and interactions. The physical sciences are merely qualitatively different attempts to give order to the underlying chaos.

Without going into depth on this subject, it is interesting to contemplate the implications of this kind of thinking when applied to social systems.

Collective Phenomena in Social Systems

In social systems, there are two contradictory characteristics. On the one hand, societies are generally conservative; their natural tendency is to preserve what exists. That, as we alluded to in Chapter 1, is in essence why cultures exist. They are like default parameters in computers; if you don't make intentional changes in a system, you revert to its cultural defaults. On the other hand, a society also has a latent capacity of changing very fast, in nearly quantum leaps. That is a result of collective action on the social system.

Societal collective action requires a stimulus, a trigger or catalyst. Nazi Germany, the Cultural Revolution in China, the revolution in Iran—all had identifiable triggering events that precipitated chaotic outcomes. The progression of events that was triggered in each case had two important characteristics: each was nonlinear and each was very sensitive to the initial or environmental conditions. For these reasons, the results of collective action, once triggered, are usually unpredictable.

At least in physical science, the mystery in thermonuclear fusion was recognized as part of the turbulence question. As a matter of fact, many of the early papers on chaos were written for the problem in thermonuclear fusion. Today, social science and management science have a tendency to attempt to treat collective phenomena on an analytical basis even in the presence of turbulence—and with knowledge of the phenomenon much weaker than what is typically available in the natural sciences.

We are living in a world in which collective action is becoming increasingly important because of technological advances in communication and information systems. Increased global interaction on all levels—cultural, economic, political, even spiritual—has increased the turbulence of the environment exponentially. This is magnified when you consider that the internal environment of the organization is nearly as subject to collective action and chaos as is its external environment. Therefore, if one wishes to manage one's organization in this new environment, it is essential that the organization's latent potential to change be rapidly developed. That is why it is so important to try to manage the organization according to the principles of social model systems, which, as we have discussed, maximize the creativity, intelligence, and *flexibility* of the system.

For more reading on the subjects of collective action and chaos theory as they relate to the physical world and/or social systems, the best place to start is probably James Gleick's *Chaos: The Making of a New Science* (New York: Viking, 1989). Another worthwhile work is Jack Cohen and Ian Stewart's *The Collapse of Chaos: Discovering Simplicity in a Complex World* (New York: Penguin Books, 1994).

There are collective phenomena in both natural sciences and social sciences. One must always be cautious in not extending analogies inappropriately between the two classes of phenomena. (This happened when quantum mechanics was first developed, and the results were not helpful.) But we find these books helpful in the understanding of organizations. Sometimes, we need to understand the phenomenon of chaos more as an analogy in the organizational sphere; the conditions of chaos may not be met in their entirety in organizations. Gleick's discussion of turbulence, including Heisenberg's comment on his death bed (p. 121), does illuminate confusing phenomena such as those we encounter in companies. Heisenberg was asked whether he was looking forward to asking God about the great questions of physics. "I think God has the answer to relativity," he said, "but maybe not to turbulence."

Conversation Competence

David Walden

In this book, we have emphasized the importance of engaging employees and managing the interactions of everyone within the company.
In particular, the social model requires people to understand each
other, to coordinate actions with each other, and ultimately to build
trusting relationships.

Of course, there are many methods, formal and informal, for seeking understanding, coordinating actions, and building relationships.
However, in this appendix, we report on one set of specific methods
that several CQM member companies, particularly Analog Devices,
Inc., have been experimenting with and using.[1]

The Importance (and Difficulty) of Conversation

Conversation is the primary way we find out what is happening and
create action in our organizations. In fact, for almost all complex
problems (or opportunities), most of the data we have is language data
and most of the thinking and planning we do is done through conversation or using language.

For instance, using language, customers signal us that there is a
problem. Using language, we discuss and agree with each other within

our organization that there indeed is a problem. Probably through conversations, we collect more data to help us understand the problem. Through conversation, we plan a tentative solution, we coordinate carrying out the solution, and so forth. Even attempts to resist the solution (which sometimes happens in our organizations) typically involve language.

More particularly, the most frequent task or activity of many people in a business, especially managers, is attempting to communicate and coordinate with each other. In fact, if we think about what managers do, their primary tool is conversation. This also is the primary way they find out what's happening and the way they create action. We sometimes think of managers as being powerful people; this power results directly from their ability to create (or prevent) specific actions of others; and the tool that managers use as leaders, coaches, and initiators of action is conversation.

Ideally, this communication and coordination is aimed at advancing the purpose of the business. However, much of the time, we are confused and either do the wrong thing or do the right thing badly. If we investigate the source of this confusion and the resulting inefficiency, we discover that we frequently fail to make or keep the commitments necessary to take advantage of an opportunity, miss opportunities altogether, or generally operate in an environment of mistrust.

Consider the following equation, which suggests that available effort can be spent on useful work or is wasted:

$$Effort = Useful\ Work + Waste$$

If we ask the typical manager how much time he or she spends in meetings or other conversations, we typically gets estimates of from 30 to 90 percent. When we ask how much of the time spent in meetings or conversation is time spent on useful work, we typically get estimates ranging from 25 to 50 percent. In other words, of the 30 to 90 percent of the time we spend in meetings and conversations, 50 to 75 percent of the time is wasted. We are probably wasting between 30 and 40 percent of all our time, and maybe more. And the time we waste results in things not getting done or not getting done correctly, which results in more waste in the form of rework or rebuilding of relationships.

Finally, all this waste often causes subsequent damage in related areas, and we miss opportunities to be doing other productive things.

The point is that poor use of conversation and language can result in massive waste. It's hard to think of improving any other single activity that could have as much benefit as improving the way we use conversation and language.

The methods we typically use to seek and investigate opportunities and to make and keep the commitments necessary to successfully pursue an opportunity are methods of communication and coordination we have learned mostly unconsciously since our childhood. They let us down as much in private life as they do in business. The fact is that most of us have seldom or never worked effectively to improve these largely implicit and unconscious methods. As discussed elsewhere in the book, one of the first lessons we learn about improving the way we manage is that it is difficult if not impossible to improve the intangible—that we must begin an improvement effort by making the process or system visible to ourselves. Thus, if we hope to improve the way we communicate and coordinate in business, we must seek to make more tangible what we are doing when we try to understand each other and coordinate action.

This leads us to the CQM Study Group on Conversation, which is also an example of mutual learning.

The CQM Study Group on Conversation

Since its founding, the Center for Quality of Management's approach to improving management methods has been to identify weaknesses in existing management systems, to find management methods to address these weaknesses, and to integrate the new skills into the existing methods, making the new methods as operational as possible so that they can be widely disseminated. Skill in conversation is a critical void in the management methods that the CQM companies have been applying.

Having recognized the weakness in conversation, we could not find a single source for adequate tangible, operational methods that could be applied to improve the way we converse. Therefore, in 1995, the CQM initiated a study group to investigate available methods relating to language and conversation. The group included participants from Analog Devices, Intel, Keane, the U.S. Navy, W.R. Grace, and Boston College School of Business.

Members of the study group read widely, listened to expert presentations, and wrote analytic notes to each other summarizing the connections they saw among available methods. By the winter of 1996, a synthesis model had been created and the study group had recommended and undertaken three major initiatives:

1. The synthesis approach was taught and tested in practice in CQM's TQM course for senior executives.
2. A study was initiated to see how the methodology could be used to redesign complex business processes, specifically, the new product development process.
3. New courses were designed to teach managers how to use the methodology in their roles as coaches and leaders.

The model created is a synthesis, in approximate order of their influence on us, of ideas from the business philosopher Fernando Flores,[2] the psychologist Chris Argyris,[3] the biologist Humberto Maturana, the general semanticist S. I. Hayakawa, the physicist David Bohm, and the anthropologist Jiro Kawakita. We have also brought to bear our many ideas from TQM.

The rest of this appendix sketches the integrated model that was developed and that has since been practiced in a number of our CQM member companies. Note that our purpose was to develop a model that could be made operational, that could be taught, and that could be improved on based on experience. Thus, we sought explicit models and step-by-step process—specific rules-of-thumb, however simplistic—to let people begin to practice and gain actual experience and work their way toward the mastery that enables one to deal with complex, real-life situations.

We have made a lot of progress in achieving this operationalization, and there is more work to be done. This appendix only begins to sketch out some of the techniques and the full power we believe can be cracked open through investigation and integration in this area.

Some Types of Conversations

In the model we developed, we have found it useful to think about five basic types of conversations, although these are by no means the only types of conversations that we have:

Conversations for conversations
Conversations for relationships
Conversations for possible actions
Conversations for coordinating action
Conversations about breakdowns

Conversations for conversations are used to decide what type of conversation we should be having. We have all had the experience of being in a situation with another person when we are having different conversations. For instance, if I am in development and you are in sales, you might come to me and ask if some special option for the product was possible, and I might tell you that it is. Later, you might discover that I have not assigned anyone to work on this special feature. After an acrimonious discussion, we might discover that, when we first talked, you thought we were having a conversation for action, and I thought we were having a conversation about possible actions. So, having a conversation to decide what type of conversation you should be having can save a lot of trouble.

(Before going on to talk about the other four conversations, we must mention that some types of conversations are often not very productive and are better avoided, for instance, conversations of judgments and stories about who did what to whom in the past are unproductive and best avoided.)

We can think about *conversations for relationships, conversations for possible actions,* and *conversations for coordinating action* as being related, as shown in Figure D.1, where each oval and key word repre-sents one of these three types of conversations.

We begin with *conversations for relationships* (the outside oval). When we meet each other for the first time, we usually start by begin-ning to build a tentative relationship. We introduce ourselves to each other, we say what a nice day it is, we mention something about some current event in the news that morning: "How about those Red Sox. They don't usually begin their annual collapse so early in the season." We are looking for early signs of what we may have in common. Basi-cally, we are trying to determine if it's safe (physically or emotionally) to be near the other person. Think about what happens when some-one you have never met comes up to you on the street and begins a conversation. We are very chary as we figure out if this person wants something we are willing to give (such as directions to a nearby loca-tion), or if it's better to try to get away before he or she tries to take something we don't want to give. Once we have decided that it's a good idea to have a tentative relationship with the other person, we may try to discover if there might be some actions we might usefully take together.

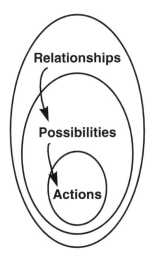

Source: Courtesy of Dr. Beebe Nelson.

Figure D.1   Three Conversations on Which Relationships Are Built

In other words, we might begin a *conversation for possible actions* (the middle oval). This part of the model should feel very familiar to anyone in sales. If we discover an action that we might usefully take together, then we need to move on to a *conversation for coordinating action* (the innermost oval), which we'll return to in a minute. Notice that jumping straight to the conversation for coordinating action without having a conversation for possible actions or building a relationship can be counterproductive. We may not have sorted out enough about our relationship or individual concerns to be able to develop sufficiently matched expectations that will result in completed actions that both parties will be satisfied with.

At any time, there can be a mismatch in expectations that leads to a breakdown in the communication or action and that requires a *conversation about breakdown* as part of the recovery process.

Conversations for Action via the Atom of Work

Once we begin to try to coordinate action, there are all sorts of problems that can defeat our intentions and often leave a bad taste in our mouth. For instance, all of us have frequently made a request of someone else or had a request made of us, thought a commitment was made, and ended up with a result that left someone disappointed.

For example, I recently asked a clerical person to edit a document for me by a certain date and time, and the person said he would. However, the person's press of work was so great that he was unable to get to my work as promised. Therefore, I was unable for several days to do the next step in the process I was involved in.

Here is an example in which I didn't perform as well as someone else expected. Recently, I was asked to produce a document by a certain date and said I would. However, I had trouble figuring out how to do the project and didn't get it done by the expected time. Therefore, it was unavailable to the person who needed it for a trip he had to make.

Sometimes, people will do more than requested. I asked my secretary to ask the company library for any available information on a particular subject, hoping to get anything that was easy for the library to find. My secretary made the request of the library, and the library did an online search for which I eventually received a charge of many hundreds of dollars. Because I was not clear that my interest was only casual, I had to pay much more for the information than it was worth to me.

Finally, which of us hasn't given someone advice only to have the person say, "Who asked you?" In other words, we sometimes respond to requests that haven't been made, and people resent this.

To provide a way to improve the quality of our conversations for action, let's explore a model or process called the *atom of work*, which we will use to hold conversations to coordinate action and which will enable us to make requests and commitments that will be more successful. Just as a physical atom is the smallest possible unit of an elementary substance, so an atom of work is the smallest possible unit of business tasks.[4] The atom of work is a schematic representation of the possible paths of making a request or offer, agreeing to a promise, carrying out the promise, and finally, evaluating how well the job was done.

The atom of work, represented in Figure D.2, starts with a requester or speaker who typically makes a request of a performer or listener; it involves four stages, numbered 1, 2, 3, and 4 around the circle, and fifth and sixth elements called "breakdowns" and "shared concerns." Figure D.3 depicts the location of the atom of work within the conversation for action. Each element of the atom of work is described below.

STAGE 1

The first stage of the atom of work is the preparation stage. During this stage, the requester communicates the context in which the request and promise are set. The stage ends with a request. Unfortunately, though most of us are very facile at making requests, the requesst themselves often are not very clear. Here are some of the things we need to think about to assure that things don't go wrong when we make requests.[5]

Most simply, there needs to be a speaker and a hearer. It is not sufficient to make a request to no one in particular: "Someone needs to fix the copier." It's also no good being disappointed or angry because

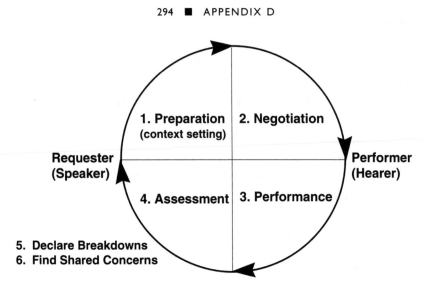

1. Preparation (context setting)   2. Negotiation

Requester (Speaker)

Performer (Hearer)

4. Assessment   3. Performance

5. Declare Breakdowns
6. Find Shared Concerns

Figure D.2   Atom of Work

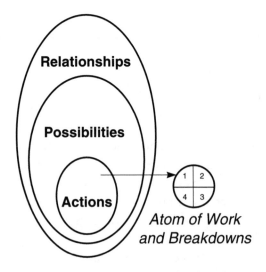

Relationships

Possibilities

Actions

1 | 2
4 | 3

Atom of Work and Breakdowns

Figure D.3   A Model for Conversations for Coordinating Action

the person we thought should carry out the action didn't, if we never made an explicit request; who hasn't done this at one time or another? And, we must be careful not to assume a request when no one is making one.

We need to be clear about what is missing. For instance, if I say, "I'm out of touch with the situation with customer X," am I worrying that I am not in control of the situation with customer X, or am I concerned that I don't have information about the situation with customer X? Let's assume that I mean the latter: I am missing information about the situation. Then, we need to specify the future action to address what is missing. Do I want a report from our customer representative, a conversation in the hall next time you and I meet, or do I want a meeting with the customer to get back up to speed on the situation?

Next, we need to be clear about the conditions of satisfaction: What do I want and how? And we need to be clear about the time frame. Time frame could be listed as part of the conditions of satisfaction; we list it separately because it is so important and because it is so often not specified—we just say we want something and don't specify the time.

We also need to be sure we have a shared *background of obviousness.* My background of obviousness is all the things that are so obvious to me that I don't think about whether I need them to be clear to you. For instance, I may hate reports that are longer than one page, or my concerns about customers may always be strategic and I leave the tactical issues to the people in day-to-day contact with the customer account.

You need to know if you can trust me when I make a request. Am I sincere and really in need of this information, or I am in the habit of making casual requests and then not really caring about the answer?

In our course on this subject, we investigate the elements of a request more deeply, and we also role-play making good requests to develop skill with requests that we currently lack.

STAGE 2

The second stage of the atom of work is the negotiation phase. This stage should end with a promise, or at least a clear statement of what will happen.

Unfortunately, just as we often make unclear requests, we also often make nonspecific promises. You ask me to do something, and I say, "Sure" or "As soon as I get a moment" or "Why not?" It's not clear whether I'm making a serious commitment; as time passes, it may become more and more clear that I haven't made a serious commitment. Or, if I made a serious commitment and carry out what I thought you wanted, I may discover later that I did the wrong thing.

During the negotiation phase of the atom of work, the potential performer needs to get straight exactly what the request is, and the requester and performer need to sort out any mismatches in expectations.

Depending on how well the performer carries out the commitment, the requester will form a judgment about the performer and whether or not to depend on this person at another time. This is why it's so important that we get clear requests and make good commitments and carry them out successfully. If we do not, we cast doubt on our capability for future opportunities.

Each of us is judging how much we trust each other every time we make a request. We can look at trust as consisting of three components: sincerity, competence, and reliability. If I make a request of you and you make a commitment to accomplish the request, based on past experience I may judge you as quite sincere, fairly competent, and usually reliable, and decide to take a chance on you. Or I may judge you as very sincere, very competent, and always reliable, in which case I won't be taking any chance at all. Or I may judge you as very competent but not sincere or reliable, in which case I may let you make the commitment but I certainly won't depend on it very much.

The judgments we make about each other make clear why seeming to make commitments that we can't or won't live up to is such a problem. Unfortunately, many of us don't feel we can decline a request, and as managers, many of us make our people feel that they can't decline a request. The best time to hear that someone can't or won't be able to succeed in a commitment is at the time of the request, when there is a possibility of finding someone else who can or will be able to accomplish the request.

If we are to have people reliably live up to commitments, they need other options during the negotiation phase besides simple acceptance. People need to be able to negotiate, make counteroffers, commit to commit later, and even decline. And, as managers, we need our people to be able to take these alternative moves if we want to build a culture of making good requests and commitments.

STAGE 3

The third stage of the atom of work is the performance phase. During the performance phase, the person who made the commitment carries it out. When done, the person declares the task complete.

Unfortunately, declaring performance complete is another thing that is often not done explicitly. Each of us has probably experienced a case when something we wanted done was completed but we didn't know about it. For instance, on Friday, I left some work with the graphics department for a presentation I would be giving Tuesday, and they promised completion by Monday morning. However, on account of another job being canceled, they finished my work by the end of the day on Friday, and then they put it in the interoffice mail to get to me Monday. Of course, had they called me Friday and told me it was already done, I could have picked it up on my way home and checked it over on the weekend. Had I found any errors, they could have been easily corrected before I caught my plane to the presentation site on Monday evening. However, by not getting the material until Monday, I didn't get to look at it until I got on the airplane Monday evening, and by then it was too late when I found an error.

Another thing we often fail to do is to declare at the earliest possible moment that we will be unable to perform according to the promised conditions of satisfaction or time frame. From the point of view of the customer, we would all like suppliers to tell us at the earliest possible moment when they think they may not be able to deliver as agreed. Yet, when we are suppliers, we routinely don't give the earliest possible warning of a problem. This is the point of the fifth element of the atom of work, the declaration of breakdown, on the part of the performer or the requester, at the earliest possible moment.

Some of the time, we can simply carry out alone a commitment we make. However, much of the time, we need help. Figure D.4 shows how one atom of work can spin off consequent atoms of work. For instance, if, as a salesperson from my company, I promise to deliver a

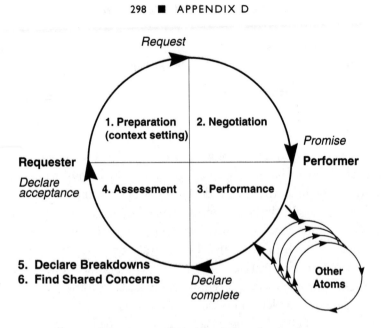

Request

1. Preparation
(context setting)

2. Negotiation

Promise

Requester

Performer

*Declare
acceptance*

4. Assessment

3. Performance

5. Declare Breakdowns
6. Find Shared Concerns

*Declare
complete*

**Other
Atoms**

Figure D.4   Atom of Work with Consequent Atoms

product to you, I will probably have to make requests of and get commitments from others in my company to actually get the product delivered to you.

In fact, a whole network of atoms of work can be spun off the first atom of work. In Figure D.5, the branch office salesperson makes a commitment to deliver a product to the client company. Then the branch office salesperson makes a request of the home office order entry and shipping person to enter the order and ship the product. The order entry/shipping person in turn makes a request of an outside credit-check service to be sure the customer's credit is good, and, finding that the customer's credit is good, ships the product. The branch office salesperson then has to make a request of the branch office installation person to install the product at the customer site. When this is done, the salesperson is finally in a position to declare the delivery commitment complete to the customer.

Other atoms of work can be spun off any stage of an atom of work. For instance, in the primary atom of work in Figure D.5, the branch office salesperson could have made a request of the company contracts

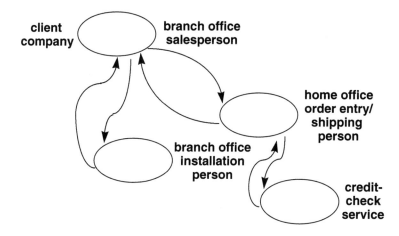

Figure D.5 Network of Atoms of Work

department to help with the negotiation phase of the atom of work. This new commitment is depicted in Figure D.6.

The figures above illustrate that it is possible to think of the activities and processes we carry out in our organizations as being *networks of requests and commitments*. This is a powerful and flexible way to look at many of the things we do, more powerful in many cases than more traditional flowcharting and input-process-output models.

STAGE 4

The fourth stage of the atom of work is the stage during which the customer assesses satisfaction with the job done by the performer. Without a specific model, the activities of this stage are activities that we typically don't carry out, which means that we don't learn how to do things better in the future, even if things need to be improved in

Figure D.6 Another Commitment May Be Required at Any Stage

the future. In fact, many people complain that they seldom know if their supervisor is satisfied with what they do. In many other cases, a performer assumes satisfaction that isn't there.

Stage 4 ends with the customer's declaration of acceptance or declaration of nonsatisfaction, which means that the atom of work may have to be rerun.

Conversations about Breakdown

Let's now ask ourselves, "Where in the atom of work can there be a problem?" The answer, clearly, is anywhere. Problems can and do arise in every stage. This brings us again to the issue of breakdowns.

We have already mentioned the importance of declaring breakdowns as soon as we know we cannot complete a commitment. We would never ride along in our vehicle with a flat tire, blithely ignoring it, with smiles on our faces. However, we do this all the time in our organizations; we sit in meetings, smiling agreement with what the boss is saying, without stating that we know what is being proposed is a bad idea and won't work and even that we may not intend to follow through as requested. Then, perhaps, after the meeting, we whisper to each other in the hall something like, "What a terrible idea. We are wasting so much effort that could be spent more usefully."

It is terribly important to our organizations that we validate having conversations about breakdown. These can occur in any stage of the atom of work, or as part of any of the other conversations. We need to declare a breakdown and decide which conversation to have next. Do we go back and clarify a portion of the atom of work? Do we need to have a conversation for possibilities? Do we need to have a conversation for relationships?

Shared Concerns

Figure D.7 completes our sketch of the atom of work. For the atom of work to work well, the parties to it need to understand what their

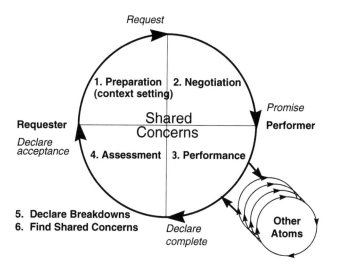

Figure D.7 Shared Concerns Provide Context for the Atom of Work

underlying concerns are (their own and the other party's) and understand the compatibility between these concerns.

If your concern is reducing costs and my concern is that I think I may be the cost you intend to reduce, I probably won't do a great job of carrying out your request that I determine how my job might be done more efficiently. (I once led an engineering group in a company that was doing significant downsizing, but where our viability was critically dependent on our getting products to market faster. Some members of the development staff deliberately did their work more slowly than necessary because they assumed that their jobs would be eliminated as soon as they finished their current project.) However, if we can find shared concerns, then both requester and performer can be working toward compatible ends.

Figure D.8 illustrates the concept of shared concerns. The figure makes clear that our mutual concerns don't have to be wholly overlapping; in fact, they don't exactly have to overlap at all. For instance, you may want a routine job done, and I may want an entry-level opportunity; this compatibility (if not "sharedness") of concerns will be sufficient for us to succeed together.

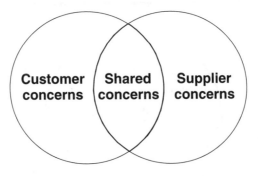

Figure D.8   Intersecting Concerns

Conversations for Possibilities Are Key to Discovering Shared Concerns

The idea of shared concerns begs the question of how we discover them, and this leads us back to our model of various types of conversations. As shown in Figure D.9, our conversation for possible actions may develop our shared concerns, and these in turn will then be available when we operate the atom of work as our tool for holding conversations for coordination of action.

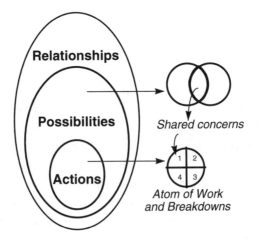

Figure D.9   Conversations for Possible Actions Develop Shared Concerns

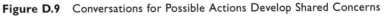

On the other hand, in some cases, we may have started the atom of work without developing a sufficient understanding of our shared concerns. Then, we may have to go back and have a conversation for possible actions to develop the shared concerns and then feed these shared concerns into the atom of work (see Figure D.10).

However, our principle of trying to develop explicit methods that we can improve for "softside" functions requires us to understand where our feelings about a situation and concerns come from and to develop a model for developing those shared concerns, if it is at all possible to do so.

Viewpoints

For any situation with any material amount of complexity, many of us don't think about the possibility of, or aren't concerned with, any viewpoint other than our own. We call this a uniview.

For instance, a circle indicating my uniview about a situation is shown in the top left corner of Figure D.11.[6] There are a couple of ways one can move regarding one's uniview of a situation. Frequently, we see the task ahead as trying to argue others into believing our uniview. We often do this in meetings or conversations where we spend a lot of time talking past each other, even to the

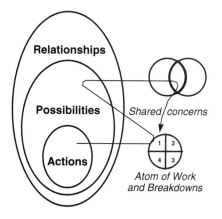

Figure D.10 Possibilities May Need Investigation before Actions Are Taken

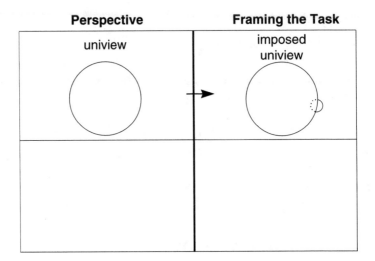

Figure D.11 A Typical but Nonproductive Path

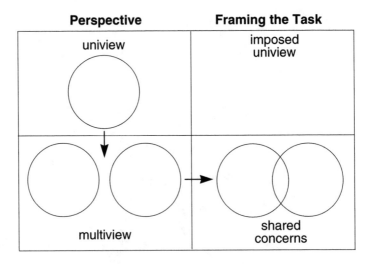

Figure D.12 A More Productive Path

point that we may be downright rude in our statements about each other's viewpoints.

For instance, in the top right corner of the figure, the little circle is the tiny value I give to your uniview, as I try to blot out your viewpoint with my own, much more "significant" viewpoint. We call this the imposed uniview.

Another direction I can go from my own uniview is down. In the bottom left box of Figure D.12, I try to discover the multiview. This means recognizing that you have a uniview of your own, and also discovering the validity of your uniview from your point of view.

With this multiview—this understanding of my own uniview as well as yours—each of us may be in a position to see some overlap between the elements of the multiview. Especially if you have been doing the same thing with regard to my viewpoint, we may be able to develop our shared concerns.

How We Reason

Where do our univiews about a given situation come from? Let's look at a model for how we reason about a situation (Figure D.13). First, we have some facts available to us. We select some of these facts. We may make some inferences based on the facts we select. We probably will make some judgments. Finally, we will draw some conclusions. Based on these conclusions, we may take some actions.

However, typically, we don't do these steps of reasoning slowly and thoughtfully. Rather, we zip through the steps almost unconsciously at the speed of neurons. Quicker than we can explicitly think, we select some facts, make inferences, judgments, and conclusions, and take action. This rapid reaction is necessary most of the time. When we see a cardboard box in the road while driving at high speed, we don't have time to analyze whether the box is empty and we can safely drive over it, or whether it contains something that is dangerous to hit. We see the cardboard box and jerk the steering wheel to avoid it. If we reasoned everything out step by step in business, we'd never get anything done.

Actions taken

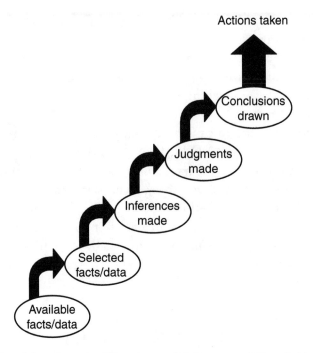

Source: Adapted from the work of Chris Argyris, Bob Putnam, and Diane Smith.

Figure D.13 Ladder of Reasoning

This rapid-fire reasoning with almost unconsciously drawn conclusions about the situation is where our uniview about a situation comes from (Figure D.14).

But there is something behind this reasoning: the observer that each of us is (Figure D.15).

Each of us is able to see different things when we look at a situation, based on our individual beliefs, experiences, emotions, mental models, and assumptions. These are so natural to each of us that, not only do we often fail to explain them to someone else, we are often not even conscious of them ourselves.

Some of the way we observe things is visible to others. However, much of the way we observe things is invisible to others, and often, part of it is invisible to ourselves as well. However, what we don't see, we still get. The observer-that-one-is is with each of us all the time, influencing how we reason.

Perspective   **Framing the Task**

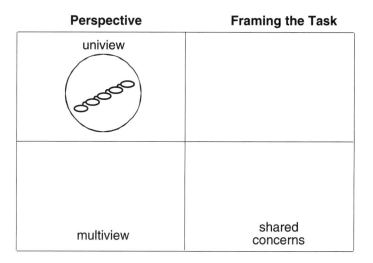

Figure D.14   The Way We Reason Determines Our Uniview

The observers-that-we-are influence the very facts that we have available to us. A marketing person typically has different facts available to him or her than does a financial person. The observers-that-we-are influence which facts we select, the inferences we make, the judgments we make, the conclusions we draw, and the actions we take (see Figure D.16).

But it works the other way, too. Not only do the observers-that-we-are influence each step in our reasoning, but each step in our reasoning

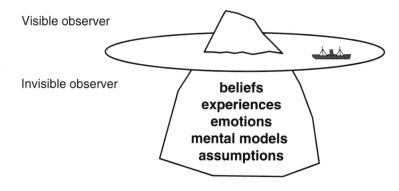

Figure D.15   The Observer-That-One-Is

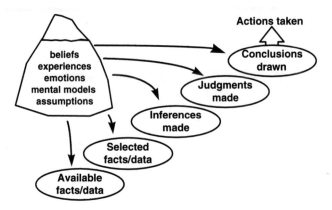

Source: A synthesis from Action Design, CQM, and Newfield Group

Figure D.16 The Observer-That-One-Is and Ladder of Reasoning

tends to confirm the observers-that-we-are. Humans have a wonderful capability to construct and reinforce internal coherence. We make a particular inference based on the way we look at things, and then the inference seems right to us and confirms to us that we really are thinking about things in the right way. We call this entire combination of the reasoning steps and the observer-that-one-is the *cycle of reasoning* (Figure D.17). As already mentioned, the reasoning cycle operates at tremendous speed, almost without thinking.

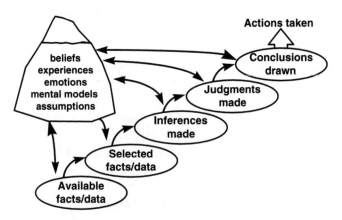

Source: A synthesis from Action Design, CQM, and Newfield Group

Figure D.17 Cycle of Reasoning

How We Can Create a Multiview

Based on our cycle of reasoning, each of us has a uniview about every situation. The problem we need to solve is how to figure out what the other person's reasoning cycle is (and make our own clear to ourselves) so that we can discover the multiview (Figure D.18). To do that, we ourselves need to change the observers-that-we-are-to become more open observers.

The solution is a set of tools that we are teaching in CQM courses or are being developed through research in our CQM member companies. We organize into a few categories the tools for becoming a more open observer to enable discovery of the multiview:

1. Defer making judgments about the viewpoints of others.
2. Create/collect tangible artifacts.
3. Become aware of your inner dialogue.
4. Inquire broadly (listen/observe, don't advocate), e.g.,
   —concerns
   —distinctions

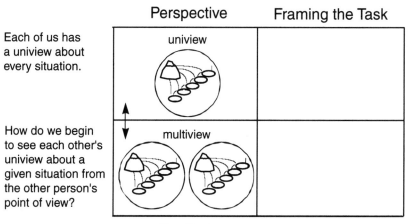

Figure D.18   Our Cycle of Reasoning Determines Our Uniview

—emotion

—facts vs. judgments vs. declarations

—commitments

5. Reflect on how to do better next time.

A first important principle is to defer assessments about the viewpoints of others, to give ourselves a chance to understand their point of view rather than just trying to convince them of ours.

Second, it helps to write down what the other person says, or even the entire conversation. Give yourself a tangible artifact that you can study and learn from.

Third, it helps to become aware that you yourself are observing the situation from your own particular point of view, to become aware of the observer-that-you-are and your own inner dialogue.

Fourth, an important distinction that helps us defer assessments is the distinction between *inquiry* and *advocacy*.[7] Inquiry usually has to do with trying to put ourselves in the other person's shoes and see his or her viewpoint. Advocacy usually involves trying to get the other person to see our viewpoint.

A number of the tools that we use as part of TQM have built into them methods of deferring assessment and including a healthy dose of inquiry. For instance, during voice-of-the-customer visits, we ask open-ended questions, don't argue back, take verbatim notes, and use active listening to draw out and confirm that we understand what the customer is saying.

There are a number of other ideas that help one see the other person's point of view that we won't go into beyond the following mention: listening for the other person's concerns; listening for the particular distinctions the other person is making; observing and listening for the emotion in the situation; clarifying when the other person is making a declaration, a judgment, or a statement of fact; and listening for what commitments the other person is making in what he or she is saying.

Finally, as in all efforts to improve our skills, after a particular effort to be a more open observer and to discover the multiview, it is important to reflect on how effective our efforts were and how to do better next time (see Figure D.19).

Perspective   Framing the Task

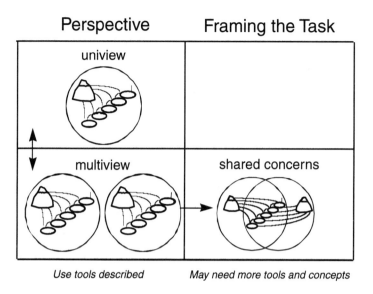

Use tools described   *May need more tools and concepts*

Figure D.19   Sharing Cycles of Reasoning

How to Find Shared Concerns

Thus, we can use a variety of tools to become more open observers and to discover the multiview. We are left with the need for additional tools to find the shared concerns. Once we have heard and understood what the other person is saying, we can move beyond finding the multiview and on to finding shared concerns. The five steps for finding shared concerns are:

1. Become an open observer.
2. Balance advocacy and inquiry.
3. Use structured (explicit) process when possible.
4. Take responsibility for what the other person hears and for your hearing what the other person says.
5. Reflect on how to do better next time.

The first presumption, of course, is that we are already working at becoming more open observers. Second, it is now time to use both advocacy and inquiry and constantly maintain them in balance.

Third, where possible, it is helpful to use structure discussion tools such as the LP method, Dialog from David Bohm, Net-touching, and so on. In fact, the seven steps, Concept Engineering, and other tools we use in various applications have built into them ways of structuring the conversation to help us move from the uniview to a multiview to shared univiews.

Fourth, it also helps if each party takes full responsibility for understanding what the other person means and for making sure the other person understands what one means. There are many tools to help with this. For instance, important sets of tools for developing a multiview and finding shared concerns center around the pair of ideas of making language concrete and making reasoning explicit to each other. Unless we make language concrete, it's hard to even know what we are saying and thinking, much less know it with any precision and have it conveyed from one person to another. Unless we make reasoning explicit, we will not begin to understand the way each other reasons and our backgrounds of obviousness about particular situations. For instance, we can use Hayakawa's principles of semantics to move from affective language to more concrete report language. We can make reasoning explicit by looking at the reasoning cycle and asking ourselves questions: What facts were available and what facts weren't available? What facts did we select and what facts didn't we select? What inferences did we make? What judgments did we make? What conclusions did we draw? We can also make various distinctions that let us better see our backgrounds of obviousness. In the one- to three-day courses on this subject that we are developing, we introduce some of the relevant tools; in some instances, we do substantial role playing with various tools.

Fifth, we once again emphasize the importance of reflecting on how we have practiced, if we are in fact going to improve our skills.

In summary, we can use the techniques above for moving around the uniview-multiview grid to hold conversations for possible actions and thus leave ourselves a proper context for conversations for coordinating action.

Conversations for Relationships and Building Trusting Relationships

In the previous sections, we introduced an explicit model for making and keeping commitments (i.e., for successfully undertaking action) and an explicit model for investigating possibilities. We finish with a model of how conversations for relationships relate to conversations for possible actions and conversations for coordinating action. The three models for the three types of conversations are illustrated in Figure D.20.

As shown in Figure D.21, we start with a tentative relationship; this builds a little trust.[8] With a bit of trust, we may be willing to share enough about our own situations to look for some possible actions. This sharing of possible actions may generate a bit more trust. The next step, in turn, could lead to coordination of action. If the action can be carried out successfully, this generates substantial trust, which leads to a stronger relationship because we see that we actually can

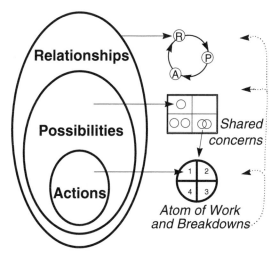

A refers to actions.
R refers to relationships.
P refers to possibilities.

Figure D.20   Each Conversation Has Its Own Model

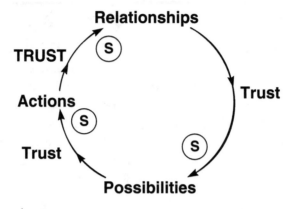

S refers to same direction

Figure D.21   Trust Loop

accomplish things together through this relationship. With a stronger relationship, we may feel able to share with each other more about ourselves and the way we reason, which could lead to more interesting actions. If we can successfully coordinate and carry out these actions, our relationship will be further improved.

We now see the importance of setting up the proper context for action and carrying out the actions successfully. If we do so, we can get into an upward spiral of greater and greater power to perform to-gether. However, if we cannot successfully coordinate action, either because we don't have tools like the atom of work, or because we don't properly set the context using techniques such as those to move from univiews to shared univiews, then trust and relationships are damaged. We will be less likely to look for possible actions together. If we fail again to carry out action successfully, our relationship may be com-pletely fractured, and no further action may be possible.

Summary

The social model requires that people understand and coordinate with each other. Getting better at doing this requires continuous improvement. Making continuous improvements requires making processes, models, and systems explicit, so that they are visible and can be improved.

Integrating methods from a variety of experts and areas, we have created an explicit set of models and methods to allow people to get better at understanding each other and coordinating with each other. Since their creation, these methods have themselves undergone several improvement iterations. The methods include:

- A specific model—the atom of work—for making and keeping commitments
- A more general model—the uniview and multiview grid—and tools for investigating possibilities to find shared concerns that lead to the possibility of keepable commitments
- A still more general model—the trust loop—for how one builds trusting relationships through finding the right possibilities and effecting successful action

Notes

Preface

1. The companies were Analog Devices, Inc.; Bolt Beranek and Newman Inc.; Bose Corp.; Digital Equipment Corp., the Aircraft Engine division of General Electric; Polaroid Corp., and Teradyne Inc.
2. Shoji Shiba, Alan Graham, and David Walden, *A New American TQM: Four Practical Revolutions in Management* (Cambridge, MA: Productivity Press, 1993). The forthcoming new edition will be titled simply, *Four Practical Revolutions in Management.*
3. Nam P. Suh, *The Principles of Design* (New York: Oxford University Press, 1990).
4. Kenneth Atchity, *A Writer's Time: A Guide to the Creative Process from Vision through Revision* (New York: Norton, 1986).

Chapter 1   The Theory and Practice of Integrated Management Systems

1. For more detail, see Appendix A.
2. Coauthor Thomas H. Lee worked with Lewis during this study.
3. Jack Cohen and Ian Stewart, *The Collapse of Chaos: Discovering Simplicity in a Complex World* (New York: Penguin Books, 1994).
4. David Packard, *The HP Way* (New York: HarperBusiness, 1995). We learned about the ten-step method from a private communication between HP and Analog Devices that was subsequently donated to the Center for Quality of Management library.
5. Peter Senge, *The Fifth Discipline* (New York: Doubleday Currency, 1990).
6. See Eliyahu M. Goldratt, *Theory of Constraints* (New York: North River Press, 1990), and Donald Reinertsen, *Managing the Design Factory* (New York: Free Press, 1997). There are many disputes among scientists and philosophers over exactly what constitutes truly scientific methodology. We do not attempt to address those issues here. It is enough to agree with the rough, intuitive understanding of the scientific method discussed above to understand the role of the scientific method in the organizations we examined. A dictionary definition can be helpful in sorting out whether any given approach follows the

scientific method. The *American Heritage Dictionary of the English Language* defines "scientific methods" as: "principles and empirical processes . . . generally involving the observation of phenomena, the formulation of a hypothesis concerning the phenomena, experimentation to demonstrate the truth or falseness of the hypothesis, and a conclusion that validates or modifies the hypothesis."

7. See Kyioshi Uchimaru et al., *TQM for Technical Groups* (New York: Productivity Press, 1993), for a discussion of NEC's Integrated Circuit and Microcomputer Systems Division.

8. See Shoji Shiba, Alan Graham, and David C. Walden, *A New American TQM* (New York: Productivity Press, 1993), p. 64.

9. This is traditional wisdom from statistical process control.

10. For a basic introduction to the plan-do-check-act cycle, see Shoji Shiba, Alan Graham, and David C. Walden, *A New American TQM* (New York: Productivity Press, 1993), pp. 45ff.

11. For methodologies that make it possible to utilize the plan-do-check-act method in large, proactive improvement projects, see Center for Quality of Management, *Concept Engineering*, 1998, and Center for Quality of Management, *9-Step Project Planning System*, 1998 (available from the Center for Quality of Management, Cambridge, MA).

12. W. Edwards Deming, *Out of the Crisis* (New York: MIT Center for Advanced Engineering Study, 1986). Late in his life, Deming began to refer to the cycle as "Plan, Do, *Study,* Act." We feel that either Plan, Do, Check, Act or Plan, Do, Study, Act provides a good quick summary and guide to the scientific method. We have used the phrase Plan, Do, Check, Act in this book because it is the phrase that had the widest influence on the organizations we studied and on other organizations around the world.

13. Eric von Hippel, *Sources of Innovation* (New York: Oxford University Press, 1988).

14. See J.H. Gill, *Saying and Showing: Radical Themes in Wittgenstein's On Certainty* (New York: Religious Studies, 1974).

15. For an introduction to the systems concept of collective action, see Appendix C.

16. See Appendix A.

17. See Edgar H. Schein, "Three Cultures of Management: The Key to Organizational Learning," *Sloan Management Review* 38, no. 1 (Fall 1996): 9–20.

18. See Appendix B.

19. For further discussion of the role of the leader, see *A New American TQM*, pp. 307ff.

20. D. MacGregor, *The Human Side of Enterprise* (New York: McGraw-Hill, 1960).

21. Andrew S. Grove, *Only the Paranoid Survive* (New York: Currency/Doubleday, 1996).
22. See Dave Nelson, Rick Mayo, and Patrick Moody, *Powered by Honda* (New York: John Wiley & Sons, 1998).

Chapter 2 Pioneers in Integrated Management Systems

1. The LP method is based on ideas originally developed by S.I. Hayakawa and Jiro Kawakita. See S.I. Hayakawa and Alan R. Hayakawa, *Language in Thought and Action*, 5th ed. (New York: Harcourt Brace, 1990), and Jiro Kawakita, *The Original KJ Method* (Tokyo: Kawakita Research Institute, n.d.).
2. See Mike Bradley and John Petrolini, "How a 7-Step Process Reduced Roadblocks Impeding Quality Improvement Teams at Teradyne," *Center for Quality Management Journal* (Winter 1993): 7–17.
3. Steven C. Wheelwright and Kim B. Clark, *Revolutionizing Product Development* (New York: Free Press, 1992).
4. See Shoji Shiba et al., *A New American TQM*, 162–165.
5. The Quality Maturity System has been revised since the version illustrated here, but the basic principle remains the same.
6. As mentioned in Chapter 1, Hewlett-Packard decided to spin off its measurement and medical products groups in 1999 to focus on the computer products that had evolved as its mainstay.
7. Responsible Care is a registered service mark of the Chemical Manufacturers Association.
8. Gary Hamel and C.K. Prahalad, "Strategic Intent," *Harvard Business Review* (May–June 1989).

Chapter 3 The Service Industries

1. Michael Rothschild, "Mapping Your Web," *Forbes ASAP* (December 1994).
2. See Victor S. Aramati and Toby Woll, "TQM in Service: A Report by the CQM Study Group," *Center for Quality of Management Journal* (Fall 1997): 5–27.
3. J.M. Juran, *Quality Control Handbook*, 4th ed. (New York: McGraw-Hill, 1988).

Chapter 4 Achieving Diverse Purposes

1. Quoted in Chester E. Finn Jr., *We Must Take Charge: Our Schools and Our Future* (New York: Free Press, 1991), 14.
2. Uri Treisman, "Studying Students Studying Calculus: A Look at the Lives of Minority Mathematics Students in College," *The College Mathematics Journal* (November 1992).

3. An Ishikawa cause-and-effect diagram, developed by the Japanese quality teacher Kaoru Ishikawa, is a tree-shaped chart that lists and classifies possible causes of a problem.

4. Nominal group technique is a highly structured form of brainstorming, used to give all members of a large group an equal voice in generating and ranking ideas. After the question for group consideration has been stated, each individual writes down his or her ideas. Then the facilitator goes around the room asking each person for one idea at a time. If an individual has no more ideas, he or she can say, "Pass." Finally, individuals give multiple votes to indicate which ideas they consider most important.

5. This account is based largely on Treisman, "Studying Students Studying Calculus," 362–372, and Jacqueline Pinsker McCaffrey, "A Report on the Development and Evolution of the Mathematics Workshop Programs," draft report submitted to the National Science Foundation, Charles A. Dana Center for Mathematics and Science Education, University of Texas at Austin.

Chapter 5   Managing the Most Complex Processes

1. See, for example, Institute of Medicine, *Assessing Medical Technologies*, Washington, DC: National Academy Press, 5 (1985).

2. Intermountain Health Care, *Annual Report*, 1993.

Chapter 6   Better Lives for Sailors and Continuous Improvement Processes

1. The Army and Air Force have been making similar efforts to create new integrated management systems. We haven't studied those efforts, but a book by former Army Chief of Staff Gordon R. Sullivan *Hope Is Not a Method* (New York: Broadway Books, 1996), deserves to be read along with this chapter by nonmilitary people who hope to understand the military's lessons in management.

2. A Pareto chart is one that lists types of problems in order of frequency. It focuses people on the most common problems, thus speeding improvement.

3. Lloyd Dobbins and Clare Crawford-Mason, *Thinking about Quality: Progress, Wisdom, and the Deming Philosophy* (New York: Times Books, 1994), 214.

4. W. Edwards Deming, *Out of the Crisis* (Cambridge, MA: MIT Center for Advanced Engineering Study, 1986), 24.

Chapter 7   The Challenge of Intransigent Organizations

1. This section draws on the previously unpublished work of one of the authors, Thomas H. Lee, on a National Research Council panel that

studied the EPA's quality assurance and Total Quality practices. The panel was originally asked to study management quality assurance practices, but expanded its examination to the whole of the agency's Total Quality Management effort. In the end, the draft report was not published because it went beyond the assigned scope of the analysis.

Chapter 8   Act Locally

1. G. Clotaire Rapaille, *Conclusions on Leadership,* study sponsored by General Motors, Center for Quality of Management, and others, 1996.
2. Ikujiro Nonaka and Hirotaka Takeuchi, *The Knowledge-Creating Company: How Japanese Companies Create the Dynamics of Innovation* (New York, Oxford University Press, 1995).

Chapter 9   Think Globally

1. Thomas H. Lee, Ben C. Ball, and Richard D. Tabors, *Energy Aftermath* (Boston, MA: Harvard Business School Press, 1990).
2. Four dimensions of development—truth, plenty, good, and beauty—are described by Russell Ackoff in *Creating the Corporate Future* (New York: John Wiley & Sons, 1981). In the summer of 1992, during a three-day workshop between CQM and INTERACT, discussions surrounding these concepts redefined the dimensions as power (authority), beauty (emotion), knowledge (method), wealth (measurement system), and values (conflict resolution).
3. A causal-loop diagram is one of the tools used in system dynamics. It shows not only how variables in a system are interrelated in localized loops of cause and effect, but also how those localized loops interrelate to one another systemwide. Structural Process Improvement accomplishes breakthroughs by combining TQM language-processing methods with system dynamics tools like causal loop diagrams and well as with system science as taught by Russell Ackoff and Jamshid Gharajedaghi.
4. Michael Goodman, *Study Notes in System Dynamics* (Cambridge, MA: MIT Press, 1974).
5. See, for example, Peter Senge et al., *The Fifth Discipline Field Book* (New York: Currency/Doubleday, 1994).
6. Hoshin management principles and practices are outlined in Shoji Shiba, Tom Pursch, and Robert Stasey, "Introduction to Hoshin Management," *CQM Journal* 4, no. 3 (Fall 1995): 22–33.

Appendix A   The Systems Theories of Russell Ackoff

1. The most rigorous description of the ideas that underlie Ackoff's arguments appear in R.L. Ackoff and Fred E. Emery, *On Purposeful Systems* (Chicago: Aldine, Atherton, 1972). A more popular treatment appears in R.L. Ackoff, *Creating the Corporate Future* (New York: John Wiley &

Sons, 1981). The implications for management are examined in Jamshid Gharajedaghi and R.L. Ackoff, "Mechanisms, Organisms, and Social Systems," *Strategic Management Journal*, 5 (1984): 289–300.
2. Ackoff, *Creating the Corporate Future*, 15.
3. *Detroit News*, 14 November 1916, cited in James C. Collins and Jerry I. Porras, *Built to Last: Successful Habits of Visionary Companies* (New York: HarperBusiness, 1994), 53. Ford's biographers make clear that this was not mere rhetoric. For example, before he was successful, Ford frequently quarreled with financial backers who wanted him to make a more expensive—and therefore more profitable—car.
4. Peter Collier and David Horowitz, *The Fords: An American Epic* (New York: Summit, 1987), 60.
5. A clear exposition of the management-by-objectives system, helpful in analyzing its weaknesses, is in George S. Odiorne, *Management by Objectives* (New York: Pitman Publishing, 1965). The following discussion of the role of the top manager indicates how the top manager was viewed as the "brain": "It is he who decides that sales should increase, products [be] developed, costs cut, or quality improved; and it is he who puts in the brains, the drive, and the leadership to bring these things about. . . . He is apt to be more adaptable and flexible than any specialist could possibly be. His expertise lies in analyzing situations, classifying problems, seeing causes, and identifying proper courses of action for others" (10–11).
6. The Center for Quality of Management is using many of Ackoff's ideas in its work. See, for example, Thomas H. Lee and Toby Woll, "Creating the New Center for Quality of Management," *Center for Quality of Management Journal*, 4, no. 2 (Spring 1995): 3–18.
7. Coauthor Shoji Shiba has studied Ackoff's method of idealized design, and he has studied how a number of companies have mobilized themselves to accomplish a breakthrough without using Ackoff's method. Appendix B describes a model for leading breakthrough that Shiba has developed based on observations of successful companies. It is influenced by Ackoff's model of idealized design.

Appendix B   Leadership and Breakthrough

1. Some of these lectures were given at MIT to the students in the Leaders for Manufacturing program, and some were given at various meetings of people from CQM member companies. We asked our colleague, Dave Walden, who was present at those lectures, to summarize them for this appendix.
2. These two paragraphs paraphrase the introductory remarks of Fred Schwettmann to a CEO roundtable on leadership at CQM's West

chapter in August 1998, at which Shoji Shiba presented the content of this appendix.

3. See, for instance, the description of the WV Model in Shoji Shiba et al., *A New American TQM* (Portland, OR: Productivity Press, 1993), 47–58.

4. *Ibid.*, 161–169.

5. For a sketch, ibid., 153–156; for more details, see the *Concept Engineering Manual*, Center for Quality of Management, Cambridge, MA, 1997.

6. Four key concepts of semantics are: the dual function of language, distinguishing report language (to convey logic) and affective language (to convey emotion); differentiating between opinion and fact; moving up and down the "ladder of abstraction"; and using multivalued rather two-valued data.

7. For instance, skill with the LP method of having a team of people understand and organize a body of qualitative information, or skill with the concept engineering method of having a team of people gather and understand the qualitative voices of the market and from them derive and agree on new product and service concepts.

8. One model for communicating with an entire organization is the 7 Infrastructures (see chapter 11 of *A New American TQM*).

9. Koji Kobayashi was president and later chairman of Japan's giant NEC Corp. in the 1960s to the 1980s. He foresaw the convergence of computers and communications, and strongly promoted convergence as NEC's corporate mission and "C and C" (computers and communications) as NEC's corporate slogan. To this end, he wrote *Computers and Communications: A Vision of C&C* and *The Rise of NEC: How the World's Greatest C&C Company Is Managed*.

10. See Chapter 6 of *A New America TQM*.

11. Perhaps even more relevant to Figure B.4 is a piece by Albrecht Dürer that shows a woman lying on a bed on the left side of a vertical gridwork of transparent small squares; on the right side, looking through the gridwork and using it to estimate relative relationships in the tableau of the model, an artist copies what he sees onto a large piece of canvas also marked off in a grid of squares. (The literal English translation of the Japanese translation of the title of this print is "Diagram of Drawing a Nude." We are unsure of the proper English translation.)

12. Shiba states that Japan needs this guideline, but notes that many people in U.S. companies may already have sufficient skill in this area.

13. Letter from Esaki to the faculty of Tsukuba University, January 1992.

14. See Figure 7.11 on page 184 of *A New American TQM*.

15. From David Packard, *The HP Way* (New York: HarperBusiness, 1995, 124–125).

16. Shiba acknowledges that he developed this model for breakthrough as he worked to understand Ackoff's concept of idealized design, mentioned elsewhere in this book.
17. This description is from Shoji Shiba's article "On Leadership," *Growing Companies* (September 1998): 16–17.
18. Notice the parallel with the left-to-right arc of business rise and fall in Figure B.9.

Appendix D   Conversation Competence

1. This appendix was drafted from CQM internal papers and courses from 1995 to 1997; in turn, in some cases, these drew on lessons learned from others listed in the notes of this appendix.
2. We learned the concept of several types of conversations and about the atom of work from people who have studied with Fernando Flores and from the publications of Fernando Flores and his associates. In particular, we have worked with Rafael Echeverria, who was a student of Flores and Humberto Maturana. After the internal paper on which this appendix is based was drafted, we heard about them for the first time from Flores himself.
3. We also worked extensively with Bob Putnam, who was a student of Chris Argyris.
4. The atom of work figure, including the "shared concerns" element shown in a later instance of the figure in this appendix, was first drawn for us by Jack Reilly, who also called it by that name. We believe Jack Reilly learned the method from Fernando Flores and from Jack's book with Business Design Associates.
5. Our initial understanding of these elements of a request came from the Newfield Group.
6. All initial version of the viewpoint diagrams was developed by Dave Walden, Gary Burchill, and Ted Walls; later, Rafael Echeverria of Newfield Group and Bob Putnam of Action design helped refine the figures.
7. We learned this distinction between inquiry and advocacy from Bob Putnam of Action Design.
8. Gary Burchill first sketched the trust loop.

Index

Account managers/application
engineers/service engineers
(communication), 44
Ackoff, Russell, 213–215, 216, 218, 221,
222, 223, 224, 239, 241–254
structural dimensions (five crucial) of
operating environment, 225
systems theories of (Appendix A),
241–254
Action science, 222
Activity-based accounting, 216
Alaska, Sitka: Mount Edgecumbe High
School, 117–121, 125, 127, 195,
204
Alaska Department of Education, 121
American Federation of Teachers, 106
Analog Devices, Inc., 220, 286, 289
Applied science, management as, 6,
209–210, 236–237
Argyris, Chris, 205, 222, 240, 289
Arizona State University, 118
Artzt, Edwin, 31
Assessment, environmental, 227–231
Assessment processes, 209, 299–300, 310
Assumptions, 66, 217
A.T. Kearney (consulting firm), 79
Atom of work, conversations for action via,
292–300, 313, 315
assessment stage, 300
negotiation stage, 295–297
performance stage, 297–299
preparation stage, 293–295
Atom of work, diagrams:
another commitment may be required at
any stage (Figure D.6), 299
atom of work (Figure D.2), 294
atom of work with consequent atoms
(Figure D.4), 298
each conversation has its own model
(Figure D.20), 313
intersecting concerns (Figure D.8), 302
model for conversations for coordinating
action (Figure D.3), 294
network of atoms of work (Figure D.5),
299

shared concerns provide context for
atom of work (Figure D.7), 301
AT&T, 12
Authority/power, 225
Awards:
Baldrige National Quality Award, 55, 78,
87, 88, 138, 171, 193, 209
Deming Prize, 10, 177, 212, 274
Excelsior Award, New York State, 108
Harding Award, 161
President's Quality Award, 171, 178
Awards/incentives, nonmonetary, 112, 260

Babson College, Management Consulting
Field Experience (MCFE), 219
Balanced scorecard approach, 5, 216
Baldrige National Quality Award, 55, 78,
87, 88, 136, 171, 193, 209
Balistreri, Ted, 174
Bataldan, Paul, 132, 150
Bell Atlantic, 125
Benchmarking, 14–15, 177, 182
Berwick, Donald, 147, 150
Bigelow, Michael, 178
Biological model of management (vs.
mechanical/social), 18, 21, 22, 55–56,
247–248, 283
Bohm, David, 222, 240, 289, 312
Bolt Beranek/Newman, 221
Books on quality management, 31–32
Borch, Fred, 4
Bose Corp., 102, 202
Boston College School of Business, 289
Bourne, R. Wiley, Jr., 78
Bradley, Mike, 39, 41, 43, 44, 45
Braun, Joel, 153–154, 156
Breakdown, conversations about, 300, 313
Breakthrough, 265
key factors in (Figure B.17), 277
model for, 275–278
steps for (Figure B.16), 276
transition questions (Figure B.8), 269
two phases (mental/technical), 277
Bryant, Nelson, 97
Burchill, Gary, 96, 223–227, 231–233